BRITISH CONSERVATISM

DOCUMENTS IN POLITICAL IDEAS

General editor: *Bernard Crick*

BRITISH CONSERVATISM

Conservative Thought from Burke to Thatcher

Frank O'Gorman

LONGMAN
London and New York

LONGMAN GROUP LIMITED
Longman House, Burnt Mill, Harlow
Essex CM20 2JE, England
Associated companies throughout the world

Published in the United States of America
by Longman Inc., New York

First Published 1986

BRITISH LIBRARY CATALOGUING IN PUBLICATION DATA

O'Gorman, Frank
    British conservatism: conservative
    thought from the 1790s to the 1980s.
    – (Documents in political ideas)
    1. Conservatism – Great Britain –
    History
    I. Title   II. Series
    320.5′2′0941   DA42
    ISBN 0-582-29643-9

LIBRARY OF CONGRESS CATALOGING IN PUBLICATION DATA

O'Gorman, Frank.
    British Conservatism.

    (Documents in political ideas)
    Bibliography: p.
    1. Conservatism – Great Britain – History – Sources.
2. Great Britain – Politics and government – 1789–1820 –
Sources.   3. Great Britain – Politics and government –
19th century – Sources.   4. Great Britain – Politics and
government – 20th century – Sources.   5. Political science –
Great Britain – History – Sources.   I. Title.   II. Series.
DA520.046   1986   320.5′2′0941   85-23809
ISBN 0-582-29643-9

Produced by Longman Group (FE) Limited
Printed in Hong Kong

CONTENTS

PART SEVEN: LATE VICTORIAN CONSERVATISM TO THE FIRST
WORLD WAR

PART EIGHT: THE INTER-WAR YEARS

EDITOR'S PREFACE

Students of political ideas will be familiar with the debate among their teachers about texts and contexts, whether the study of political ideas primarily concerns the meaning of a text or an understanding of the main ideas of an epoch. Both should be done but not confused; and texts need setting in their context. Yet it is easier for the student to find and to read the texts of political philosophers than to be able to lay his hands upon the range of materials that would catch the flavour of the thinking of an age or a movement, both about what should be done and about how best to use common concepts that create different perceptions of political problems and activity.

So this series aims to present carefully chosen anthologies of the political ideas of thinkers, publicists, statesmen, actors in political events, extracts from State papers and common literature of the time, in order to supplement and complement, not to replace, study of the texts of political philosophers. They should be equally useful to students of politics and of history.

Each volume will have an authoritative and original introductory essay by the editor of the volume. Occasionally instead of an era, movement or problem, an individual writer will figure, writers of a kind who are difficult to understand (like Edmund Burke) simply by the reading of any single text.

B. R. C.

AUTHOR'S PREFACE

Conservative writers and politicians are fond of claiming that theirs is the tradition of moderation, flexibility and pragmatism. British Conservatism, we are told, is not 'ideological'; its principles do not arise from a set of abstractions and it does not consist of logically related propositions. Unlike some modern ideologies, we are informed – presumably Liberalism, Socialism, Communism and Fascism – Conservatism does not primarily depend upon particular beliefs about man and society. It is a gospel for all seasons. What define it are less its intellectual qualities than its instincts, habits and feelings. Conservatism appeals to the whole man or woman. Consequently, it is argued, British Conservatism has had a continuing appeal for successive generations.

There is, no doubt, a certain amount of truth in all of this. Conservatism does lack a logical and systematic set of beliefs. It is neither predictive, visionary nor utopian. It does accept the world – especially the social structure and the distribution of property – largely as it is. It does not seek to impose an order upon it but seeks to conserve the order which is in being. Unlike certain ideologies, Conservatism lacks universal application. British Conservatism, indeed, is very different from its continental counterparts, which enjoy much greater intellectual precision and which have normally endorsed authoritarian political regimes.

Nevertheless, strong recurrent themes may be detected in British Conservatism in the two centuries of its existence. There has been, in short, a Conservative way of thinking about politics and society. This Conservative tradition[1] has emerged and developed through the statements, explanations and rationalisations offered by conservative writers, politicians and propagandists, through the calculated glorification of the legacies of certain individuals (especially Burke and Disraeli) and through the recurrent celebration of key 'Conservative' themes (Patriotism and Imperialism, to name just two). In all this, as we shall see later, we may detect an underlying consistency of attitude towards Man (permeated by the doctrine of the Fall of Man), towards Society (viewed as a living organism), towards the past (venerated as a store-house of wisdom and the source of political legitimacy) and towards social and political action in the present (aimed at the conservation of the existing social structure and, not least, social and political institutions). To treat Conservatism as some commentators – especially Conservative commentators – have done in fact reduces it to the level of incoherent opportunism. The view of man-in-society expressed by Edmund Burke at the end of the eighteenth century in response to the theories, revolutions and wars generated by events in France is generally agreed to be the initial statement of Conservative principles. Many generations of Conservatives have found Burke's philosophy compelling and, with necessary adaptations, serviceable. It is by no means clear that they have ever for long departed from its essential tenets, still less found themselves in clean contradiction with it. Furthermore, each generation of Conservatives has been aware of the *corpus* of Conservative principles and they have been ready to venerate it and relate the legislative and political issues of the present to the legacies of the past. Were the political crises of 1831–32, 1846, 1866–67 and 1886, for example, simply inspired by legislative questions? Was not more, very much more, felt by Conservatives to be at stake?

Inevitably, variations in British Conservatism, within and between the decades, may readily be found but is not the same true of the vicissitudes of Whiggism from the seventeenth to the nineteenth centuries, of Liberalism in the nineteenth and twentieth and Socialism in the twentieth? Is British Conservatism demonstrably more opportunist, more pragmatic and more disposed to ignore questions of principle than the other great mainstreams of British political thought and practice? As Professor Hearnshaw observed half a century ago, Conservatism 'tends to be silent, lethargic, confused, incoherent, inarticulate, unimpressive'.[2] Nevertheless, Conservatives have never been unwilling to engage in controversy, to defend their actions, to explain their objectives and to criticise the schemes of their opponents. We should not take too seriously the carefully fostered impression of a safe, pragmatic and thoroughly non-doctrinaire Conservatism as the last word on the subject.

Like all political groups and parties, British Conservatives have *used* political ideas. They have used them to attract support for their campaigns to secure power or to maintain it. They have used ideas to procure moral acceptance ('legitimacy') of a particular kind of authority, especially when that authority was being challenged (e.g. the authority of the landed interest in the first half of the nineteenth century). They have used ideas to promote national unity in periods of national danger and insecurity (from the Napoleonic wars down to the Falklands conflict, Conservatism has never been far removed from patriotism). They have used ideas to reconcile conflicting demands upon the power of the state, especially since that power began to increase in the nineteenth century (Disraeli's appeal to 'One Nation' is by no means the only example). And they have used ideas to slow the development towards mass democracy, to moderate its impact and to discipline its operation. (The Conservatism of Lord Salisbury is only the most spectacular and transparent such instance.) It is essential to keep these points in mind during the sections that follow in order to understand the significant, yet sometimes subtle, impact of Conservative ideas upon the political development of Britain, and not merely the history of the Conservative Party, during the last two centuries.

At the beginning of the Introduction I outline the basic defining themes of British Conservatism. The chronological sections which follow relate these ideological verities to the political questions and policy debates of particular periods.

I am acutely aware that in such a brief work it is impossible to do justice to two centuries of Conservatism. I have, for the most part, confined myself to the mainstream of Conservative political ideology, endeavouring to present to the reader some idea of the major developments in Conservative thought. I have not, however, confined myself to the Conservative party but I have frequently found it necessary to relate thought to action, philosophy to politics. Consequently, I have tried to provide a representative and balanced account of different trends within Conservatism at any particular time by including a wide variety of sources, philosophical and political, official and unofficial, upper class and lower class, poetic and practical.

I hope that an independent presentation of British Conservative ideas and their history will fill an unaccountable gap in the literature. Such a volume must be timely in view of current reconsiderations of the nature of Conservative ideology. If it tempts and encourages others to investigate this peculiarly British tradition then it will have served its purpose.

I should like to acknowledge here the assistance of Conservative Central Office in general, and of Mr G. D. Block in particular, for permitting me generous access to their materials on the history of the British Conservative Party. Furthermore, Dr M. Milne of the Polytechnic of Newcastle-upon-Tyne allowed me to benefit from his unrivalled knowledge of *Blackwoods* in the first half of the nineteenth century. To these, and to other scholars whose work I have made use of, I am indebted. Finally, I would like to acknowledge the generous advice and assistance of the General Editor of the series, Professor Bernard Crick.

Frank O'Gorman
Manchester
August 1985

NOTES

1. Of course, all political movements manufacture and sustain their own 'traditions', a process which undoubtedly involves the idealisation of historical personages. The refurbishing and renewal of political traditions is the work of every generation and the Conservative tradition has been enthusiastically cultivated for two hundred years. It is my impression, furthermore, that the Conservative tradition is not markedly less protean than that of the Labour Party: it has manifested at least as much consistency and arguably more cohesion.
2. F. J. C. Hearnshaw, *Conservatism in England* (1933), p. 6.

ACKNOWLEDGEMENTS

We are grateful to the following for permission to reproduce copyright material:

Associated Book Publishers Ltd for an extract from *The Spirit of Conservatism* by Sir Arthur Bryant; B.T. Batsford Ltd for an extract from *Freedom and Reality* ed. John Wood; Macmillan Accounts and Administration for extracts from *The Conservative Opportunity* by Blake and Patten, *Tides of Fortune* and *The Middle Way* by Harold Macmillan; Newnes Books Ltd for an extract from pp 48–9 *Lord Randolph Churchill, Vol II* by Winston S. Churchill, originally published by Odhams Press Ltd 1909; Penguin Books Ltd for extracts from pp 10–13, 24–7 *The Case for Conservatism* by Quinton Hogg 1947; The Political Quarterly and the Author, and Rt. Hon. J. Enoch Powell for an extract from an article in *The Political Quarterly Review* Apr.–June 1953; Routledge & Kegan Paul Ltd and The University of Chicago Press for an extract from pp 22–6 *Studies in Philosophy, Politics and Economics* by F. Hayek 1967.

To Else, Annelise and Adam

INTRODUCTION

MAJOR THEMES IN BRITISH CONSERVATISM

Conservative attitudes and assumptions about man in society and man in politics derive from a group of fundamental ideas. As a coherent set of principles these were first expressed by Edmund Burke at the end of the eighteenth century. Taken separately, these ideas can be shown to be much older than Burke but it was he who brought them together into a recognisable 'Conservative' synthesis. For present purposes, it may be useful to highlight four of these recurring ideas. *Firstly*, Conservative writers are usually at pains to emphasise the *inherent evil* which resides in the characters of countless men and women. This idea of the imperfection of human nature, this impression of inherent and irremoveable weaknesses in the human make-up – envy, greed, violence, selfishness – leads Conservative writers to scorn the possibility of successful social and political engineering. Ambitious schemes of reform and radical change fail to take account of the inability of man to overcome his weaknesses [1.1].* This sombre conviction of the frailties and complexities of man arose directly from contemporary religious beliefs about the Fall of Man but they did not always depend upon them. Indeed, as the nineteenth century wore on the problems of population increase, urbanisation and industrialisation became ever more daunting and threatening to the established order. Conservative writers from Coleridge onwards adopted a secular version of the Fall of Man which was no less powerful than its predecessor. Conservative writers of the twentieth century,

---

* References to material in this anthology are given in the text inside [square] brackets, indicating the number of the document in this book in which the extract occurs. Other references are given in the normal way, and are listed at the end of this introduction.

furthermore, continue to have serious doubts about the rationality and perfectibility of Man and the social order in an age of war, persecution, slavery and mass starvation.

Secondly, many Conservative writers profess an *organic theory of society*. According to this belief, society is enormously complex, far more than the sum of its parts and the simple mass of its relationships. This is so because a society is a living and growing *organism* of incalculable delicacy, constantly renewing and developing itself according to a pattern unintelligible to man himself. It is, therefore, to the survival and healthy growth and development of this complex organism that political activity is to be directed, not towards the establishment of some theoretical maxim. It is to this ancient yet continuing social order that the individual is committed, not to some legal or contractual idea of 'the body politic'. Obviously, this organic theory of society has enormous implications for Conservative political ideas, especially insofar as it presumes an attachment to existing forms of social and political arrangements and at best a cautious outlook upon the pace of political and social change [1.2].

Thirdly, Conservatives profess enormous attachment to *historical tradition* in social and political life, as instinctive 'affection for the proliferating variety and mystery of traditional life, as distinguished from the narrowing uniformity and equalitarianism and utilitarian aims of most radical systems'.[1] Institutions and practices derive a very considerable part of their legitimacy from their usefulness to successive generations. True statecraft, then, must be founded upon a recognition of the importance of precedent and an appreciation of the abiding legacy of the past to the present. What this meant in practice was that the British constitution itself was founded upon historical rights and traditional practices. As Burke put it:

> You will observe that from the Magna Charta to the Declaration of Right, it has been the uniform policy of our constitution to claim and assert our liberties as an entailed inheritance derived to us from our forefathers, and to be transmitted to our posterity. We have an inheritable crown, an inheritable peerage; and an House of Commons and a people inheriting privileges, franchises, and liberties from a long line of ancestors.[2]

The first business of politics, then, was to look to this inheritance so that the people might continue to enjoy its benefits [1.3].

It is, therefore, a very simple and logical step to the *fourth* principle, which we wish to stress, that of *conservation*. The conservation of the existing structure of society, its estates and classes, especially the ruling class, and, not least, its distribution of property, is a positive virtue to Conservatives. This is so because, as they argued in the eighteenth and nineteenth centuries, only such a distribution of property, power and wealth can guarantee the future survival of such constitutional rights and popular liberties as existed [1.4]. The true reason for this lies in the threat to liberty from an over-mighty state. The existence of large blocs of private property and wealth can, indeed should, rival and even surpass the resources of the government itself. An emphatically unequal distribution of property and the perpetuation of enormous social inequalities amount to the substantial price which Conservative thinkers are prepared to pay to safeguard society from an authoritarian State. 'If there is no private property, there will be no freedom: the State will be unchallengeable and supreme.'[3] A twentieth-century version of this way of thinking may be seen in Conservative attachment to the idea of a property-owning democracy. This is, to Conservatives, the only form of democracy which can survive. Consequently, radical attempts to upset the distribution of property, wealth and consumption in the direction of greater equality must be viewed with the greatest reserve.

We are now in a position to understand one of the most fundamental of all differences between Liberalism and Conservatism. Whereas to the former political liberty is the most prized of all political values to the latter it occupies a less elevated position. To be sure, Conservative writers pursue the goal of political liberty but they believe that it is only attained as a consequence of certain prior social and political arrangements. These include the preservation of existing institutions, the perpetuation of inequalities of property ownership and the maintenance of social order. 'British liberties', affirms Gilmour 'are the outcome of a highly complex combination of traditions, ideas, laws and historic rights and institutions.'[4] For the Conservative, then, the justification of political authority does not lie in the majority principle, nor does it derive from the fact of election. Political legitimacy does not arise out of the 'will' of a certain number of people. Rather, it must conform to what Burke termed 'the steady maxims of faith, justice and fixed fundamental policy' [1.5]. In the last analysis, it is not what people want that must be the final arbiter in politics but what they ought to want in the context of the historical evolution of their society. Lying outside the area of individual and human choice, then, exist certain ethical standards which serve at the theoretical level as the ultimate criteria for political action and political behaviour. How seriously Conservatives observe these standards as conscious objectives while engaged in political action is obviously a matter for debate.

THE WORLD OF CONSERVATIVE POLITICS

In the Conservative world the place of politics is at best a restricted one: the importance of politics in human affairs should not be exaggerated. Politics as an end in itself should not be taken too seriously nor treated with undue reverence [2.1]. Ever suspicious of political 'solutions' and constantly concerned about the power of the state, the conservative statesman seeks to preserve and even extend the non-political sphere, the sphere of private and personal agency. 'Many of the greatest crimes and the greatest failures of history have been due to the attempt to realise the highest human ideals through political authority.'[5] Significantly, too, the Conservative statesman will not depend merely upon political organisations for his power. He will look for a wider, 'non-partisan' source of popularity and approval. He seeks to earn the gratitude of the whole community and mobilise the patriotism of all the people. Politics should not be about the narrow and determined enactment of a party manifesto but the steady enlargement of the area of private activity and personal morality. Conservative politics do not depend upon any one version of social or political arrangement because they do not believe that the state has or should have the final power to determine the lives of the people. And because Conservatives repudiate the contractual obligation of individuals to the state the Conservative Party can prosper under different types of regime: monarchical, oligarchical or democratic. Indeed, the concerns of Conservative politicians must include the successful negotiation of the transfer from one type of regime to another and its subsequent stabilisation. It has undoubtedly been one of the great strengths of the British Conservative party that it has not tied itself to any particular type of political and social regime, still less to any particular mode of economic production.

In all the ringing declarations of principle of this type there is naturally an element of special pleading, of pious hoping and even of wishful thinking. These are not necessarily accurate descriptions of what Conservatives have actually done. We need, in short, to preserve a sense of proportion and, to some extent, to retain our critical instincts. Conservatives have not, for example, been conspicuously successful in ensuring that government plays a minimal role in British life. In the nineteenth century it was normally conservative governments – not Whig and Liberal ones – which preached and practised the virtues of protection, paternalism and intervention. In the twentieth century, too, Conservative governments have been usually prepared to perpetuate a goodly proportion of war-time or socialist collectivism. Throughout its history, indeed, the Conservative Party has been prepared not merely to preach and practise the values of private philanthropy but to augment such voluntary activity with State or State-sponsored assistance in many fields. Nor is this in the least surprising. If it is an essential feature of Conservative politics to encourage the individual to emancipate himself to act upon his own moral agency then the state must surely conspire to create the circumstances in which this becomes possible.

Nevertheless, there can be no gainsaying the fact that Conservatives have constantly preached against the creeping menace of state centralisation in all its guises. Burke, for example, was fond of emphasising the claims of loyalty to one's family, village, town and country. In the nineteenth century Conservatives associated Whig politics with centralisation, monopoly and corruption. Even in the twentieth century Conservatives continue to idealise the local community because the defence of local interests, the power of local elites and the utility of local paternalism all conspire to create a balance against the claims of central government and its agencies.

How, then, has modern British Conservatism come to be so closely associated with loyalty to national institutions and with the sentiments of patriotism? In all this it is important to remember that Conservatives emphasise civic responsibilities rather than personal rights and that they advocate the enjoyment of the latter in the context of the former. Furthermore, the organic notion of society strongly underlines the unity of the community, albeit in a theoretical and abstract manner. Conservatives recognise, nevertheless, the existence of divisions within society but they refuse to take them too seriously. Such divisions are an integral feature of any human society. The task of the statesman is not to remove them but to render them tolerable. Class loyalties, for example, are perfectly normal and natural but they are not the supreme allegiances. What unites all classes is loyalty to the nation and what touches men of all ranks is symbolic representation of the nation: the monarch, the flag, the anthem [2.2]. Men must be ready to fight and die for these causes. 'In the final resort the soldier's is the noblest of all professions', wrote a popular twentieth-century Conservative pundit.[6] The close association between the Conservative Party and the armed forces on the one hand, and between the Conservative mind and the traditions of the armed services on the other, should not be taken lightly. Patriotism, then, is something more than an affirmation of the harmony of social groups and classes. Patriotism is a celebration not merely of individuals and institutions but of a way of looking at society and history, a way of feeling about public life. 'The nation, not the so-called class struggle, is therefore at the base of Conservative political thinking. Harmony not struggle is its ruling political objective.'[7]

In international affairs the Conservative keynote is a vigorous defence of national interests rather than an ideologically inspired or fashionable internationalism. The Conservative view of the world envisages a group of powerful nation states all defending their political and economic interests. Among these the British nation must hold its head high by plain speaking to its enemies, by keeping its word to its friends and by fulfilling its international (treaty) obligations. All this presupposes a strong sense of national cohesion, a vigorous defence policy and formidable armed services. The defence of the national interest may be undertaken by Britain itself or within some larger grouping of political units. There is, therefore, nothing in the slightest degree illogical in the fact that the party of patriotism and national unity was at the same time in the nineteenth and for much of the twentieth century the party of empire. (The two greatest exponents of imperialist politics, Benjamin Disraeli and Joseph Chamberlain, were both Conservatives [2.3].) Nor is there anything in the least surprising that it was the party of patriotism which was responsible for the entry of Britain into the European Economic Community. These vastly different institutions in their own way represent valid examples of the defence of Britain's interests but, still more, structures within which Britain can display her moral energy. As Lord Hugh Cecil put it: 'As in our relation with foreign countries so also in respect to the dominions and dependencies of the Crown beyond the seas, the purpose of national policy must be the fulfilment of the national vocation.'[8]

Interestingly, the development of a Conservative tradition within these islands coincided with the emergence of a *British* political structure. Wales had been integrated into England in 1536, Scotland in 1707. The United Kingdom was completed, however, in 1801 with the Act of Union of Ireland with England. After 1801 any emphasis upon purely *English* sentiment and interests would have endangered the delicate balance of the Union itself. Consequently,

English statesmen discovered a *British* nation and proceeded to establish a *British* empire. In all of these developments, Conservative politicians and publicists were closely involved.

A party which spends its time looking to the national destiny does not have much patience with the pettiness of party politics. Conservative writers and politicians love to claim that they rise above mere partisanship, especially when 'the Conservative cause is the national cause'.[9] Sometimes they even affect a certain guilt over their own status as party politicians. Now, we have to exercise a little care just here. The Conservative party has never been slow to protect its own. It is not at all clear that the Conservatives have acted in a less partisan manner than their Whig, Liberal and Labour counterparts nor that their supporters have seriously wished them to do so. Nevertheless, since the time of Disraeli at least the Conservative Party has been, or expected to be, the party government. Consequently, Conservatives may have been more disposed to speak the language of national unity than their opponents. They have certainly been more ready to play the patriotic card than their opponents, whether Liberal or Labour, both in war and in peace time.

Within this securely established national structure Conservatives place a high priority on maintaining and conserving the institutions of the State, especially those which embody national unity – the monarchy, parliament, the established Church. Necessary change and modernisation must be engrafted on to solidly established foundations. Conservatism therefore offers a solid institutional framework within which change, adaptation and reform may be rendered acceptable. To what extent Conservatives really have pursued reformist and modernising objectives over the period of their party's existence is, no doubt, a matter for endless debate. The point is that British Conservatism has rarely for long presented a totally reactionary appearance.

In some ways, then, Conservatism operates at two levels. On the one hand there is the Conservatism of sentiment, nostalgia and symbolism while on the other there is the Conservatism of reason, necessity and political reality. An example may be helpful. The Conservatism of sentiment has never been more in evidence than in the remarkable veneration of the monarchy which Conservatives have exhibited in the last hundred years. The monarchy, of course, embodies Conservative instincts surrounding the defence of hereditary institutions and the unity of the nation and empire. Yet it is more than a purely symbolic association. Conservatives are apt to immerse themselves in the majesty and mystique of the monarchy because it dramatically embodies in one family the values of the existing political *and social* system. In the same way, Conservatives have tended to identify themselves with the ceremonies, forms and rituals characteristic of certain professions, especially the armed services. The significance of this sort of behaviour lies in the shared, public vindication of the authority of the state and shared public acceptance of its hierarchies, institutions and professions [2.4]. The monarchy, the professions and national institutions have not always been treated with humble respect by leading Conservative politicians. This is where the second, purely political, level of Conservatism becomes relevant. Powerful images of ermine robes and rolling acres should not obscure the ability of Conservative political leaders to break with the past and to embark upon uncharted seas and sometimes very disturbing adventures. The actions of Wellington in 1829, of Peel in 1846 and of Disraeli in 1867 were the hallmark of ruthless and determined men. They arose from motives of political advantage, calculation and opportunism and owed nothing to sentiment and nostalgia. Yet Conservative political leaders have to respect the sentiment and nostalgia which permanently grip the party and, not infrequently, to agitate it. There is, then, in Conservative politics a unique counterpoint between the nostalgic expectations of the party faithful and the political dilemmas of the party leadership.

Moreover, as Disraeli said, 'the Constitution of England is not merely a Constitution in State, it is a Constitution in Church and State'. Until recent decades one of the most powerful of all Conservative appeals was the defence of the Church establishment. The conception of an alliance between Church and State, the function of the former in consecrating the latter, and the function of the latter in defending the former have been integral elements in the Conservative conscience in Britain. In the same way that Conservative philosophy has always been imbued with powerful ethical elements so too Conservative politics has never been far removed from Anglicanism and the purposes of Conservative statesmen have included the defence of the Church against a succession of enemies: Jacobins, Catholics, Radicals, Liberals, Nonconformists and Communists [2.5]. It would be a serious mistake to treat Conservatism too narrowly, to regard it exclusively as the public statements of a political party. British Conservatism has been closely involved with the defence of social and religious as well as political establishments. To the development of this ideology it is now time to turn.

THE PRE-HISTORY OF CONSERVATISM

Enthusiastic commentators have occasionally been tempted to endow British Conservatism with the lengthiest pedigree imaginable, occasionally even stretching back into the Middle Ages.[10] It seems farfetched to permit such an ascription, however, before the establishment of the modern British political system based on national independence, constitutional monarchy, parliamentary sovereignty, cabinet government and the rule of law. Even then it is all too easy to mistake superficial resemblances to certain general Conservative attitudes – appeals for order and social discipline, for example – for a body of coherent Conservative ideas. Anthony Quinton, for example, assigns 'chronological primary' to Richard Hooker in whose *Laws of Ecclesiastical Polity* (1594), apparently 'the main Conservative convictions are prominent and explicit'.[11] Professor Huntington agrees: 'Here, two hundred years before Burke, was delineated every significant strand of Burkean thought. The substance of their Conservatism is virtually identical.'[12] No doubt apologists for the Elizabethan settlement demanded obedience to authority and submission to the monarchy and the Church. No doubt they adopted a defensive and conserving attitude to the institutions and practices under attack by their puritan opponents. But their arguments lack both the organic theory of society and the historical perspective on social and political institutions proper to modern Conservatism. Conservation may be a defensive theory but it is surely not *any* defensive theory.[13]

It is more rewarding to note the emergence of a specifically 'Tory' attitude to politics in the second half of the seventeenth century than it is to wrangle over spurious pedigrees. After the Restoration of 1660, the Church and King party acquired the label 'Tory', notably over attempts to exclude the Catholic James, Duke of York, from the succession to Charles II. In the Exclusion crisis of 1679–81 the name 'Tories' was finally given to those who opposed the exclusion of James from the succession as a direct challenge to royal authority. As a term describing a distinct set of principles, practices and methods, bred of the long alliance between Church and King, 'Toryism' was first used in 1682. Most of these Tories, however, were sufficiently staunch Anglicans to resist James II's attempts to reintroduce Roman Catholicism. The Glorious Revolution of 1688–89 thus seriously damaged Tory commitment to divine right monarchy and the duty of passive obedience, though it by no means destroyed it. Thereafter, the Tories tended to become a Country party of opposition to Whig goverments, seeing themselves as the squirearchy opposed to the interests of Whig grandees, critical of the exercise of power and hostile to the expensive war policies of their rivals.

After the Hanoverian Succession of 1714 the Tories were condemned to a future of almost permanent opposition to the Hanoverian monarchs and their ministers. During this political wilderness their political and theoretical mentor was Viscount Bolingbroke, whose writings, together with those of other publicists, did much to assert a distinctly Tory tradition of politics with which to confront the Whig propaganda purveyed by the writers employed by Walpole. With the benefit of hindsight, certain of these 'Tory' themes were to form an integral part of later Conservative theory. *First*, Bolingbroke adopted a sceptical attitude to the role of abstract theory in political life. For Bolingbroke the principles of the British constitution could only be understood historically and by reference to experience rather than to abstract theory. *Second*, Bolingbroke understood that man is naturally sociable and that his existence occurred within families, groups and occupations. Man was not a legal or abstract entity but a social person. *Third*, Bolingbroke believed that the rights and liberties enjoyed under the British constitution had a prescriptive and historical foundation, not a contractual nor abstract origin. The constitution was as much the product of the common law tradition stretching back over centuries and conditioning the customs and habits of Englishmen as it was of particular legislative enactments. Whig theorists shared many of these historical and traditionalist qualities but found it exceptionally difficult to abandon their belief in some form of contract theory. *Fourth*, in his repudiation of Walpolean political methods, his rejection of corruption and influence and his affirmation of the purity of country politics, Bolingbroke was depicting an ideal political order that was at once rural, hierarchic and static as opposed to urban, individualistic and dynamic. Built into Bolingbroke's 'Tory' mentality was a nostalgic vision of an ideal society which had never really existed but one which Bolingbroke wished to restore.

The other great Tory theorist of the eighteenth century had little to do with the Tory party. Nevertheless, David Hume shared some, though by no means all, of Bolingbroke's concerns – a nice commentary upon the danger of issuing labels like 'Tory' or 'Conservative' too freely in this period. Nevertheless, like Bolingbroke's, the essence of Hume's philosophy is his rejection of abstract reason as a method of political argument and his repudiation of contract theory as a source of political obligation. For Hume adopted a pessimistic view of man, arguing that his 'limited generosity', his innate selfishness and a scarcity of material goods made social progress unlikely. Furthermore, Hume's scepticism was more comprehensive than that of Bolingbroke and, in the last analysis, was to be of considerably more significance in the history of British Conservatism. Hume cast mordant philosophical doubt upon the existence of any coherent meaning, pattern or rhythm in history. He doubted, moreover, that statesmen had the capacity to impose order upon the will and impulses of mankind in the mass. These pessimistic attitudes were to be taken up later by Conservative thinkers after Burke. Hume argued, for example, that men obeyed authority not because of morality or duty but because it was to their advantage to do so. Like Bolingbroke, although from a very different standpoint, Hume sought to preserve and defend the Glorious Revolution and a society of ranks and orders. Ultimately, however, he defended it not for prescriptive nor for moral reasons but for reasons of general advantage and benefit. In other words, it was possible for 'Tory' writers like Bolingbroke and Hume to reach similar conclusions by different – sometimes *very* different – routes.

The real difficulty with using labels like 'Tory' or 'Conservative' in the early and mid-eighteenth century is that such unmistakably 'Tory' or 'Conservative' values as the defence of authority, the continuity of institutions, the rights of property and the rule of law within the context of a rapidly observed social hierarchy were so widespread that the description becomes almost meaningless. Samuel Johnson was unquestionably a 'Tory' in his hostility to corruption, to war and to empire but he lacked Bolingbroke's prescriptive outloook and he was angered by the scepticism of Hume. How much, then, does the word 'Tory' explain and clarify if it may be so variously construed? Only when the dramatic ideological disputes of the later eighteenth century stimulated challengingly novel theories of men and society did more specific and distinctive definitions emerge. Indeed, customary attitudes – to hierarchy, obedience and order, for example – required little in the way of detailed philosophical defence before the Enlightenment and the French Revolution issued their own challenges to the intellectual foundations of the *ancien régime* in Europe. 'Tory' attitudes and arguments may readily be detected in Britain in the seventeenth and eighteenth centuries but not yet a coherent and self-conscious Conservative philosophy.

EDMUND BURKE: A FOUNDING FATHER (1765–1797)

Edmund Burke may confidently be treated as the most important Founding Father of Conservative ideas. It was Burke who laid down in a reasonably systematic form the fundamental philosophical, political, social and religious ideas upon which later Conservatives developed more specific details of policy and practice. The Conservative canon has, of course, been extended since Burke's day to incorporate, for example, the love of empire. At the same time, not all of Burke's dogmas have been retained by later Conservatives (e.g. his distaste for greater religious toleration), but most of them have. The Burke of the 1790s in particular has been recognisable to later Conservative writers and politicians as a source of inspiration and wisdom. The Burke who attacked the underlying principles and the horrifying practical consequences of the French Revolution by upholding the ordered liberty fostered by the British constitution has struck many a chord in later writers, wrestling with the bewildering problems presented by complex social and political changes. There can be no question, then, that Burke's ideas do represent the starting point for the continuous elaboration and development of a characteristically Conservative ideology.

One of the main reasons for this lies in Burke's approach to political issues. Throughout his career as a Whig politician Burke constantly repudiated the validity of certain types of abstract political thought. His defence of the American colonists in the 1760s and 1770s proceeded from practical considerations concerning the growth and development of American society, customs and institutions and the impracticality of maintaining British supremacy. (Burke did not defend the Americans because they were fighting for an abstraction like 'liberty'.) He was always an advocate of reforming institutions, of purifying them and returning them to their original purposes and principles. He opposed visionary and radical schemes of reform, preferring to work with the known and the familiar [3.1]. For Burke, the constitution of the country and its institutions were essentially sound and required little significant reconstruction, although occasional reforms and renovations might be required. Burke believed in the aristocratic political system of the day. He spent the first half of his career defending it from the Crown and the second half from radical reformers. Although later Conservatives have normally identified themselves with the later Burke, the Burke who in the 1790s denounced the French Revolution and the atheistic and democratic principles upon which, according to Burke, it proceeded, there is a recognisable continuity in his ideas. His main concern was thus to preserve the balanced constitution of the eighteenth century, with the separate spheres of influence apportioned to King, Parliament and People no matter from whatever quarter a threat to it might appear[14]. No wonder, then, that when the fabric of British and even European institutions came to be threatened by the pressures unleashed by the French Revolution then these predisposing elements in Burke's thinking were developed into a generalised Conservative philosophy of man and society.

The starting point of Burke's – and indeed any – Conservatism may be found in his conviction that politics was a concrete rather than a speculative activity. As far back as 1769 he had complained that 'Politics ought to be adjusted, not to human reasonings, but to human nature, of which the reason is but a part, and by no means the greatest part'. Political statesmanship required experienced judgement, not dry, abstract calculation [3.2]. It required a grasp of the instincts, loyalties and prejudices which went with ancient institutions. Men were not primarily rational beings and to try to make a man, still less a multitude of men, conform to some predetermined abstract category was not only absurd but dangerous. Men could not re-order the world around them and to attempt to do so might subvert the social stability and political order upon which civilised society and the enjoyment of political liberties depended. In the *Appeal from the New to the Old Whigs* (1791) he pronounced: 'The awful author of our being is the author of our place in the order of existence; and that having disposed and marshalled us by a divine tactic, not according to our will, but according to his, he has . . . virtually subjected us to act the part which belongs to the place assigned to us.' Vast areas of social existence, therefore, were not open to rational analysis or criticism.

In the same vein, Burke's version of the social contract emphasised the realities of social living. In the eighteenth century most writers, and certainly most reformers, believed that men had been truly free in the state of nature which preceded the formation of society. They had voluntarily surrendered the exercise of certain of these freedoms to the state at the time of the original contract when the state came into existence. Burke, however, did not believe the myth of the voluntary and historic contract. For Burke, the state of nature was anarchic and primitive from which civilised social life was a thankful deliverance [3.3]. It was membership of society which gave men contractual obligations to their fellow men, to the state and, ultimately, to God. Burke's contract theory emphasised the duties of men. It was binding and timeless and had permanent moral force. Society and its institutions – in spite of what certain radical writers were affirming – did not threaten man's freedom. They created it. Men did not have the moral right to ignore or to infringe these duties of loyalty and obedience to civil society. For Burke the real rights of men were the benefits of living in society – however imperfect its institutions and however unequal the distribution of wealth and property. To argue, as some radicals did, that men had a right to consent over who governed them, still more, rights of resistance and rebellion, struck at the heart of his conception of society. Men had basic social rights – to the unhindered possession of their goods and labour, to order, justice and security – but their political rights depended upon the constitution of the state as it existed. The claim of institutions in demanding and deserving the loyalty of citizens did not depend upon the opinions of these citizens. The will of the people, whether represented in elections, mob-rule, violence or insurrection, was not the origin of political rights. Men were obliged to obey legitimate (i.e. prescriptive) and legal authority so long as the state did not itself threaten its own legitimacy.

Inevitably, then, the general purpose of Edmund Burke's political ideas was to conserve the society with which he and his contemporaries were familiar. This meant two things. It meant protecting the social structure and the ownership of property exactly as it was [3.4]. At the political level, it meant protecting the existing political order. Of Britain he wrote: 'All the Reformations we have hitherto made have proceeded upon the principle of reference to antiquity.' The Glorious Revolution, he roundly claimed, 'was made to preserve our ancient, indisputable laws and liberties' and he went on:

> We are resolved to keep an established church, an established monarchy, an established aristocracy, and an established democracy.

His further observation that these were to be preserved 'each in the degree it exists *and in no greater*' (my italics) underlines the importance of conserving a prescriptive constitution. From time to time it may be necessary to reform some part of it in order to retain its intrinsic qualities but it will rarely ever be necessary to remove and replace it, short of some unimaginable calamity. Burke thus denied the relevance of any external criterion of the worth of institutions. They have a prescriptive legitimacy in their own right and from having existed from time out of mind not a legitimacy arising from some external criterion such as efficiency, modernity or humanity [3.5].

Burke's retrospective ideas of reform and conservation blurred his grasp of social change and continuity. At times in the 1790s when he struggled with rising anxiety to preserve the fruits of British history he seems to have stopped the clock at the time of the Glorious Revolution. He found it hard to tolerate, except in theory, any changes in the political structures then established. He was much more conscious of the diversity and complexity of society than he was inclined to understand the growth and development of a society.[15] He saw that this diversity and complexity could nevertheless be reconciled into effective social harmony. The individual was not the basic social unit. In a hierarchic society, individuals lived in groups, each one of which had its own history, its own rights and its own persona. The individual owed his loyalty to the timeless demands of his family, his community, his church, his nation. Loyalty was directed to groups within society, not to individuals and not to abstract ethical ideas. His frequently quoted remarks in the *Reflections* about the social contract as 'a partnership not only between those who are living, but between those who are living, those who are dead, and those who are to be born' certainly tremble on the verge of an organic theory but do not seem to me fully to describe one. Nevertheless, Burke certainly prepared the ground for later, organic theories by opening a time dimension in discussions of social change and by shifting the stuff of political thought away from mythical ideas of contract to the society in which men actually lived [3.6]. At times, Burke does seem to admit the inevitability of perpetual change in society and he does leave the door open for the emergence of new prescriptions. In doing so, he drags himself clear of the old cyclical mentality which assumed the perpetual rise, decay, fall, renovation and subsequent decay of societies and moved towards a linear conception of social change. Burke stressed the need for preservation, permitted some degree of growth and accumulation but stopped well short of a theory of progressive development. In his earlier career he had taken account of the rights of the individual and had even acknowledged rights of resistance to the authority of the state. In his later writings directed against the French Revolution he came to emphasise the powers of the state and the necessity for obedience to it. Burke never entirely ruled out the justifiability of revolution, especially if the rulers of a state themselves destroyed the legacy which it was their function to preserve, and he never discounted the possibility that democratic forms of government might be found suitable for certain societies at certain times. It was not for men, however, in a rash and wilful aggression, to destroy the political legacy of the centuries. The statesman, then, must take account of the wishes of those he rules but he must not be led by votes of the majority – still less by the vociferous protests of a minority – to undo the work of the ages for temporary gain and transient popularity. Burke hated tyranny but most of all he hated the tyranny of the majority [3.7].

The defence of an oligarchical *political* system had economic and social implications. Edmund Burke defended the divine right of the Whig aristocracy less against the dangers of state centralisation – that was a distant and unlikely prospect in eighteenth-century England, although it may not have been in Europe – than against the much more likely prospect of mob rule, revolution and anarchy. To Burke it was natural that men of great property, proud traditions, adequate leisure, education and a sense of public responsibility should constitute a 'natural aristocracy' with an automatic title to rule. Their political as well as social and economic supremacy would provide continuity and stability to the life of society. Consequently, their social eminence and their private property should be carefully respected. Burke argued that 'the plunder of the few' would benefit the multitude very little because such a redistribution would lead to violence and anarchy rather than to a state of blissful equality. No wonder that Burke's theory of a natural aristocracy has been employed by successive generations to vindicate the rights and privileges of the existing ruling order.

These are familiar conclusions but two further observations should be borne in mind. The first is that Burke, like many eighteenth-century writers, assigned a very broad meaning to the word 'property'. It did not merely include possession of property but also the rights which went with that property (to charge a rent, levy a fine, influence a voter, exercise the power of an office, exercise chartered rights, etc.). It may be claimed that Burke was defending not merely the existing distribution of property but, what is far more significant, the complex cluster of customs, practices and attitudes which had grown up around it. The second point worth making is that the phrase 'landed orders' conjures up bucolic visions of nostalgic simplicity. In fact the British landed interest of the eighteenth century were a thriving entrepreneurial class who had in the previous century begun to capitalise agriculture and who were now closely involved in the drive to industrialise. Edmund Burke's defence of property may with some justification be represented as the defence of industrial and commercial as well as landed property. As Burke himself remarked in 1770: 'There is no such thing as the landed interest separate from the trading interest.'[16] It would be entirely mistaken to view Burke's Conservatism simply as nostalgic, reactionary feudalism.

There can be no doubt that Burke believed, like his friend Adam Smith, in the profit motive, in free trade and in a minimal role for government. Burke defended the capitalism of a society and economy dominated by the landed interest. As early as 1769 he was repudiating the value of mercantilist restrictions upon industrial growth and a year later was laying down the maxim that the interests of producer and consumer were identical.[17] Towards the end of his life he summarised his economic thought in *Thought and Details on Scarcity* (1795). Here was a flinty statement of non-intervention by the state. ('To provide for us in our necessities is not in the power of government') [3.8].

Such an attitude is little more than the conventional wisdom of the age. Yet Burke approached society and politics with reverence for their historical origins and treated politics as the art of stable conservation and steady continuity. He stressed the power of custom, habit and instinct in the life of man. He understood the complexity and fragility of societies and consequently the role of prudence and pragmatism in statecraft. He offered a powerful – if at times superficial and hysterical – critique of enlightenment beliefs and the privileged status which reason occupied among them. This is not to say that Burke was able to anticipate later developments of Conservative thought in any detail. His preoccupation with corruption and his somewhat brittle and insensitive approach to social problems were quite characteristic of eighteenth-century thinking. His obsession with prescription weakened the future orientation of his thought. He trembled on the verge of an organic theory of the state and wallowed in a conspiracy theory of revolution (in his French thought, at least). He lacked many aspects of the Romantic Conservative imagination: the idealisation of Medievalism, the desire to recapture the spirit of the age, the search for national origins, the worship of the peasant and the nostalgia for rural simplicity. Burke was not a Romantic Conservative but many aspects of his thought – his traditionalism, his reassertion of hierarchic values and sentiment and his idealisation of custom and precedent – prepared the way for Wordsworth, Shelley, Coleridge and Scott.

It is well to remember that Burke was a Whig politician all his life who moved eighteenth-century Lockian Whiggism in a Conservative direction. He moved away from seventeenth-century Whig ideas on the state of nature, on the social contract and on the nature of man to advance the cause of certain concepts which have become part of the Conservative tradition. Burke's position in the Conservative Pantheon is, justifiably, a very important one.[18] In the twentieth century it has shown disturbing signs of becoming more important that it really deserves. New Conservatives in America have used Burke as the champion of Christianity and capitalism in their own cold war against atheism and communism. Just as revolutionary Jacobinism threatened to engulf an embattled *ancien régime* in Christian Europe in the late eighteenth century so now American and Atlantic civilisation was believed to be threatened by pagan ideology from the East. Can Conservatism endure, wondered Russell Kirk 'when two of the three great powers in the world are ruled by Marxist doctrinaires, and while technological and economic and cultural change continue to tear apart the cake of custom everywhere'.[19] Burke's generalised wisdom lent itself to such usage, especially to authors and groups seeking moral certainty in troubled times. He expressed with timeless eloquence the principles of the free enterprise system, the ideal of civilised leadership, the growing fear of mob rule and the revulsion from mass society and, not least, the human craving for safety and security in an era revolution. No wonder that Burke's Conservatism has been a fruitful source of inspiration for two centuries.

ROMANTIC CONSERVATISM 1790–1830

Europe reacted to the shock of the French Revolution by defending its ruling order, reviving its Christian traditions, idealising its feudal chivalry, reacting against the threat of democracy and strengthening the forces of law and order. An age of warfare, revolution and reaction rang to the clash of conflicting ideas (faith *v.* reason, progress *v.* reaction and oligarchy *v.* democracy) and conflicting interests (agriculture *v.* industry, capital *v.* labour, state control *v. laissez-faire*). A Europe which did not understand, and did not know how to control the bewildering complexity of political revolution, as well as social and economic change, was a certain breeding ground for Conservative attitudes. Among others, Adam Muller, the great Austrian Conservative, advocated a return to medieval practices and institutions, especially the spirit of war, sacrifice and heroism. The early decades of the nineteenth century may, therefore, conveniently be termed a period in which 'Romantic Conservatism' flourished.

British Romantic Conservatism, however, lacked the clarity and logical rigour of its continental counterparts. Probably because political polarisation was not as marked in Britain and because no consistently serious threat either to the Hanoverian regime or the existing social structure existed, it was a somewhat shapeless and indistinct form of Conservatism. Nevertheless, its main features can be described as the elevation of the spirit of man and nation set against an idealised version of the past. The Romantics were brimful of enthusiasm for the Church, the Middle Ages and the Nobility. Romantic Conservatives derived their inspiration in present politics from imagined utopias in the past. Clearly, they owed much to Burke and often used him as a conscious point of departure but they infused life and colour, fantasy and sentiment, nostalgia and idealism into his political theory.

In this process the context of politics was of enormous significance. Britain was at war with France from 1793 to 1815 and the country was swept by surges of dynastic patriotism during the epic conflict. This was not simply a case of rallying around the throne. The rising tide of radicalism in the 1790s elicited a 'Tory reaction' on the part of Pitt's government in which basic civil liberties were suspended for the duration of the war. At the same time a loyalist 'Tory' opinion swept the country. Around 1,500 Loyalist societies sprang up everywhere, carried out political and religious witch-hunts, committed acts of petty discrimination against radicals, circulated Loyalist literature and in all this acted with the positive approval of the state and the Church. In this war of ideas the initial victory went to those who manned, administered and supported the 'Tory' polity of the 1790s. Radicals and reformers largely vacated their customary 'patriotic' stance, leaving patriotic values to be associated with support for the government and the existing political and social system. Loyalty to the person of the monarch and to the institution of the Church was quite rapidly transformed into a significantly new type of political and social patriotism. Now that hatred of the old national enemy, France, was at its height the new Patriotism of the 1790s changed old John Bull into a flag-waving, French-hating Church and King Tory. A poet like Wordsworth who had originally celebrated the new era ushered in by the French Revolution now settled down to emphasise the Burkean values of loyalty, constitutionalism and tradition, to rally to the national banner the simple political and religious faith of millions of ordinary people [4.1]. Pitt's government identified itself with these patriotic sentiments. Those who supported it ultimately formed the Tory party of the early nineteenth century.

Defence of the state involved, even required, the defence of the Church. The one was the first line of defence for the other. The Church still enjoyed great moral authority. Its pulpits were a source of loyalty, propaganda and deference for the secular arm. Its offices were an indispensable source of ready patronage and wealth. Its bishops were a reliable source of ministerial support in the Lords. 'Thus did the ecclesiastical constitution of the country harmonize with the political', commented one great historian.[20] Yet the Anglican Church was threatened with the rivalry of the reviving churches of Old Dissert and the astonishing growth of new Methodism. The emerging Toryism of the turn of the century was necessarily an Anglican Toryism. In particular, its repudiation of the claims of both Disserters and Roman Catholics to a greater degree of religious toleration laid the basis for that aggressive Anglicanism which was to be a hallmark of nineteenth-century British Conservatism. In particular, popular hostility to Catholic Emancipation fanned the great Tory slogan 'No Popery'.

Patriotic sentiment in the present was reflected in patriotic sentiment in the past. Romantic Conservatism emphasised Burke's veneration for history but transformed it into a living reality. The past of the nation became a treasure house of inspiration for the present. The adventures of great and patriotic heroes became constant subjects for novels, poems and pictures. Burke had not conveyed the emotional empathy for the Middle Ages which swept the country in the early years of the nineteenth century. Nostalgia for medievalism, for castles and chivalry, knights and ladies, heroism and mystery, armour and honour – a past utopia in the history of the nation – gripped the soul of the Romantics.

The creation of this chivalrous utopia was nothing more nor less than the impact of industrialisation and urbanisation upon some of the more defensive and nostalgic elements in the old society. The fantastic unreality of medievalism was a direct repudiation of the values of commercial society, an assertion of feeling in place of commercial calculation, of intuition against reason and science, of religion against atheism, of imagination against reality. The idealisation of a past society with its stable community life and the harmony of its social groups remained one of the most compelling political and social visions in the history of Britain in the nineteenth century. As the new middling orders threw in their lot with the old aristocracy and identified their interests with those of the old oligarchy they bequeathed a tradition of Tory resentment. The 'Tory Radicalism' associated with William Cobbett rested on the myth of a society in which the classes were united by sentiment rather than by fear. In demanding social reform and manhood suffrage, Cobbett was not consciously behaving like a modern democrat; he was simply demanding the restoration of ancient practices and the return to the Englishman of his birthright. Now that the landed interest had abandoned its paternalistic responsibilities there was nothing for it but for the common man to demand the restoration of his lost inheritance [4.2].

The most prolific and influential writer to popularise these values was Sir Walter Scott. His Waverley novels, published at the rate of approximately one per year between 1814 and 1832, reached an enormous audience. In novels such as *Ivanhoe* and *The Talisman* Scott touched the very powerful medieval chords of his reading public. In others, such as *Redegauntlet* and *Waverly*, Scott depicted the recent history of Scotland in a compelling and patriotic manner. In all his novels, however, Scott embellishes the themes of loyalty to monarchs, conformity to institutions, their rules and rituals, acceptance of hierarchy and the social system [4.3]. Scott idealises History, recognising the sources of social order in the veneration of antiquity and the springs of patriotism in the preservation of national institutions. Of social progress, popular rights and economic progress nothing is heard. Indeed, Scott, like almost all the Romantics, hated the new economics. 'They hated Bentham and James Mill and their associates because Utilitarianism stood for the age of the machine, the hell-hole city, and the barrenness of liberal morality.'[21] They also hated them because the new economic order degraded and demoralised the masses.

What Scott did for the past, the Lake Poets did for the natural world in the present. Their poetry is motivated by the desire to experience vivid, varied and lasting impressions and, at its most ascetic, a mystic-like state of tranquility. Nature fascinated the Romantics and offered man the highest form of experience.

Wordsworth had reached Burke's conclusion – albeit by a different route – that society, like nature, was not created artificially but proceeded according to a mysterious design through the ages. In a series of political sonnets begun in 1802 Wordsworth evoked the love of home and the love of country in a burst of poetic patriotism. In the *Tract on the Convention of Cintra* he affirmed that Napoleon could only be defeated by arousing the patriotic sentiments of the masses of Europeans. Patriotism arises out of love of nature. In spite of his earlier approval of the French Revolution he came to see Britain as the sanctuary of all true freedom in an oppressed and tyrannical world. Like any true Tory, Wordsworth gloried in the overthrow of Napoleon and swelled with pride at Britain's achievement in maintaining her national independence and freedom. This achievement, like his poetry, did not merely appeal to the literate middle and upper classes. All citizens could share in its appreciation. As early as his preface to the 1800 and 1802 editions of the *Lyrical Ballads* he set out 'to make the incidents of common life interesting by tracing in them . . . the primary laws of our nature'.

> Low and rustic life was generally chosen because in that situation the essential passions of the heart find a better soil in which they can attain their maturity, are less under restraint, and speak a plainer and more emphatic language, because in that situation our elementary feelings exist in a state of greater simplicity and consequently may be more accurately contemplated.

This veneration for popular culture as embodying enduring human values was to be a powerful theme in popular nineteenth-century Conservatism.

Yet Wordsworth and other Romantic poets and writers were not content to affirm the beauty of nature and the bucolic wisdom of the rural masses. At the intellectual level, the Romantc revolt was a protest against the rationalistic philosophies of the Enlightenment of the eighteenth century. Following Burke closely and deliberately, S. T. Coleridge affirmed that man was altogether too complex and irrational blandly to obey the dictates of arbitrary secular concepts. These tended to exaggerate human capacities. Man could only fulfil his responsibilities to the institutions and customs of the society to which he belonged. Like Burke, Coleridge recoiled from the individualism of Paine and believed that only by men keeping faith with their obligations could a common national community come about. Only by restoring religion to the primary position which it had once enjoyed could this be achieved. For Coleridge, religion was the foundation of politics. To conserve the political constitution it was necessary to preserve the religious constitution. Coleridge came to see that the ultimate ends of man and society are beyond his grasp, understanding and reason [4.4]. More than any other early nineteenth-century thinker, Coleridge reaffirmed Anglican ideals. Indeed, for Coleridge, the alliance between Church and State was the first line of defence for a prescriptive constitution against the great enemies, Reason and Progress. Coleridge dreamed of a 'National Church' bestowing spiritual leadership and moral example and through the ministrations of the Clerisy (a group of secular intellectuals) raising the educational standards of the citizenry.

For Coleridge, then, religion had a vital role to play in the life of society but his is not an intensely emotional religion. Rather, it is a utilitarian force, a cultural and sociological necessity in a changing and unsettled world.

Like Burke, Coleridge was prepared to rouse the country against radical reformers. His *Lay Sermons*, written in 1817 and 1818, were a warning to the British upper and middle classes to beware of radicalism, to keep to the ways of the old constitution, to look to the leadership of the landed classes even in an increasingly commercial age, to obey the king and to love the church.[22] The *Sermons* are an appeal to better and more honorable living, not to better thinking, not to more radical politics. Even more than Burke, Coleridge saw the need for public morality, as well as prescriptive traditionalism, to be the foundation of social order and just as strongly as Burke perceived the necessity for the state to dedicate itself to ethical objectives. 'Men, I still think, ought to be weighed, not counted.' Coleridge was a social Conservative, believing in hierarchy, order and discipline but he emphasised the obligations which went with property, the demands of paternalism as well as the extravagance of aristocratic consumption. Nevertheless, Coleridge seems to have had a more sophisticated understanding of change and progress than Burke had. Coleridge's Conservatism, at least, was the product of the tension between the forces of change and the forces of order. The ideal State that he described in *On the Constitution of Church and State* (1830) comprised three divisions, the landed interest (to provide stability and premanence), the commercial and professional classes (to provide progress and freedom) and the Church (to provide education and civilisation). It was in the tension and in the synthesis of these divisions that Coleridge's Conservatism consisted. He saw that industrialism was threatening the old society of orders and to conserve it required harmony and balance between old and new elements. In promoting this balance, Coleridge went further than Burke would have done in the direction of State intervention. He envisaged, for example, a State system of education, a sure sign of movement away from the Burkean origins. More than most Conservative thinkers of this generation, he sympathised with the poor and the underprivileged. In some of the fiercest denunciations of the society around him penned by any British author, Coleridge deplored the breakdown of paternalism and the exploitation of the masses. He pitied the tragic casualties of *laissez-faire*. The State must intervene to protect the victims of industrialisation from the factory owners, and the gentry must exercise their paternal responsibilities to protect and to educate those more vulnerable than they. Burke's *laissez-faire* ideas meant little to Coleridge. The fact that Coleridge came out against Parliamentary Reform in 1830 does not allow us to conclude that he was a 'reactionary'. He believed that the commercial and manufacturing interest already had social influence aplenty. Like Burke, however, he believed that political power should represent property and that at the political level a balance had to be struck between the competing demands of different forms of property. Unlike Burke, however, Coleridge saw that the welfare of the poor was a legitimate area for State action. And Coleridge was much less inclined than most Romantic Conservatives to build medieval castles in the air and to retreat into rural simplicity. He does, at least, endeavour to make room for the new interests, classes and problems of the industrial revolution in his philosophy.

THE TORY PARTY AND PEELITE CONSERVATISM (1812–1846)

Romantic Conservatism was articulated as a social and intellectual response to the French Revolution and, later, to Benthamite utilitarianism. It was not primarily a political ideology and it was certainly not a party ideology because no Tory party can be said to have existed before the death of the Younger Pitt in 1806 at the very earliest. Although Pitt had tried to pilot the nation through the storm of the revolutionary period he always remained a non-party man. Although he cultivated the surge of patriotism which swept around the established order in Church and State he did not try to make party political capital out of it. Pitt was patriot, not a party politician. And although he presided over the 'Tory' repression of the 1790s he never acknowledged his leadership of a 'Tory' party. After his death, however, some of the leading members of the old governing coalition began to organise themselves into a coherent group. By the time of the ministry of Liverpool (1812–27) it begins to make sense to speak in terms of a Tory government pursuing Tory policies and appealing to a Tory public opinion. Liverpool's government conciliated the landed interest with the Corn Law of 1815 but its fiscal policies which sought to promote industrial capitalism offended against the nostalgic rural verities of Cobbett, Scott and Southey. Supporters of strong and responsible government in an age of revolution might rally round the ministry of Liverpool as they had rallied round the ministry of Pitt but they were increasingly divided on a succession of key political questions, including Parliamentary Reform and Catholic Emancipation.

Some of these tensions may be seen in the career of George Canning, perhaps the most significant figure in the development of Toryism between Pitt and Peel. Disraeli always recognised Canning's importance in the pantheon of Tory statesmen and he was unquestionably the most dynamic figure in the political circles of his generation. As editor of the *Anti-Jacobin* in the 1790s he showed that he had imbibed the Burkean fundamentals. He borrowed much, too, from the Romantic intellectuals of his time. As a very great Foreign Secretary, Canning showed that he recognised the real power of assertive nationalism, although he was horrified at the possibility of popular revolution against legitimate authority, whether in Greece, Portugal or in South America. At home, Canning, like most Tories of his day, opposed Parliamentary reform. For one acknowledged as a 'Liberal' or progressive Tory, his arguments were disappointingly negative [5.1]. There are, consequently, many similarities between Canning's position on the issue and that adopted by the Ultra-Tories in the years immediately before the 1832 Reform Act [5.2]. On the great question of Catholic Emancipation, however, Canning was prepared to wait for the opinions of his fellow countrymen to catch up with his own reformist tendencies.

For many years, of course, the issue seriously divided the Tory party and a considerable body of anti-Catholic and anti-Irish literature was produced, especially when the Catholic Association began to mobilise the Roman Catholic population of Ireland. The issue encapsulated many powerful elements in the Toryism of the early nineteenth century: the survival of the Union, the defence of the established constitution in Church and State, the place of the established Church in Ireland, the defence of property, law and order. The discussion over whether Catholic Emancipation might be conceded to the Irish as a right or as a calculated concession or not at all was ended by the Clare election and by Wellington's capitulation in 1829. He had, of course, no alternative. To have resisted further would have endangered public order in both Ireland and England. Nevertheless, Catholic Emancipation shattered the unity of the Tory forces which had governed the country for many years and made possible the passing of the Reform Act of 1832 by the Whig administration of Lord Grey.

The fact that 'Toryism' before 1832 could encompass such a wide spectrum of opinion suggests that it lacked a precise ideological as well as political focus. Peelite Conservatism[23] was an attempt to provide a coherent Conservative response to the trauma of Catholic Emancipation and the defeat and divisions suffered over the 1832 Reform Act. It was Peel's achievement at the political level to rebuild the organisation and morale of his party in opposition until the sweeping election victory of 1841 inaugurated the great administration of 1841–46. At the social and economic level Peelite Conservatism sought to bring the ideas of old Toryism into line with the new world of industrialisation and urbanisation; an attempt to generate industrial and economic growth while protecting the powers and privileges of the landed interest and preserving what could be preserved of the structure of the old constitution. It was a gospel of modernisation and reform – reform, in particular, of manifest abuses. Finally, it was an ideology intended to promote the unity of a not very disciplined party which faced the uncertain world ushered in by the Whig Reform Act of 1832.

Yet Peelite Conservatism emphasised and sought to preserve many of the traditional elements of the old Toryism. It was the gospel of strong and sound government, of law and order, of the defence of property and the preservation of the constitution. Peel's Conservatism was less the desperate rallying cry of a party in opposition than an appeal to the national interest in an age of dangerous radicalism. He preached the gospel of sound administration, governmental expertise and professionalism in politics. At the same time, he commended the institutions of the country to the nation: he revered the monarchy, the Church and the old balanced constitution but believed that the reform of diseased limbs might in the long run enable the body politic to survive [5.3]. At a time when the privileges of the established Church were meeting rising criticism Peelite propagandists stoutly defended the principle of Establishment. Peel himself regarded the defence of Church property as a touchstone of Conservatism at a time when the Whig party was committed to the lay appropriation of ecclesiastical revenues and when the Commons was no longer an exclusively

Anglican body. 'Patently in need of reform but lacking autonomous powers, it was dependent for necessary legislation on a parliament which legally had ceased to be either Anglican or Protestant. If reform was to be imposed by its enemies, the state connection which had been its guarantee might prove its undoing.'[24]

At the same time, Peelite Conservatism turned its face towards the future. Almost as soon as the Reform Act had passed it was well understood that the fortunes of the party could only be improved by engrafting on to old attitudes a genuine acceptance of the Reform Act. If Ultra-Conservatism were to triumph then the party would be faced with oblivion. Even before the Tamworth Manifesto, the major signposts of the New Conservatism were becoming clear [5.4]. Issued during the election campaign of 1834–35 on behalf of his minority government, the Manifesto was not a programme of measures but a ringing declaration of the direction which the Conservative Party must take in the new political world which the Reform Act of 1832 had created. Peel had said as much before. In this document Peel, in fact, disclaims 'the contentions of party' in favour of 'the maintenance of order and good government' which requires full public – as opposed to party – confidence. Peel was yoking the new electors of 1832 to the old constitution, assuming and preaching that their fortunes and their property might be at risk if radical reform ran riot. His economic attitudes and reforms were congenial to their interests and, on the whole, he was careful to advance no proposal which might alienate them. Schemes for social reform – on housing, working conditions and education – received little encouragement from Peel. Peel, then, had to argue from the appeal to stability through the defence of old institutions to the appeal to change through the conciliation of new interests, classes and, indeed, voters. Reform was now announced to be desirable, if 'undertaken in a friendly temper, combining with the firm maintenance of established rights the correction of proved abuses and the redress of real grievances' [5.5]. The politics of Ultra-Conservatism was repudiated by the politics of cautious reform and progress.

The quality of Peel's Conservatism was ideally suited to the needs of an industrialising economy. Peel understood the new industrial world and had a clear conception of the country's future. His great budgets of 1842 and 1845 together with the Bank Charter Act of 1844 laid the fiscal foundations for mid-Victorian prosperity. In all this Peel was no less doctrinaire than many a later Liberal or Socialist. He brought to bear on the problems of his day a remarkably rigid adherence to the 'Liberal–Tory' ideas of Huskisson, an adherence which was partly responsible for the confusion that some of his measures fell into. Furthermore his unquestioning acceptance of free trade ideas prevented any pragmatic regulation of the untidy railway boom of the 1840s.[25] Ultimately, his willingness to contemplate the extermination of the fiscal privileges of the landed interest – the structural backbone of the Conservative party – during the early 1840s confirmed the powerful suspicions of Peel, the manufacturer's son, entertained by the landed interest. Furthermore, the Maynooth grant of 1845 made loyal Anglicans shudder at this subsidy to Popery [5.6]. Nevertheless, the ultimate touchstone of commitment to the landed interest was the Corn Laws, which kept prices high and deterred imports. The failure of the Irish potato harvest led him – to some extent unnecessarily – to enact the permanent repeal of the Corn Laws in 1846 [5.7]. Peel lost the confidence of his party whose subsequent divisions consigned it to twenty years of opposition. Those who remained loyal to Peel formed a distinct party for a few years until, after Peel's death in 1850, they drifted into the Liberal party. Peel's attempt to convert the Tory party to the philosophy of Tamworth had failed.[26] Peel had always found it necessary to walk the delicate tightrope between the conflicting elements and interests in his party. This was why he was fond of playing the patriotic card, of assuming the mantle of national statesmanship rather than that of party politician. Indeed, Peel sometimes seemed uncomfortable in playing the party game, looking to the national interest, even at the cost of his own consistency (as in 1832 and 1846), and even popularity (as in 1829 and 1846).

It would, of course, be mistaken to suppose that 'Tory' or 'Conservative' ideas were confined to the official party of Peel. The early decades of the nineteenth century were particularly rich in extra-parliamentary Tory opinion. Inspired by Cobbett, a generation of Tory writers and Tory reformers recoiled in horror at the evils of industrialisation and urbanisation and sought a retreat to rural solace [5.8]. They dreamed of a golden age of rural paternalism, class harmony and community concern. But a party dominated in the constituencies by the landed interest could not conceivably tinker with schemes to increase the Poor Rate while a party wishing to appeal to manufacturers could not possibly intervene to improve working hours and conditions. Although bereft of official political support, Tory radicals launched a series of campaigns in 1831, first for a Ten Hours Bill, then, a few years later, a campaign against the

Whig Poor Law Amendment Act of 1834. There was considerable support and sympathy for such causes in Tory periodicals but their failure closed the Conservative door on such populist veins of Tory radical opinion and activity. Thereafter, they merged into the swelling stream of Chartism. Tory radicalism may have been a lost cause in the 1830s but it occupies an important place in the history of British Conservatism. Tory radicalism linked the organic Toryism of Burke and the Romantic Conservatism of Coleridge and others to the 'Young England' movement of the 1840s, and the 'One Nation' traditions of Disraeli and the Fourth Party later in the century. As a sustained critique of the theories of liberal individualism and free trade economics, it was to have a long and influential history.

Not all extra-parliamentary Toryism was of this radical variety. After the 1832 Reform Act a large number of Conservative Operative Societies sprang up to organise lower-class Conservative voters. By 1836 over one hundred such societies were in existence. Many had a charitable and even prudential aspect, although most of them were subsidised by the local gentry and, especially, Peel's Conservative party machine. What the Loyalist Associations had achieved in the 1790s the scores of Operative Conservative Associations repeated in the 1830s [5.9]. In an age of dramatic economic change and at a time of popular radicalism these societies were pledged to the defence of the old constitution and to the inculcation of deferential habits among lower class voters.[27] Even in the age of Peelite Conservatism, the old paternalism continued to flourish and the deference and obedience of the lower orders was fastidiously cultivated from above.

DISRAELIAN CONSERVATISM (1839–1880)

After the Repeal of the Corn Laws the role of the Landed Interest in what – significantly – was re-named the Protectionist party became overwhelming. As the personnel and policies of Peel drifted over to the Liberals in the 1850s the Protectionists became a reactionary party of the landed classes. Although the party of Derby and Disraeli did attract a limited amount of support from middle-class elements in the towns it was largely dependent on traditional influences: the church, the corporations, local families and, not least, on corruption.[28] On the eve of the 1867 Reform Act landed MPs outnumbered business MPs by 4:1 in the Protectionist party (in the Liberal party, they were roughly equal). The Anglican prejudices of the Tory squires were no adequate basis for a governing party and the Protectionists spent the period 1846–66 in the wastelands of opposition. It was to be Disraeli's function in the history of British Conservatism to wean his party away from its commitment to agricultural protection. After 1849, with the indispensable assistance of Derby, Disraeli steadily moved his party back into the world of the industrial revolution and endowed it with public professions which enabled it once more to become a party of government.

Unavoidably, the enterprise has been obscured by generations of party propaganda, rhetorical exaggeration, literary romance and sheer political nostalgia. 'It was left to Disraeli', writes Arthur Bryant, 'to recreate Conservatism and to lead the crusade of an ancient national party to restore the rights and liberties of the people'.[29] The customary mythology credits Disraeli with transforming and thus saving his party, of leading it in the direction of social concern and compassion ('Social Reform'), of persuading it to trust the people and meet democracy half way (the 1867 Reform Act), of exhorting it to appeal to all classes, especially the deferential Tory working-class voter ('One Nation'), and to establish a great world-wide empire (Imperialism). All this was achieved while preserving the framework of the established constitution and safeguarding the institutions of the nation. The inspiration for this compelling vision is deemed to have come from Disraeli himself. In his Young England days in the 1840s he had dreamed of uniting the classes under the benevolent leadership of an enlightened, patriarchal aristocracy. Repudiating the Liberal individualism and the free trade politics of Peel, he yearned for a revival of the traditions of Church and King in order to restore national unity and reinvigorate the people. And he lent further enhancement to these dreams at particular times of his career for particular purposes. What these ideas owe to Romantic Conservatives like Coleridge should not be underestimated: 'Fundamentally it is impossible to understand Disraeli in terms of the middle or later Victorian periods. He grew up with the Romantic Movement. His temperament was naturally in tune with it and his education and foreign travels fed the romantic vein.'[30]

There is, in Disraeli's thought, a certain cohesion and a certain consistency. These largely consist in the stylish repetition of key elements in early nineteenth-century Conservatism. Like Burke, Disraeli acknowledged the spiritual basis of society and venerated the Anglican establishment. He repudiated the philosophies of abstract rights, foremost among which he included utilitarianism. He borrowed from Burke the organic conception of society and was fond of repeating his warnings against the dangers of innovation. From this appreciation of the continuity of social life he derived the role of historical tradition in developing the national character and the institutions of a country. His account of English history, as Quinton noted, is seemingly derived from Coleridge.[31] From it, he conjured up an updated version of the hoary old prejudices against corrupt Whig lords, disloyal Dissenters and thrusting, middle-class, monied men, enjoying property and power without responsibility. Nevertheless, the powerful emphasis on elitism in Disraeli's thinking underlines the importance of talent, experience and service as well as the hereditary ownership of land. In revivifying the function of the landed interest Disraeli places so much weight upon paternalism and the obligations of property that at times he appears to be vindicating leadership for its own sake and not the leadership of the landed class.[32] Indeed, by the time of his death, the Conservative party was opening its doors wide to the new industrial elite of the towns.

Perhaps the most effective means of coming to grips with Disraeli's Conservatism is to understand the cast of mind which produced it. Throughout his life he assumed that traditional civilisation was threatened by a combination of social and political dangers. The emerging urban world of the industrial revolution threatened the old balanced constitution while the selfishness of Whig oligarchs in enriching their class threatened to provoke revolution.[33] What was vitally needed in this age of crisis was a restoration of faith in the ideals and values embodied in the old constitution [6.1]. Political initiatives ought to be directed at strengthening, not undermining, these values. This could only be done by seeking to preserve as much of the institutional heritage of the country as could safely be preserved to enable people to retain their spiritual links with the past. This, of course, required the continued primacy of the landed interest. By this he meant, not simply the territorial aristocracy but 'the population of our innumerable villages . . . the crowds in our rural towns . . . that estate of the poor which, in my opinion, has been already dangerously tampered with'. This looks dangerously like the politics of nostalgia, designed to maintain a social order dominated by the clientage systems of the landed aristocracy and gentry. To avoid the political obliteration which such a set of objectives might bring upon his party, Disraeli embarked upon a series of brilliant and bewildering ideological and political strategems designed both to satisfy the powerful political and psychological needs he was arousing while shifting his party on to more generally attractive political ground.

There was urgent need for it. Not only had the Protectionist party spent twenty years languishing in opposition. After the death of Palmerston in 1865, the Liberalism of Gladstone appeared to post an imminent threat to the traditional institutions of the country. Solid defence of the constitution from the opposition benches was now quite insufficient. Disraeli's first response, paradoxically, was the Reform Act of 1867. When his Liberal opponents failed to pass a reform measure in 1866 Disraeli, to the surprise of many, passed a measure which was not only more radical than the Liberals had envisaged but more extensive than he had himself intended. Once his objectives are grasped, however, his tactics become intelligible. He realised that modest tinkering with the franchise would merely put on the registers more liberally inclined electors. A bolder measure would bring respectable, and probably deferential, working men into the electoral system. Better to pass an emphatically Conservative Bill, outflank his opponents, and transform in the interests of his party an electoral system on which they had failed to win a single election with a parliamentary majority, with the exception of 1841. There was a further consideration, though this was uttered with the benefit of hindsight. In uniting to the landed interest not merely sections of the deferential working class but also elements of the propertied middle class, Disraeli would be constructing a broad, sober and respectable Conservative coalition. Such a coalition, in government or opposition, would safeguard the country from Liberal and Radical innovations. In this way, the surprisingly generous Reform Act of 1867 could be depicted as serving Conservative objectives [6.2]. The Act may have seen the birth of 'Tory Democracy' but Disraeli's fear of democracy should never be underestimated.

A further distinctive element in Disraelian Conservatism was the rhetorical promise of social and humanitarian reform, which he began to express in 1872. Those with wealth and property had responsibilities to the less fortunate that could be fulfilled not only by charitable and paternalistic activities of the traditional kind, but in the new industrial society, also by the State. Disraeli believed that the condition of the people was a central concern for politicians. Since the 1832 Reform Act, the middle classes had secured representation and had advanced their interests at the expense of the working classes. The Conservative Party must become the part of popular welfare [6.3]. 'Tory Democracy' concerned not merely the people's electoral rights but their welfare, providing Conservatism with both a popular and a legislative purpose. 'One nation' bound together the classes of society in a powerful web of reciprocal obligations which made inequalities bearable and elite rule legitimate. It also provided a corporate, interventionist alternative to the self-help philosophy of Liberalism at the national level. (At the local level, Liberal municipal interventionism was most marked). The object of politics was to reconcile the classes, not to foment conflict between them. Only thus could genuine sentiments of patriotism, national unity and social and political stability be guaranteed.

Historians, of course, have been keen to point to the contrast between Disraeli's rhetoric and his achievement, the failure of his second ministry to prepare a considered programme of reforms and, still more, its failure to legislate one. A few achievements were registered: minor improvements in housing and sanitation, the sale of food and drugs Act, minor factory acts and a river pollution act. The list is not a particularly long one. Historians, moreover, have at one time or another stressed the non-political origin of such legislation as did pass and the low priorities which social reform enjoyed in the cabinet, not least by Disraeli, who rapidly became involved in foreign affairs. The landed interest, furthermore, regarded the welfare of the lower orders as their – or their class's – responsibility and not that of a powerful state, which would need vast increases in taxation to fund an enormous bureaucracy. If, however, performance was less than promise it would be a mistake to dismiss the social welfare aspirations of Disraeli. If he was not able to convince his party of the need for a coherent legislation programme of reform, still less develop one himself, he had laid down the objectives and stated his lofty ambition. After all, his party in 1874 had no mandate for such a programme nor were contemporary expectations of his government equivalent to those of the twentieth century. His ministry's record, however defective, is better than that of most nineteenth-century ministries. Historians too frequently measure Disraeli's admittedly piecemeal but cumulatively impressive set of small reforms by the standards of the great national reforms of the twentieth century. Such anachronism should be avoided. So should the expectation that Disraeli – an old and a sick man by the 1870s – should have been able within a few years to convert his party and the political classes to the need for a revolution in the range of government actions. Of course, as his party began to attract urban middle class elements in the 1870s, the vision seemed to become *less* rather than *more* likely to be realised. How permanent its influence was to be we shall see later.

Perhaps the most enduring of Disraeli's bequests to the Conservative party was his vision of enlightened imperialism. To the throne and the altar was now added the British Empire. In his great Crystal Palace speech of 24 June 1872 Disraeli outlined his vision of 'a great country, an imperial country' commanding the seas and bestriding not merely Europe but the world [6.4]. This was Disraeli at his most innovative and – probably because there was little imperialist precedent in earlier Conservative literature – his briefest.

Once again, historians have shown how little Disraeli achieved in his bid to make Britain an imperial power. Nevertheless, his rhetoric had an immediate impact. As the party of Empire, the Conservatives acquired a new national purpose now far removed from the exclusive interests of the landed classes. They acquired a new electoral image which expanded their old-fashioned 'Church and King' patriotism into an up-to-date projection of nationalism. Disraeli's imperialism, intentionally or not, was an excellent political riposte to Gladstone's well-publicised moral concerns. Not that all of Disraeli's own party accepted and all of Gladstone's Liberal party repudiated imperialist objectives. Disraeli himself had described the colonies as 'a millstone round our necks' in 1852. The rhetoric of empire could be put to good political use in 1872 and after and this is exactly what Disraeli did. What he could never have envisaged was how powerfully and how thoroughly his imperialist vision was to permeate the mentality of British Conservatism.

The Conservative tradition underwent considerable change in the decades between Burke and Disraeli but it continued to focus attention upon the need to preserve traditional institutions and a prescriptive constitution, even if its preservation required surgery. Burkeian ideals of organic change were still being echoed with remarkable similarity by Disraeli nearly a century later. As he said in his Manchester speech, 'In a progressive country change is constant and the great question is not whether you should resist change which is inevitable, but whether that change should be carried out in deference to the manners, the customs, the laws and the traditions of a people or whether it should be carried out in deference to abstract principles and arbitrary and general doctrines.' As he proudly proclaimed, 'the programme of the Conservative Party is to maintain the Constitution of the country'.[34] And he revelled in the immunity from revolution which the continuity of British history made possible [6.5].

Disraeli did more, however, than re-establish the electoral fortunes of the Conservative party. He did more than equip it with a set of political objectives. What he did was to endow the Conservative party with a sense of enduring and unique national mission. As early as his _Vindication of the English Constitution_ he had announced in typically Disraelian prose:

> The Tory party in this country is the national party; it is the really democratic party of England. It supports the institutions of the country, because they have been established for the common good, and because they secure the equality of civil rights, without which, whatever may be its name, no government can be free, and based upon which principle, every government, however it may be styled, is, in fact a Democracy.[35]

Throughout his career, Disraeli continued to feed Tory prejudice, to heap flattery upon compliment, to identify the destiny of the nation with the fortunes of the Conservative party. It may be without doubt one of the most remarkable exercises in political seduction ever undertaken in the history of Great Britain. And with respect to the enormous prestige which has always attached to Disraeli's reputation – and still does today – it must be counted one of the most successful [6.6].

More of a Romantic and more of a visionary than Peel, Disraeli nevertheless preached the same message: that in the new age of industrialisation adaptation must occur but without losing sight of old values. Disraelian Conservatism marked the abandonment of the old 'Church and King' Toryism of the landed interest and the transition to a series of alliances between land and industry, government and the professions and, not least, between the classes. How far Disraeli matched action to ambition and how far a pious consistency underlay his actions are not the present issues. At the ideological level, he gave Conservatism a new content and a new direction – 'Tory Democracy', 'One Nation', 'Imperialism' – but always stressed the traditional social anchorages.[36] The historian of British government might reasonably expose the gap between ideal and reality, the contrast between promise and performance but the historian of ideas notes the enduring power of Disraelian concepts and imagery for over a century after his death in 1881. That this was far more than a piece of rhetorical pretence is attested by the party's ultimately successful adaptation to an industrial society and its concurrent appeal to middle- and working-class electors. Historians may be right in observing that whatever their rhetoric Conservative leaders in office behave like Peel but it is always the visions of Disraeli which they evoke when appealing to a popular audience.

LATE VICTORIAN CONSERVATISM – TO THE FIRST WORLD WAR

Conservatism in the late Victorian era was an ideological response to the steady march of democracy: the 1867 Reform Act was followed by the Secret Ballot Act of 1872, the Corrupt Practices Act of 1883, the Reform Act of 1884 and the Redistribution Act of 1885. As the old Liberal, Goldwin Smith, remarked in 1893, 'Under the belief that she has a monarchical government and an hereditary upper chamber, which assure her stability and safety, England has plunged into a democracy more unbridled than that of the United States under conditions far more dangerous.'[37] Nevertheless, and not a little paradoxically, the Conservatives became at this time a party of government: the Liberal split over Home Rule in 1886 brought Joseph Chamberlain's urban Liberal-Unionists over to Salisbury's landed and suburban Conservatives. A Conservative alliance of property owners was being created. Consequently, Salisbury's Conservative party was the natural party of government until the Liberal victory of 1906. Conservative ideology in this period, then, was a ruling ideology of a highly elitist and inegalitarian, landed and commercial, regime which was rapidly adapting itself to industrial capitalism. Within the shell of old orders, practices and institutions – and some not so old – new social and economic groups were being integrated into the establishment. At this period, the middle classes began to flock into the Conservative party – not merely the industrial bourgeoisie but also suburban, white collar occupational groups, especially in the provinces. Many of them identified themselves with the landed aristocracy. Consequently, this was an Indian summer for the old order. Complacent, and often very fulsome, eulogies of the ancient institutions of the country were a commonplace.

Lord Salisbury, Conservative leader from 1885 to 1902, among many others, was determined to defend those institutions. He intended to use the Conservative Party to slow down and control – it was impossible to prevent – the march towards democracy. Salisbury was no blind reactionary. He knew that to stand stubbornly in the way of progress might do more harm than good [7.1]. To resist change for the sake of resisting change might endanger the political and social order, and the civilised values which they fostered. 'Conservatism for him was not a counter-attack on the opponents of religion, property, and the social order, but a fighting retreat, stubborn and slow, involving constant rearguard actions and continual regrouping, and interspersed with brief periods of rest on a precarious equilibrium.'[38] Just as Disreali had attacked the Conservatism of Peel, so Salisbury, early in his career, reacted against the 'One Nation' Conservatism of Disraeli. He believed that popular politics, with its attendant social tensions, class groupings and surges of national excitement threatened the texture of national unity and, in particular, undermined the old mixed constitution of King, Lords and Commons. Salisbury was quite clear in his mind that the old aristocracy would have to accept some sort of partnership with the middle classes. What he doubted was the will and the capacity of the middle classes to defend their own interests in an age of working-class politics. Unlike Disraeli, Salisbury conceived of politics as a struggle of classes and interests. There is little trace left here of Burke's Conservative vision of conservation and ordered change. The ancient constitution, for Salisbury, was an embattled rampart with Liberals, Radicals and Socialists swarming all over it. He gloomily concluded that the only alternative to the ultimate domination of the country by the trades unions would be a military dictatorship.

Indeed, a distinct shifting of emphasis towards a theoretical band of right-wing politics was taking place in Conservative circles, within and without the Conservative Party. Foremost among these right-wing thinkers was Sir Henry Maine, whose very significantly titled early works *Ancient Law* (1861) and *Village Communities* (1871) whetted Conservative appetites for his serious reservations about *Popular Government* (1886). For Maine, democracy would obliterate the traditional constitution but it would not lead to the elevation of the popular will. Order and stability would be threatened by popular unrest and might have to be re-established by military force. In a popular government, power would reside with small elites of party activists [7.2]. His vindication of the existing social order was derived, then, as much from his horror of the alternatives as from his appreciation of its inherent qualities. In the work of Sir James Fitzjames Stephen we move even further away from traditions of ancestral wisdom and into avowed justifications of individualism. Stephen's most famous work, *Liberty, Equality, Fraternity* (1873), almost goes beyond Burkean Conservatism in its stress on the virtues of obedience, leadership and strong government. For Stephen, egalitarian experiments are futile. They can neither prevent groups from monopolising political power nor can they suppress the individual's pursuit of his own enhancement [7.3]. But, as Stephen remarked, 'Neither legislation nor public opinion ought to be meddlesome.' The cautious state paternalism of Disraeli was being discarded. For example, in the work of W. H. Mallock, especially his *Aristocracy and Evolution* (1898), State intervention was repudiated. Individualism and entrepreneurialism were inherently good and socially beneficial. Inequalities in society were inevitable. The welfare of the masses was beyond the power of the State to improve. The popular voice scarcely mattered.

By the end of the nineteenth century, then, Conservative voices were being raised against the evils of collectivism and Socialism. As Noel O'Sullivan has remarked: 'the conservative enemy is no longer liberalism but socialism; and what happens as a result, is that conservatism visibly begins to adopt and defend the liberal values it had formerly opposed'.[39] Indeed, within a very few years almost the entire repertoire of twentieth-century Conservative arguments against the dangers of State centralisation had been rehearsed. The historian William Lecky warned in his *Democracy and Liberty* (1898) against the bureaucratic State, against the oppressive tentacles of controls and restrictions and against the rising power of trade unions. Like so many Conservative thinkers of this age, he took a pessimistic view of class relationships, envisaging an unsettled future riddled with class conflict, from which only the authoritarian State could deliver society [7.4]. For Lecky, Socialism was destructive of liberties and free discussion. Socialism inhibited economic growth. Socialist egalitarianism impoverished the nation. Socialist principles were incompatible with free trade and commerce. Socialism asserted class loyalties in place of patriotism. Before the turn of the century the Conservative case against Socialism had been very well developed. It may be doubted whether the twentieth century has added very much to it.

With the repudiation of Socialism went the celebration of Capitalism. These tendencies were epitomised in the early years of the twentieth century by the formation and activities of the British Constitution Association. In its literature and at its meetings the Society not only railed against the stultifying effect of collectivism on a free market economy but against most other forms of State intervention: free, universal education, old age pensions, unemployment benefit and school meals [7.5]. In the age of Salisbury the Conservatives had come to believe in cheap and minimal government as fervently as the Liberals. Occasional instances of State help for the deserving poor were no substitute for self help among the working classes. Salisbury offered the defence of property, social and political stability, a minimum of government interference and the bland professionalism of the true politician which bred business confidence. 'The State, for Burke the most important pillar of Christian morality, had become for Salisbury little more than an agency to defend property.'[40] [7.6] However incomplete Disraeli's 'One Nation' welfare policies had been there had at least been something more than a pretence of defending humble people against exploitation. Disraeli, for example, had recognised the right to picket in 1871 but Salisbury refused to reverse the Taff Vale Judgement of 1901. Indeed, Salisbury openly repudiated Disraeli's sympathy for the eight-hour day in 1892. It must be said that in practical terms Disraeli's vision of a 'One Nation' society does not seem to have had much impact upon the executive Conservatism of Salisbury.

Not surprisingly, these tendencies elicited from the outset a reassertion of Disraelian Conservatism. The 'Tory Democracy' of Lord Randolph Churchill has been dismissed by a recent authority as 'a collection of postures and slogans, whose main purpose was to serve as a vehicle for its author'.[41] Nevertheless, Churchill's ideas impressed some contemporaries and they have appeared to later generations of Conservatives as exciting extensions, not merely affirmations, of Disraeli's legacy. There was, indeed, a considerable debate in Tory journals and periodicals about the direction which the party ought to take after the death of Disraeli in 1881 and Churchill and his 'Fourth Party' plunged into it.[42] Churchill had some conception of the need of the Conservative party to become more populist and more accountable. In particular, he saw the need for his party to appeal to new voters from the working classes [7.7]. Although this did not go to the lengths imagined by some contemporaries, it was a dramatic bid for the mantle of Disraeli. Churchill's resignation from Salisbury's government in 1886 thus marked the failure of his challenge, personal, political and ideological. It is a failure which should not arouse nostalgic sentiments. Churchill's credentials as a reformer were less than impeccable. He opposed, for example, franchise reform. What motivated him was the idea of *popular support for* the traditional props of Conservatism: the Throne, the Church, the House of Lords. He was not interested in decisive shifts of political power. Even in Churchill's Conservatism, then, the element of patrician reform from above was still far more compelling than the demand for change from below.[43]

This period of redefinition in the history of Conservative ideology is further remarkable for the emergence of Unionism as an influential element in the Conservative tradition. Gladstone's conversion to Home Rule for Ireland in December 1885 drove both the Whigs (led by Hartington) and the Liberal-Unionists (almost 100, led by Joseph Chamberlain) into opposition. This partnership on the issue of the Union of Ireland with England between Whigs, Liberal-Unionists and Conservatives was initially intended to be a temporary and pragmatic means of defeating Home Rule. Salisbury made the defence of the Union a powerful defining characteristic of his party. In fact it created a permanent realignment of political forces – and one, furthermore, which helped to ensure the political dominance of the Conservative party from 1885 to 1906. The impact of Home Rule was to accelerate the drift of the propertied urban middle classes into the Conservative party, which increasingly appeared to be a party of capitalism, property and order [7.8]. The claim that Chamberlain brought with him a firm commitment to State intervention may be true in the short term[44] and it is the case that his son, Neville Chamberlain, was to be an exponent of interventionism in the 1920s, but the Conservative party of the period 1885–1925 was characterised far more by its commitment to individualism and free enterprise than to State action. The record of the Salisbury administration of 1886–92 on the social side was meagre. Even the County Councils Act of 1888 was a defeat for reformers since Poor Law and Taxation reforms were ignored. In the main, the Unionist connection probably hardened Conservative attitudes against interventionism. A separate Liberal-Unionist organisation lingered until 1911 but long before then many local Conservative associations had merged with their Unionist counterparts. Early in 1912 the Conservative and Unionist party was born.

Conservatism at the end of the nineteenth century, then, concerns consolidation: of the United Kingdom, of the rights of capital over labour, of the power of the State over the nation and the rights of the ruling establishment. Most of all, Conservatism concerned the expansion and consolidation of the empire. Conservatism, in this as much else, caught the mood of the moment. The swelling of an aggressive, patriotic and imperialist sentiment was reflected in the work of men like Seeley (*The Expansion of England* (1883)) and Froude (*Oceana* (1886)) and in the jingoism surrounding the Boer War. Disraeli had bequeathed the idea of an imperial mission of 'a great country, an imperial country, a country where your sons, when they rise, rise to paramount positions, and obtain not merely the respect of your countrymen, but command the respect of the world.' His successors developed this assumption in two ways. One

(Salisbury) was to generalise his vision of the imperial mission [7.9]. The other (Chamberlain) was to outline schemes for imperial reorganisation.

This latter was to dominate the imperialist ideology of late Victorian Conservatism. Schemes for the organisation of the empire must be viewed in an economic context. British economic prosperity could no longer be automatically maintained in free competition against foreign rivals. British industry now needed protection in the shape of tariffs which made the penetration of domestic and imperial markets more difficult. Furthermore, a tighter organisation of the empire would protect British access to raw materials as well as markets. The campaign for Tariff Reform and the personality of Joseph Chamberlain provided the vehicles for the imperialist aspirations of late Victorian Conservatism. Most of all, they fastened to these economic arguments an idea of 'Social Imperialism', by which the revenue deriving from tariff reform might be put to welfare purposes at home. Chamberlain dreamed of an imperial federation and possibly, even, a federal council [7.10]. Unable to convert his party from within, he resigned from the cabinet in 1903. He then proceeded to fail to convince it from without. Nevertheless, after the election defeat of 1906, and despite the opposition of Balfour, the Tariff Reformers captured the party, and proceeded to carry out a witch-hunt against free traders. The Conservatives had become an imperialist, tariff reform party.

In the years leading up to the First World War, however, the intense and powerful emotional impulses in late Victorian Conservatism were beginning to fragment. Serious contradictions were becoming apparent within British Conservatism. How could the party of capitalism reconcile itself to policies of 'Social Imperialism'? How could the party of law and order reconcile itself to the unpleasant tendency to countenance violence on the part of Irish Protestants in Ulster, something to which the Conservative party drifted perilously close in the years immediately before the First World War? How could the party of the constitution reconcile itself to attacks on that constitution during the liberal ministries of 1906–14? Why did the Conservatives accept the social reforms of the 1906–14 period with such relative equanimity while threatening the political stability of the United Kingdom by its resistance to Liberal constitutional measures? In the years immediately before the First World War the Conservative party wore its ideological clothing less convincingly than at any other time. At the political level, at least, Conservatism had reduced itself to the protection of property, the defence of tariff reform and the rights of Ulster Protestants. As Professor Marsh has aptly commented: 'The Conservative conscience stood in need of a new formulation.'[45]

THE INTER-WAR YEARS

The experience of the First World War revived traditional Conservative values. While the Conservative party itself supported the war and formed a coalition with the Liberals to further its prosecution, the tides of patriotic fervour and imperial loyalty put an end to the disruptive tendencies of earlier years. The war, furthermore, removed some embarrassments. Within six weeks of its outbreak, Irish Home Rule was on the statute book. Within two years, indeed, the Conservatives had gone far towards overcoming their distaste for further parliamentary reform, votes for women and national conscription. At the economic level, the Conservatives dropped their horror of collectivism. During the war the State presided over a degree of superintendence of the economy which would have been unthinkable to Conservatives of Salisbury's generation. Intervening to maximise industrial production, to foster high productivity, to promote peaceful industrial relations and even to encourage industrial rationalisation in the victorious war effort, central government showed that economic efficiency, military success and a return to parliamentary government were perfectly compatible objectives.

The essential point about post-war Conservatism, however, is that it sought to articulate a reasonable alternative to the ideologies of the left (Socialism and Communism) and those of the right (Nazism and Fascism). This left ample room for the pragmatism of Baldwin and the Conservative talk of the reconciliation – not the abolition – of social classes. Baldwin evoked a 'New Conservatism' in 1924, faintly reminiscent of Disraelian Conservatism. Some of the outstanding features of Baldwin's 'New Conservatism' include the emphasis he placed upon social harmony, the identification of the party leadership with the rank and file, social reform and the protection of the weak. The practical consequences of this brand of Conservatism can best be seen in the reforms of Neville Chamberlain at the Ministry of Health between 1924 and 1929. This moderate and sympathetic approach to social questions should not be cynically disregarded. As a consequence of the huge majority enjoyed by the 'National' government at the election of 1931 and retained in 1935 Baldwin was able to ignore his own traditional right wing and embark upon 'measures of empirical nationalisation, of piecemeal social welfare, and of economic pump-priming' which might otherwise not have been possible.[46]

Consequently, to depict the Conservative party of the inter-war years as the party of the establishment is scarcely illuminating. The land, the Church, the professions, the city and local chambers of commerce were indeed 'pillars of Conservatism in thin disguise',[47] but many changes to the economic life of the country occurred in the inter-war years.

In the last analysis, Conservatism was undoubtedly defensive, protecting property and power and the political system which legitimated them. Consequently, there were few *political* innovations in the inter-war period – although economic experiments abounded – and the political and social structures exhibited remarkable continuity despite the impact of world recession.

In this process, considerable importance attaches to the massive repetition of two key Conservative themes: the virtues of patriotism and the necessities of empire. Baldwin's idealisation of the English character may have been one of the primary agencies for the transmission of the former. The unique English commitment to liberty, compromise, fairness and moderation he identified with the Conservative traditions of the nineteenth century. There seems little doubt that this was a conscious representation. In the early 1930s Conservative writers and agents were instructed to cultivate a specifically *National* spirit in the country. As Baldwin told the 1932 Conference: 'our aims must be national and not party; our ideals must be national and not party'.[48] This ambition was one from which Baldwin sought personally and politically to profit as he revelled in the image of the rural squire, glowing with serene honesty. More distantly, the appeal of a simple, rural – and now threatened – social polity may have been enormously compelling both to a comfortable middle class which could readily identify with its values and to sections of the working class which might aspire to do so. His speeches are peppered with appeals for national unity, for government to be responsive to the needs of the people and for the people to heed the words of government [8.1]. In some ways, Baldwin's rhetoric is unctuous and platitudinous. It is, however, quite unlike that of most pre-1914 Conservative politicians.

Similarly, Conservative commitment to imperialist values soared after 1918 in inverse proportion as the political texture of the empire became weaker. Conservative obsession with imperialist issues, events, symbols, personalities and wars may be seen as a yearning for a world of magic, make-believe, fantasy and escapism for a society embattled by alien ideologies and apparently insoluble economic problems. More seriously, it reaffirmed the strength of hierarchical and militaristic tendencies which had powerful nostalgic effect. Baldwin, to be fair, was less conspicuous as an imperialist than as a patriot. Reforms in the government of India, for example, proceeded steadily after 1924 in spite of vociferous opposition within his own party. He was personally identified with the Imperial Conference of 1926 which laid down the principles of Commonwealth co-operation and thus the beginnings of the transition from Empire to Commonwealth [8.2]. His approach to imperial questions was pragmatic and realistic. His commitment to protection and imperial preference in October 1930 was a reaction to the world financial crisis, not a doctrinaire decision. As he said in a speech in Scotland in July 1934:

> Unionists were anxious to know whether what was being done by the government was always consistent with what they called Unionist principles. There were no political principles of any kind that had ever been laid down or ever supported by the party which could cope with the kind of problems this Government had to cope with to-day, and therefore the sheet was quite clean.
>
> The more these problems were tackled, the more interference it must mean with old habits. These interferences were neither Socialist, nor Liberal, nor Unionist. They were interferences that any Government that was really bold enough to tackle these problems must make.

These years witnessed a rapid retreat from, and then a cautious advance towards, the practice of State intervention. The increasing power of the State, the threat of competing ideologies at home and abroad and the seemingly irreversible growth in the size of economic units in capitalist society conspired to effect a new Conservative emphasis upon individualistic and libertarian values. It is not too much to affirm that in the 1920s the Conservatives raided the Liberal cupboard in their attempt to keep the Socialist wolf from the door.[49] War-time controls, of prices, investment, transport, food distribution and even of direct labour, were rapidly abandoned after the war. The economic policy of the 1920s, indeed, most of the inter-war period – free trade, a return to the gold standard, balanced budgets, lower taxes and reduced government expenditure – was a total repudiation of the collectivisation of the war years. This is not to suggest that individual Conservative measures lacked progressive merit nor that individual Conservative ministers lacked compassion and concern. Winston Churchill at the Exchequer from 1924 to 1929 and Neville Chamberlain from 1932 to 1935 angled many of their budget measures at the least privileged. Chamberlain's Chancellorship enjoyed notable successes in Housing, Factory legislation and Pensions. Nevertheless, official Conservative thinking stressed the helplessness of the country in the grip of world recession and market forces.

Hostility to State control was unquestionably one of the most familiar hallmarks of Conservative party propaganda in the inter-war period. At the political level, a nebulous 'freedom' from bureaucratic interference was deemed the supreme ethic insofar as it made possible the full expression of talent and the realisation of individual – and thus national – potential. At the economic level, the price mechanism, left to itself, would satisfy consumer demand and reward labour. Political liberty in a democracy was thus a function of a fully developed system of competitive capitalism [8.3] Such confident rhetoric could not be sustained after 1931. If unregulated market forces had brought the British economy to such a catastrophe, then there seemed little point in pursuing an economic policy based upon unregulated marked forces. In 1931, under enormous pressure from his party, Baldwin was forced to resume a policy of protective tariffs, a policy which he had abandoned in 1924 [8.4]. 'The power of the free export of capital and the free import of goods now accrued to the state.'[50]

The 1930s were not, however, to be remarkable only for the re-establishment of Protection. Gradually, but inexorably, the Conservatives abandoned the policy of minimal State intervention in industry. Even in the 1920s the government had taken upon itself the reorganisation of the railways and the subsidising of wages and profits in the coal mines. Government had created a single civil aviation organisation, a nationalised electricity grid and a public broadcasting monopoly, the BBC. Structural changes in the economy were prompting and promoting greater government intervention in economic life. The development of new industries, organised in large corporate units, often dependent upon shareholder capital, assured markets and government assistance, constituted a significant source of pressure upon government to inaugurate and expand protectionist policies and to become ever more closely involved in economic problems. To such industries as the petro-chemical, chemical, motor car and electricity industries unregulated and unrestricted free competition was unacceptably hazardous. The Great Depression made government aid and rationalisation more urgent. The National Government, therefore, not only established import quotas but managed and massaged the currency, regulated prices and output, influenced the location of industry, offered subsidies to some industries, supervised the rationalisation of others and even conducted sales drives through central agencies in yet others. Industries both new and old were caught up in this retreat from *laissez-faire* and the doctrines of nineteenth-century Liberalism.

Such a decisive transition in the economic philosophy of Conservatism did not occur without considerable head-shaking, enormous resentment and considerable discussion. The decisive intellectual inspiration, however, was the 'Middle Way', a tendency associated with Harold Macmillan and other Conservative MPs, some of whom, like Macmillan himself, represented industrial constituencies beset by the worst of the recession. In 1927 they published their *Industry and the State*, which declared that the gospel of planning was the necessary solution to the problem of the recession. Thereafter, Macmillan's ideas developed. He envisaged a National Plan, a Public Investment scheme, plans for industrial reconstruction and minimum wage legislation [8.5]. Such tendencies were reflected in the creation of PEP in 1931 (Political and Economic Planning) and in 1935 the creation of 'The Next Five Years Group'. The group called for collective action, affirming that 'the community can and must deliberately plan and control . . . the economic development to which innumerable individual activities contribute'. Such a system of regulated capitalism represented an enormous departure from nineteenth-century traditions of free enterprise.

Notwithstanding, and possibly because of, these increasingly powerful tendencies in inter-war Conservatism, bitter denunciations of Socialism remained a permanent feature of innumerable speeches, pamphlets and books. The relationship betweeen the Conservatives and their Labour opponents was in truth a delicate matter. Once the Labour party had replaced the Liberal party as the effective alternative to the Conservatives, Baldwin was anxious to accept them as legitimate constitutional rivals. At the same time, he wished to restrict the powers of trades unions while outbidding Labour for the working-class vote. Indeed, in the inter-war period, the Conservative party did not attract a large proportion of working-class *members* but the anxieties of Tory MPs in marginal constituencies together with the continuing power of deference encouraged the support of large numbers of working-class Tory voters. Baldwin was walking a tight-rope. In 1925 he commendably exerted his influence to stop a bill promoted by a Tory back-bencher which attacked the political levy. Yet the limits of Conservative tolerance of Labour were soon to be revealed. The General Strike of 1926 had to be defeated in the interests of national unity. Some Conservatives – Churchill in particular – were bellicose and even spiteful. Baldwin played the patriotic card with flexibility and moderation. Nevertheless, the collapse of the strike was followed by the Trades Disputes Act (1927) which outlawed sympathy strikes and provided for contracting-in, as opposed to contracting-out, of the political levy. Although the Conservative party was unquestionably drifting into collectivism, there should be no mistaking its deadly serious intention of discrediting and weaking its Labour opponents, 'pledged' as the National Manifesto of 1935 put it, 'to a number of revolutionary measures'. Even after five years of coalition government between 1940 and 1945 a distinguished Conservative theorist could still depict the Labour party as a party of incipient totalitarianism [8.6]. The potency of ideology and propaganda is well illustrated in the ability of the Conservative party in the inter-war years to project themselves to the country as a party of national unity, economic reconstruction and 'the Middle Way' and to their own supporters as the hammer of the left.

THE NEW CONSERVATISM (1940–1975)

The Second World War confirmed and quickened collectivist trends in Conservative ideology. The need for war-time planning promoted collectivist ideas while the need for loyalty in war-time revitalised Tory traditions of national patriotism and imperial mission. The Coalition government led by Churchill and dominated by Conservatives launched an unprecedented programme of social legislation which included social security, family allowances, the Education Act of 1944, Keynsian budgetary techniques and policies of full employment. These met, on the whole, with a lukewarm acceptance in the Conservative party. In May 1943 the Conservative Party Conference considered that the Beveridge Report 'accorded with sound principles for the improvement of the condition of the people within the framework of the existing economic and political system'. With a few slight amendments it passed Conference with only six dissentients. Conservative party commitment to a National Health Service, however, was much more guarded. Churchill wanted the Coalition to continue after the war in order to continue this work. It was the Labour party which forced the election of 1945, recognising that it might benefit from the new mood of aggressive equality among the electorate. In any case, it may also have seen that little room for further, future agreement with the Conservatives existed.

Collectivist pressures had been unleashed by the war and some Conservative politicians had seen the need to adjust to them. This provoked a backlash of free enterprise sentiment. *Aims of Industry* was founded in 1942 and other groups within the party mobilised in order to agitate for the dismantling of State control of industry after the war. Yet the threat of war, the importance of national defence and the need for State involvement in programmes of economic recovery tended to make State intervention in the economy just as vital after 1945 as it had been before. There would be no reversal of the trends towards greater collectivism after 1945 as there had been after 1918. To manage these powers in accordance with *Conservative* ideals rather than with *executive* needs was the objective of the Tory Reform Committee. Raising their standard against the liberal Conservatism of the 1920s, they demanded a return to the traditions of Disraelian Conservatism and One Nation. The State should retain in peace-time the superintending powers it had exercised in war-time. This ideological cutting edge to Coalition collectivism ultimately became known as 'The New Conservatism'. New Conservatives seized control of the policy-making organs in the party and, on the whole, captured its leadership. How far they captured the heart of the Conservative rank and file is less certain. Certainly the harsh and abrasive manner in which Churchill fought the General Election campaign in 1945 was reminiscent of the Conservatism of the 1920s and the party consequently received little credit for the progressive features in its manifesto [9.1].

Indeed, it was to take time for the New Conservatism to outweigh the lofty and patriotic themes generated by the war and articulated so powerfully by Churchill. Borne along the confidence generated by victory in war, the Conservatives adopted the somewhat complacent view that as the natural party of government they should be allowed to get on with the job of administration. To a nation which had not forgotten the privations of the Depression during the sacrifices of war-time – nor the Conservative record on Appeasement during the 1930s – such an assumption seemed almost offensive. Nevertheless, to a party which treasured such ideals, patriotism and imperialism hung heavy over the party. 'We are', stated a motion at the 1948 Conference 'an Imperialist power or we are nothing'. Such sentiments continued to appeal to Conservatives even when India and Pakistan attained independence in 1947 and Burma in 1948. No wonder that the 1948 Conference included a verbal celebration of Conservative imperialism. Imperial preferences were to be retained and an imperial economic partnership was envisaged. Nevertheless, the transformation of 'an empire into a commonwealth was proceeding. [9.2].

The central element in 'The New Conservatism' was the redefinition of the role of the State in a free enterprise economy. Tactically, it was necessary to present a clearly defined alternative to Labour's policies of nationalisation and welfare while at the same time maintaining the impetus established by the economic policies of the Coalition government. It also had to carry the right wing of the party and the broad support of loyal Conservatives in the country. Overcoming the considerable resistance in the party to *any* positive statement of policy, the right progressives captured the 1946 Conference and Churchill agreed to the establishment of an industrial policy committee. The following year, the Industrial Charter was unveiled, debated and accepted as the basis of the party's new economic policy. At all costs, the party was determined to obliterate the reputation of recession and unemployment which the memor' 'f its policies in the 1930s continued to evoke. By 1949 a general policy statement based on the Industrial Charter, edited by R. A. Butler and touched up by Churchill, was issued as *The Right Road for Britain*. This remained the foundation of official British Conservatism for over twenty years. [9.3].

Much has been written about the Industrial Charter. It is, indeed, a remarkable document. It combines the now customary Liberal-Tory emphasis on the merits of private enterprise with the heavy commitment to state direction of industry. (The State *control* of industry was left to the Labour party.) Industries already nationalised – coal, the railways and the Bank of England – were to be left alone but road transport was to be denationalised. The Charter, furthermore, committed the Conservatives to policies of full employment and social welfare combined with some reduction of government expenditure. It emphasised the virtues of greater individualism and co-operation within a context of firmer central planning.

The 'New Conservatism' in economic affairs could be presented as an extension of earlier Conservative tendencies rather than a direct repudiation of them [9.4]. The new role of the State could be depicted as a development of the interventionism of the 1930s. Similarly, the desire to establish harmonious relations between employer and employee is reminiscent of the 'One Nation' ideals of

Disraeli. Indeed, Disraeli and Lord Randolph Churchill were cited by Churchill in his Foreword to *The Right Road for Britain*. Significantly, however, as the 'New Conservatism' became better defined and indeed approximated more closely to the Labour Party's manifestoes, so the rhetoric of anti-Socialist argument intensified. Nationalisation was likened to Soviet expropriation. Socialism eroded individual responsibility and State control threatened personal freedom [9.5]. As the 'New Conservatism' equipped the Conservative party not merely with a set of objectives but also a definable and credible managerial style they began to argue that they could manage capitalism more efficiently than the Labour party. And became they could manage it more efficiently then, consistent with the traditions of Conservatism, they could manage it more humanely.

For the 'New Conservatives' the purpose of modern economic policies was social reconstruction. As Leo Amery put it in 1954 'the Treasury should not be the master but the faithful steward of the Productive departments'. Commitments to vast social programmes implied an abandonment of the balanced budgeting of the inter-war years. Nothing less, however, would remove the impression, ceaselessly fostered by Labour, that the Tories were a cruel and heartless party. Consequently, the Conservatives had accepted as early as 1943 not only the Welfare State but a much broader system of insurance and benefits for old age, illness and unemployment together with an Education Act and Family Allowances. Such policies, inevitably, were presented as the quintessence of paternalist and Disraelian Conservatism. Nevertheless, it was the Labour government of Attlee which put them on the statute book. In response to the Conservative Party's need to issue a new and distinctive manifesto on social welfare the 'One Nation' group emerged in 1950, including Iain Macleod, Edward Heath, Angus Maude, Enoch Powell, Robert Carr and a handful of others.

The 'One Nation' group wished to cast Conservative social welfare policy in a new mould, at once humane and classless but also efficient. The State should not act as the dispenser of endless benefits and subsidies. It should concentrate help on those most in need. The State must provide the infrastructure of civilised modern life – in housing and in health – without excessive centralisation or bureaucracy. A pluralism of services, State, private, local, voluntary, remained the ideal of 'One Nation'. Consequently, the scope of voluntary and charitable work should be extended. Although nineteenth-century traditions of voluntary charitable benefaction were not abandoned, the 'One Nation' group believed that the State should be used, as Disraeli had foreseen that it should, as an agency of social reform and a means of achieving minimum standards of social comfort [9.6]. It would be entirely mistaken to regard the group as crypto-Socialists. Although they believed in the beneficient power of the State, they also believed in the ability of the individual to pull himself up by his (educational) boot straps. Clearly, many of the 'New Conservatives' believed in an unequal society in which merit rather than birth earned financial and social rewards. The social order was unequal but it permitted mobility according to merit. Individuals profit not through innate qualities or claims of right but through will, effort, merit and the badge of progress – the acquisition of property. The State should lay the foundations for social harmony by laying down certain basic standards but it should not seek to level down.

There can be no doubt that the 'New Conservatism' amounted to an impressive and modernised re-statement of Conservatism but yet one which consciously, even remarkably, looked to its own antecedents. Although the extension of State control of the economy and of welfare was significant, it was not unlimited. State control must not distort the market nor weaken initiative nor impair creativity. The essence of Conservatism remained less a commitment to collectivism than a modernisation of capitalism and the regeneration of free enterprise. The capital market, free competition modified, reformed and regulated) and the private ownership of the means of production – not State control – remained the mainsprings of economic growth, the primary means of distributing wealth and the ultimate guarantee of social stability and political freedom. Free enterprise was the life-blood of an industrial and commercial society. The 'One Nation' group, in particular, was addicted to the view that the key to national wealth was the return to free enterprise. Even the Industrial Charter had preached the view that reductions in government spending could finance reductions in taxation. Furthermore, it had roundly condemned restrictive practices on both sides of industry and suggested the abolition of the closed shop. The liberal or libertarian element in the 'New Conservatism' is no less powerful than the collectivist. New Conservatism concerns the tactics of intervention in a reformed and invigorated capitalist polity. It is not a means of establishing a new, or even significantly transformed, system. Even in the welfare services people were exhorted to provide for themselves and their own above a minimum standard. 'New Conservatism' was a new way of making Capitalism work. It was most emphatically not the first step towards Conservative collectivism.

Although contemporaries could not be aware of it, New Conservatism depended for its political feasibility upon the continued fulfilment of certain conditions. The first was that the wealth of the country would continue to increase sufficiently to finance the expansion of non-productive services. The second was that there would be no significant increase in the demand for these services. Thirdly, wage and price inflation would need to remain low to enable the State to afford the desired expenditure. Finally, there would be no significant increase in the effective competition for those funds. By the middle of the 1970s not a single one of those conditions could be sustained indefinitely.

THE NEW RIGHT

Long before then, disillusionment with the political and electoral consequences of the New Conservatism was growing. Indeed, the New Conservatives had never monopolised ideas in the Conservative party. Even before the end of the war, there was disquiet that high spending programmes of social reform might threaten individual liberties and lead to a frightening enlargement of the State sector.[51] The late 1940s was a period of fervent anti-Communism both in Britain and America and Cold War attitudes inevitably fostered these latent anxieties. In America this bred a spate of Conservative literature – stimulated by Peter Viereck's *Conservatism Revisited* in 1949 and Russel Kirk's *The Conservative Mind* in 1953. Whether such tracts inspired imitators in Britain is doubtful. What they did do was to arouse latent anti-collectivist suspicions and foster a black and white way of looking at the world and at politics.

Under the surface of orthodox 'New Conservatism', therefore, emerged a developing critique of 'collectivism' in Conservative thought and action. The immediate intellectual inspiration was Friedrich A. Hayek's *Road to Serfdom* which had been originally published in 1944. Hayek was an ex-patriate Austrian who had become a British subject in 1938. He is noteworthy, above all, for both his repudiation of collectivism as an attack upon personal freedom and his close association of capitalism with democracy. For Hayek, personal freedom and democracy best thrive in a climate of competitive capitalism. It is, however, a popular misconception that Hayek is attached to a philosophy of complete *laissez-faire*. In fact, he envisages a large number of regulatory functions for the State which are needed to protect people from the consequences of blind economic forces. As long as the government does not purport to establish a monopoly of a particular service then its activities may be legitimate. Most of all, the State must establish the conditions for competition even if this requires State intervention against monopolies. What is so striking about Hayek is his conviction – published at exactly the moment that war-time collectivism was inspiring a generation of British Conservatives to extend economic planning into peacetime – that collectivism would establish totalitarianism, that creeping collectivism would crush the competitive instinct [10.1]. The type of Conservatism which Hayek has inspired[52] assumes that political liberty and a free constitution can only endure in a free enterprise society where the creation of wealth depends on private rather than public initiative. Such an idea had been a common-place in Conservative circles in Britain between the wars. Faced with the welfare and nationalisation programmes of the Attlee government, the economic interventionism of Conservative governments in the 1950s and the need to present a distinctive approach to economic issues after the electoral defeat of 1964, Conservatives began to take Hayek very seriously indeed.

Probably the most notable exponent of such free-market views – and certainly the most well-known – was Enoch Powell. Although originally an exponent of the 'New Conservatism' he had always been a keen advocate of efficiency and competition. Although he had been a member of Macmillan's government, he began in the mid-1960s to denounce its interventionist policies and to advocate free market economics. He denounced State control of the economy as unwise on the grounds of its impossibility. The information available would be inadequate, the practical complexities too great, the bureaucratic instruments too insensitive. Free enterprise had at least two advantages. First, it released energy, promoted inventiveness and stimulated growth. Second, it offered freedom of choice to the individual man or woman. Powell would deny that such a doctrine was either cruel or heartless. Economic growth could provide the wealth with which to alleviate poverty and to minimise social suffering. Capitalism, for Powell, produced the prosperity necessary for a wide distribution of property and wealth – and thus promoted freedom and democracy.[53] In a famous remark, Powell stated: 'Often when I am kneeling down in Church I think to myself how much we should thank God, the Holy Ghost, for the gift of Capitalism.'[54]

What Powell added to Hayek's justification of capitalism is a powerful, patriotic sentiment. For Powell, patriotism is the retreat of the wounded imperialist. A declining imperial power must look to her own defence, her own resources and her own traditions and she must cherish her own institutions and her own way of life. From this proposition followed many of the stances which made him one of the most prominent politicians in the country in the late 1960s and early 1970s – his hostility to coloured immigration, his dislike of the Commonwealth and his opposition to British entry into the Common Market. Few individuals did more to influence the climate of opinion in Britain, and within his party, against the prevailing progressive liberalism of the post-war consensus and the 'New Conservatism'. His populism, his patriotism and his evident relish for personal consistency, occasionally taken to logical extremes, were the hall-marks of a fresh approach to politics and one which evidently had popular appeal. In some ways, Powell stands in a direct line of descent from those great Tory leaders – Disraeli, Chamberlain, Baldwin and Churchill – who spoke to the working classes and refused to apologise for doing so. For Powell claimed to have stratagems designed to reverse Britain's 'decline' and restore her national greatness [10.2].

Of more immediate and direct relevance to the emergence of a new right wing brand of Conservatism than the theories of Hayek and the speeches of Powell were the political difficulties into which the Conservative party enmeshed itself in the 1960s, not least the two electoral defeats of 1964 and 1966. Much was heard about the withdrawal of the State from industry in the second half of the decade – the Selsdon mentality – but the Heath government of 1970–74 left the structure of the nationalised industries virtually intact. Although it initially abolished the Prices and Incomes Board and removed some features of state control of the economy it nevertheless retained others.[55] Heath wished to achieve competitiveness by a dash for growth rather than mark a change in the nature of the British economy. He returned to a policy of wage and price controls and maintained high levels of public spending. Two election defeats in 1974 led to the overthrow of Heath's leadership – and the gradual removal of his closest supporters from positions of influence within the party. The election of Mrs Tatcher to the leadership early in 1975 marked the repudiation of centrist policies and the assertion of competitive virtues of low taxation, low inflation, the disengagement of the State from the control of incomes and prices, and the assertion of market freedom. The party policy statement, 'The Right Approach' (1976) revived the Selsdon spirit with its call for tax cuts, the restoration of the free market economy, the reduction of trade union privileges and the need for efficiency [10.3]. The document is also remarkable, however, for its emphasis upon the need for sacrifices, the abandonment of established practices, the need for a return to traditional values and, not least, the necessity for cuts in government spending in both welfare and non-welfare services – something which Enoch Powell had not originally demanded. Nevertheless, we should not exaggerate the suddenness of the transition inside the Conservative party. It took several years to nail all the policy planks into a platform and much of the process occurred as a reaction to the events of the Labour government of 1974–79. For example, *The Right Approach* did not envisage legislation against the trade unions but the experience of the Winter of Discontent in 1978–79 led the party to propose such legislation.

As soon as these tendencies became evident the exponents of the New Conservatism began to shift anxiously. As early as the summer of 1975 the Tory Reform Group revived. This marked the amalgamation of several established groups dedicated to the Disraelian element within the British Conservative tradition, to One Nation, to planning and to increased government spending. A reassertion of these values seemed desirable in the face of the energy, vision and crusading zeal of the 'New Right' which sought nothing less than the reversal of Britain's economic, and, to some extent, social and psychological, decline by a repudiation of the values of the New Conservatives. Indeed, the New Right burned with resentment at the disastrous consequences of a generation of consensus politics, of deals between big business, big unions and big government, of planning and high taxation. The spirit of independence and personal initiative upon which free enterprise depended had been almost fatally weakened by decades of welfare, bureaucracy and compromise. Economic ruin confronted the nation.

The New Right, then, wished to revive simple, old-fashioned verities in order to emancipate the individual and to revive the economy [10.4]. There was always something populist in New Right propaganda, an indignant retreat into common sense, a dislike of 'experts', civil servants, do-gooders and intellectuals. The old establishment of comfortable Labour and compromising Conservative politicians had to be challenged, the old orthodoxies defied. The old politicians had spoken the language of democracy and conformed to the requirements of political accountability but they had thrust measure after measure down the throats of the electorate: immigration, decimalisation, entry into the Common Market, National Health Service reform and the reorganisation of Local Government boundaries. No wonder that in the mid-1970s people were turning to fringe, extremist and sectional parties in their abhorrence of the old parties. The time for change had come. Politicians had to conform to the popular will. The economic decay which had built up over several decades had to be tackled. National regeneration could occur only through hard work, thrift and self-reliance. Easy, comfortable options could no longer be tolerated. The time for sacrifice and suffering had come. The sins of the past had to be purged in the present.

At a time of rapid technological change, economic uncertainty and social tension such an appeal has undoubted attractions. Wrapped up in patriotic sentiment, so powerfully released during the weeks of the Falklands War in 1982, it became something of a minor crusade.

The 'New Right' is strident, vociferous, firm. It talks the language of confrontation; its posture is aggressive, its values those of courage and resolution, not those of compromise and conciliation. It appears to be more exciting, more polemical and more innovative than it really is. It is confident, populist, radical and authoritarian. Indeed, there is much poll evidence to indicate that on a series of issues – law and order, immigration, trade union power, the control of inflation – the 'New Right' had considerable public support. The attitude, the appearance and the emotion is quite central to the politics of the 'New Right' [10.5].

The success of the New Right depended upon the effectiveness of its economic policies. Retreating from a system of State control of the economy which had by the mid-1970s succeeded in promoting 'Stagflation' – economic stagnation accompanied by rising inflation – the 'New Right' argued for a drastic reduction in State control. Since the war, both parties had agreed to a vastly enlarged public sector in which governments were responsible for economic policy in areas as diverse as finance, the balance of payments, the exchange rate, ownership of and investment in basic industries, the establishment of an energy policy, the maintenance of full employment, the State regulation of regional subsidies and aids. At the same time, governments of both parties were substantially committed to high spending welfare programmes. It was now argued that government intervention – in the shape of inefficient and run-down nationalised industries, subsidies, loans and assistance for inefficient and uncompétitive firms and a taxation system which appeared to penalise entrepreneurial skill and success – had actually accelerated the very decline it was supposed to arrest. 'For the Tory party to be the guardian of national continuity is one thing; for it to be the guardian of national failure is quite another.'[56]

The British 'New Right' found stimulus in the writings of the American economist Milton Friedman. He argued that economic growth occurs despite, not because of, State intervention. The heavy hand of the State stultifies activity and initiative while encouraging lavish expectations of welfare and support on the part of the population. Consequently, government expenditure gets out of control. While failing to satisfy the expectations it arouses, government intervention worsens economic performance by promoting inflation, raising prices and interest rates. It is not wage-push nor even rising import prices which leads to inflation but the readiness of government to print the money which the nation's economic performance has not earned. These themes constantly recur in the writings of speeches of the New Right. By the mid-1970s the idea that inflation was caused by budget deficits and by an excessive amount of money in circulation had taken hold of the Conservative Party. To the groundswell of reaction against the politics and economics of the New Conservatism was now added the conviction that financial and economic salvation depended upon achieving reductions in the rate of growth of the money supply [10.6]. If this could be done, inflation would fall and prices and taxes could be reduced. What needs always to be remembered, nevertheless, is that these discussions did not merely concern the technical question of controlling inflation: they concerned the sort of society that Conservatives envisaged, the role of the State and the welfare services and the status of the individual in society. The Labour government in 1976 adopted certain monetarist tactics but it did not abandon basic Keynesian techniques of economic management – incomes policies, regional aid, subsidies, investment, budgetary deficits, etc. A monetarist approach to State spending did not necessary entail the abandonment of other aspects of State intervention. In the politics of the New Right, however, crusading zeal to reverse national decline has involved the rolling back of the powers of the State on all fronts. [10.7].

To what extent is the ideology of the New Right compatible with the traditions of Conservatism? There is, of course, nothing new in upholding the place of economy, thrift and efficiency, in valuing competition and individualism and in prizing the consequences of freedom from government interference. Yet the almost biblical commitment to monetarism sits a little oddly on a party which has normally distanced itself from magical cures and remedies. The monetarist view of a rational economic man steadily pursuing his, and therefore the community's, interest does not square with the traditional Conservative view of the imperfections of man. In general, the power of market forces appears as an agency for the cure of rather too many ills rather than one among a wide variety number of other Conservative strategies. This lack of restraint arises from the urgent need to repair the fabric of an ailing capitalist economy in an unfriendly world when time – and North Sea oil – are not unlimited. Yet a sense of proportion needs to be maintained. The assumption that market forces are, in a sense, self-stabilising and that they are a natural concomitant both to political liberty and political and social stability are not self-evident propositions. The old Conservative verities of stability, continuity, compassion and moderation have been most in evidence when State intervention has been used to moderate and to cushion the impact of market forces. The examples of Germany, Japan and France suggest that the right kind of State intervention directed towards specific objectives can achieve remarkable results. To what extent, indeed, is the very concept of 'market forces' of relevance in the oligopolistic economies of the late twentieth century? As Edward Heath wrote in February 1985: 'I don't believe that what we've got now is true Conservatism. It's 1860 Laissez-Faire Liberalism that never was.'[57]

The rhetoric of the New Right has to be distinguished from social and political reality. Much is heard of the national interest, the spirit of patriotism and the need for discipline. Much is seen of the monarchy and much use is made of the appeal to law and order. Yet the appeal of the New Right is sectional: to white, southern, suburban and rural England. Even at the height of its electoral success in 1983 the Conservative Party found little support in the urban areas of the North, Midlands, Wales and Scotland. At the time of writing (May 1985) the degree of success of the economic policies of Thatcher's Conservative party cannot be predicted. Yet something can be said after almost six years of monetarism. The decline of Britain has not been arrested, nor even slowed. The sceptic might remark that steady decline has become rampant collapse. Now, it may be that the foundations are being laid for recovery and that the future is brighter than the present. Even if this were to be so, however, it may be that the damage that has been done to the social fabric – especially in terms of unemployment and the alienation of the young – has created problems worse than those which two Thatcher administrations have attempted to solve.

Nevertheless, the libertarian rhetoric of the New Right, its emphasis upon personal responsibility and independence, serves several purposes. It rallies the party faithful and it affirms an ultimate political and even ethical objective. The language of freedom and patriotism must be set beside the Socialist objectives of egalitarianism and totalitarianism. Freedom involves the freedom of the individual to decide whether to participate in the benefits of an unequal social order. The New Right fosters the illusion of national community through the effective deployment of royal ceremonial, patriotic celebration and emphasis on the military strength and independence of the nation. In times of depression and uncertainty, such symbols appear compelling and even inspirational. Behind them, however, lies the traditional Conservative objective of the salvation of the existing social and political order which might even have been recognisable to Edmund Burke [10.8].

CONCLUSION: BRITISH CONSERVATISM IN THE TWENTIETH CENTURY

In a century of unprecedented change and almost unintelligible developments and transformations the role of Conservatism is easy to misconstrue. Its preoccupation with into history can easily appear as indulgent and irrelevant nostalgia. Conservatives, however, would argue that their basic principles and instincts – those, in fact, with which we began this book – were never more important than in this age of uncontrollable change. Acceptance of familiar institutional landmarks and their recognition as symbols of deeper values contribute something to continuity and social stability. Conservatives, arguably, have not, on the whole, violated their ancestral conventions about ordered and natural change as key elements in the preservation of the social and political fabric. In a mass democracy, moreover, the reform of political structures and the provision of welfare should proceed on a sensible, pragmatic and realistic basis and not as a result of abstract speculation. Serious inequalities in the possession of power and the distribution of property, similarly, should be tolerated and accepted. When economic growth permits, of course, wealth and property can be spread more widely and, consequently, political and social freedoms guaranteed against the invasions of the State. In these, and in many other ways, the Conservative tradition has been of use in the twentieth century, although, as Anthony Quinton writes, 'the older Conservatives' devotion to ancestral wisdom seems to have come to an end'.[58] Reverence of the past for its own sake, cultivation of historic communities which never existed and a belief in the doctrine of prescription in the Burkeian sense are no longer to be found within the Conservative tradition. The political system and the social structures which underpin it can in the twentieth century – indeed, must in the twentieth century – be defended on alternative grounds. Principles of leadership, obedience and social discipline can be maintained more convincingly than on the standard arguments which Burke used two centuries ago.

The major departures in twentieth-century Conservatism from the traditions which it inherited lie unquestionably in the economic sphere. Conservatives have become the party of free enterprise capitalism. At the same time, they have had to recognise that in a mass, urban society the underprivileged can not adequately be protected from the ravages of social and economic misfortunes by local, voluntary philanthropy. State intervention is needed to rescue the poor, the weak and the sick. At the same time, a wide range of services ranging from the provision of education to the provision of a water supply require constant State intervention. This tension between free enterprise and State control lies at the heart of twentieth-century Conservatism. What Conservatism wishes to conserve, then, are the financial and economic structures of liberal capitalism, together with their supportive (and much older) political, institutional and, to some extent, social and occupational structures. Beyond these objectives, Conservative governments wish to provide the services and facilities proper to a civilised society in the modern era. Their philosophy, their political theory, is often defined as a reaction to Labour's centralism. The Labour party wishes to introduce the centralised State while the Conservative party wishes to preserve constitutional freedoms: the Labour party threatens the disposal of private wealth and property while the Conservative party promises to enhance it: the Labour party weakens the national defences while the Conservative party aims to improve national security. Consequently, the underlying tensions in the political ideas of British Conservatism have never been resolved. In the New Conservatism of the post-war era both the old Conservative traditions of Disraelian 'One Nation' politics as well as the newer libertarian economic ideals were combined. The present emphasis in Conservative thought is unquestionably in the direction of the latter. Whether the Conservatives will be left to conserve an economically shattered and a socially divided Britain or whether the crusade of the New Right will revive the nation into a new era of prosperity and self-confidence cannot at this time be foreseen.

REFERENCES

1. Russell Kirk, *The Conservative Mind from Burke to Santayana* (1953), p. 8.
2. Edmund Burke, *Reflections on the Revolution in France* (1790), Pelican Classics (ed. Conor Cruise O'Brien), p. 119.
3. Sir Ian Gilmour, *Inside Right* (1977), p. 149.
4. *ibid*, p. 147.
5. Lord Eustace Percy, 'The Conservative Attitude and Social Policy' in *Conservatism and the Future* (1935), q. R. J. White, *The Conservative Tradition* (1950), p. 33.
6. Sir Arthur Bryant, *The Spirit of Conservatism* (1929), p. 172.
7. Quintin Hogg, *op. cit.* p. 32.
8. Lord Hugh Cecil, *Conservatism* (1912), p. 213.
9. Sir Ian Gilmour, *op. cit.* p. 166.
10. Professor Hearnshaw not only does this (*op. cit.* pp. 19–20) but speculates on its occurrence in Ancient Greece and Rome.
11. Anthony Quinton, *The Politics of Imperfection* (1978), pp. 23, 24.
12. Samuel P. Huntington, 'Conservatism as an Ideology', *American Review of Political Science*, VI (1957), p. 464.
13. Quinton, in fact, comes dangerously close to arguing this (p. 24): 'Conservative belief becomes explicit only in reaction to a positive, innovating attack on the traditional scheme of things. What exists speaks for itself simply by existing. It is only when some ideal or imagined alternative is effectively set beside it that there is occasion for those loyal to the established state of affairs to justify their endorsement of it. Hooker's doctrine of Church and State is a response to the first theoretically articulate challenge to the established customs and institutions of English society. The Puritan doctrinaires he was arguing against were the first dissenting group in English history to fortify their challenge with a body of explicit theory.'
14. It is entirely typical of Burke that he steadfastly refused to entertain parliamentary reform in England while eventually conceding it for Ireland. He believed that whatever the defects of the English electoral system, it permitted the representation of opinion either *directly* or *virtually* (i.e. through non-elective

agencies). In Ireland, however, parliamentary reform was desirable because the Irish Catholics were not even *virtually* represented and if parliamentary reform were not conceded Ireland might eventually experience a Catholic rebellion and ultimately secede from the empire. To extend the franchise in Ireland would establish a propertied electorate. To extend the franchise in England would dilute a propertied electorate and pave the way for democracy and anarchy.

15. It seems to me that many commentators confuse the two. Anthony Quinton, for example, argues that 'Organicism is clearly affirmed' in the *Reflections* but his subsequent quotation refers to diversity rather than to growth (*The Politics of Imperfection*, pp. 57–8).

16. *Cavendish Debates*, 1, p. 476.

17. See *Observations on a Late Publication, Intituled The Present State of the Nation* (1769).

18. But he was by no means the *only* such writer in the 1790s. Professor Dickinson, very sensibly in my view, deals with other writers as well as Burke in his chapter 'The Conservative Defence of the Constitution' in *Liberty and Property* (1977).

19. Russell Kirk, *The Portable Conservative Reader* (1933), p. xxxii.

20. E. Halevy, *England in 1815* (1924), p. 394.

21. R. Kirk, *The Conservative Mind from Burke to Santayana*, p. 106.

22. The *Lay Sermons* of 1817 and 1818 seem to me to embody Coleridge's Conservatism. The more noteworthy *Constitution of the Church and State* of 1830, while undoubtedly more polemical and even more contentious, nevertheless is describing an *ideal type* of Constitution and not one which exists.

23. The word 'Conservative' was first used in the 1820s but its common use in a Tory context dates from 1830–31. Within a few years it had become common usage (see G. D. Block, *A Source Book of Conservatism* (1964), pp. 65–68. The account in Hearnshaw (*op. cit.* pp. 50–52) ascribing the political origin of the term to 1834 is seriously in error. In terms of nomenclature, at least, the 'Conservative' as opposed to the 'Tory' party appears during the rearguard action against the Reform Act.

24. N. Gash, *The Age of Peel* (1968), p. 7.

25. Peel is not the most popular hero in the Tory pantheon. 'His attitude to change was almost wholly responsive. He accepted the inevitable at the very last moment, and occasionally even

later. The contrast with Disraeli is marked. Disraeli's attitude to change was often anticipatory. Where Peel usually accepted the inevitable, Disraeli tried to forestall it', Sir I. Gilmour, *Inside Right*, p. 127. See also the very similar passage in Lord Hugh Cecil, *Conservatism*, pp. 66–70.

26. For an interesting, if exaggerated, view of Peel's doctrinaire economic but pragmatic political attitudes see Boyd Hilton, Peel: a Reappraisal, *Historical Journal*, 22(3), 1979.

27. Robert Stewart takes exactly this line (*The Foundations of the Conservative Party*, pp. 166–68). For the Conservative Operative Societies see the classic account by R. L. Hill, *Toryism and the People, 1832–46* (1929), pp. 47–57.

28. As late as 1865 the Protectionists won only 22 of the 100 urban seats in the UK with a population of over 50,000. Not one of the 22 was in London. C. Seymour, *Electoral Reform in England and Wales* (1913), pp. 302–6.

29. Sir Arthur Bryant, *The Spirit of Conservatism*, p. 21.

30. Richard Faber, *Beaconsfield and Bolingbroke* (1961), p. 23.

31. A. Quinton, *op. cit.* pp. 80–1.

32. Nigel Harris, *Competition and the Corporate Society* (1972), pp. 285 6.

33. Interestingly, as several commentators have noted, Disraeli sometimes looked beyond Burke back to Bolingbroke who promoted the ideal of a nation united by a 'Patriot King', untroubled by social or political divisions. Such passages may be found in chapters 30 and 31 of the *Vindication of the English Constitution*. On this theme see the unjustly neglected work by Richard Faber, *Beaconsfield and Bolingbroke*, especially pp. 19–35.

34. T. E. Kebbel, *op. cit.* ii, p. 487.

35. B. Disraeli, *Vindication of the English Constitution*, p. 182.

36. American Conservatives occasionally look back nostalgically to Disraeli's 'One Nation' ideology but not as frequently as they do to Burke. For one amusing view which regards Disraeli's paternalist aristocracy as a meritocratic ideal ('What Disraeli aimed at was quite literally the rule of the best') see Roland Hogins, 'Disraeli's Doctrine of Toryism', *South Atlantic Quarterly*, vol. 15 (1916), pp. 241–9, especially pp. 246, 248.

37. Goldwin Smith, *Questions of the Day* (1893), p. 91.

38. Paul Smith, *Lord Salisbury on Politics* (1972), p. 106.

39. Noel O'Sullivan, *Conservatism*, (1976), p. 111.

40. Nigel Harris, *op. cit.* p. 25.

41. Paul Smith, *Disraelian Conservatism and Social Reform* (1972), p. 323.

42. On this debate see R. Foster, *Lord Randolph Churchill* (1981), pp. 106–9.

43. P. E. Quinault, 'Lord Randolph Churchill and Tory Democracy, 1880–1885', *Historical Journal* 22, i, (1979), p. 143.

44. Even this is doubtful. Many of the Liberals who supported Salisbury were free-traders. Goschen is typical of many. His entire career was directed against extending the scope of State action. Significantly, he joined the Conservative party in 1893. For further discussion of Conservative free traders see W. H. Greenleaf, 'The Character of Modern British Conservatism' in *Knowledge and Belief in Politics* (eds. R. Benewick, R. N. Berki and B. Parekh) (1973), p. 197. As for Chamberlain himself, what did he demand when office beckoned in 1895? The Colonial Office for himself and a committee of enquiry into Old Age Pensions.

45. Peter Marsh, *The Conscience of the Victorian State* (1979), p. 242.

46. Martin Pugh, *The Making of Modern British Politics, 1867–1939* (1982), p. 276. For a more detailed discussion of some of these themes see John Raymond, *The Age of Balfour and Baldwin, 1902–40* (1978), pp. 208–11.

47. A. J. P. Taylor, *English History*, 1914–45 (1965), p. 264.

48. *q.* Tom Stannage, *Baldwin Thwarts the Opposition* (1980), p. 42.

49. There is an interesting account of this transition in Noel O'Sullivan's *Conservatism* (1976), pp. 120–5. O'Sullivan, however, seems to me to underestimate the traditional Conservative distaste for the power of the State, even in the Disraelian period.

50. Nigel Harris, *op. cit.* p. 53.

51. Notably the Progress Trust and the 'Signpost' series of booklets. Before 1945 it is doubtful if the New Conservatives had the support of more than half the parliamentary party. On this, see A. Gamble, *The Conservative Nation* (1974), pp. 35–6.

52. And continued to inspire. One of the attractions of Hayek for Conservative publicists has been his flexibility, his readiness to adapt his arguments with the passing of time and his preparedness constantly to put his ideas before the public. See, for example, *The Constitution of Liberty* (1960).

53. The 1960s threw up a good deal of literature of this kind. See, for example, T. Raison, *Conflict and Conservatism* (1965); M.

Wolff *et al*, *The Conservative Opportunity* (1965); R. Blake *et al*, *Conservatism Today* (1966).

54. As quoted in 'The nature of Powellism' by K. Phillips in Nugent, N. and King R. *The British Right* (1977).

55. The Industrial Reorganisation Corporation was abolished and investment grants and the Regional Employment Premium were ended. Nevertheless, the Small Business Development Bureau was retained and Rolls Royce, UCS and Harland and Wolff brought the government to give aid to lame ducks.

56. Zig Layton-Henry, *Conservative Party Politics* (1980), p. xiii.

57. *The Sunday Times* 3 February 1985, p. 15.

58. A. Quinton, *op. cit.* p. 90.

Part One
MAJOR THEMES IN BRITISH CONSERVATISM

1.1 EDMUND BURKE: GOVERNMENT AND HUMAN NATURE

Edmund Burke (1729–97) had been a Whig politician for a quarter of a century when the French Revolution challenged the fundamental principles of civil and political organisation. In a series of works, the first, and greatest, of which was *Reflections on the Revolution in France* (1790), Burke confronted the novel theories of the French revolutionists with his own synthesis of reformulated Whiggism and a series of sociological insights which lifted political philosophy to a new level of practical realism. One of the central themes in the *Reflections* is the need for government to be consistent with man's nature. Government should arise not from abstract principles but from ethical standards which are not within man's capacities to alter or to determine. Foremost among these is the recognition that government exists to restrain the imperfections in man's nature. This, as well as later, quotations from the *Reflections*, is from the Pelican edition of 1968, edited by Conor Cruise O'Brien, pp. 150–1.

If civil society be the offspring of convention, that convention must be its law. That convention must limit and modify all the descriptions of constitution which are formed under it. Every sort of legislative judicial, or executory power are its creatures. They can have no being in any other state of things; and how can any man claim, under the conventions of civil society, rights which do not so much as suppose its existence? Rights which are absolutely repugnant to it? One of the first motives to civil society, and which becomes one of its fundamental rules, is, *that no man should be judge in his own cause*. By this each person has at once divested himself of the first fundamental right of unconvenanted man, that is, to judge for himself, and to assert his own cause. He abdicates all right to be his own governor. He inclusively, in a great measure, abandons the right of self-defence, the first law of nature. Men cannot enjoy the

66

rights of an uncivil and of a civil state together. That he may obtain justice he gives up his right of determining what it is in points the most essential to him. That he may secure some liberty, he makes a surrender in trust of the whole of it.

Government is not made in virtue of natural rights, which may and do exist in total independence of it; and exist in much greater clearness, and in a much greater degree of abstract perfection: but their abstract perfection is their practical defect. By having a right to every thing they want every thing. Government is a contrivance of human wisdom to provide for human *wants*. Men have a right that these wants should be provided for by this wisdom. Among these wants is to be reckoned the want, out of civil society, of a sufficient restraint upon their passions. Society requires not only that the passions of individuals should be subjected, but that even in the mass and body as well as in the individuals, the inclinations of men should frequently be thwarted, their will controlled, and their passions brought into subjection. This can only be done *by a power out of themselves*; and not, in the exercise of its function, subject to that will and to those passions which it is its office to bridle and subdue. In this sense the restraints on men, as well as their liberties, are to be reckoned among their rights. But as the liberties, and the restrictions vary with times and circumstances, and admit of infinite modifications, they cannot be settled upon any abstract rule: and nothing is so foolish as to discuss them upon that principle.

1.2 QUINTIN HOGG: THE ORGANIC THEORY OF SOCIETY

One of the twentieth century's most articulate, influential and reflective writings on Conservatism is Quintin Hogg, Lord Hailsham's (1907–) *Case for Conservatism* (1947) pp. 24–27. Intended as a riposte to post-war Socialism in Britain, Hogg's book, nevertheless, relates the political issues of the 1940s back to the fundamental principles of Conservatism. Like Burke, and like many other predecessors, Hogg denies that Conservatives ought to pursue simplistic yet ambitious schemes for utopian change. In these excerpts he demonstrates the continuing relevance of organic ideas of society to mid-twentieth-century Conservatism, and its assumptions concerning change and reform.

Instead of a clear-cut conception of an ideal society to which all nations should attempt to the best of their ability to conform, Conservatives believe in a somewhat more mature conception of the nature of political organisation. This theory may be described as the organic theory of society.

A human community, they would say, is much more like a living being than a machine or a house. A machine or a house can be made to conform more or less to a plan. Given the materials, each can be altered more or less at will. Neither need, unless its makers desire it, possess an individuality. If parts fall into disrepair or become outworn, they can be ruthlessly scrapped and replaced. Each has an existence relative only to the needs and purposes of their users. Each can be replaced entirely if they suffer disaster.

By contrast, living creatures are not to be so used. Making or breeding them may be a scientific study. In a sense, by studying certain biological laws, they can be bred for certain characteristics, or trained in certain aptitudes. In that sense, they may be 'planned'. But it is a sense wholly different from that in which we lay out the ground plan of a house, or a 'blue print' of a machine. Treating their ailments is indeed a science and an art, but it is a study not the least bit like engineering. At times, no doubt, surgical operations are desirable and even necessary. But such operations are never good in themselves, and often, to save life, inflict permanent loss upon the patient.

Like all analogies, this comparison must not be pressed too far. But two other distinct points of likeness can be noticed. As Burke wrote: 'A state without the means of change is without the means of conservatism.' (sic.) No living organism can remain static and alive. If Conservatism meant 'no change', clearly the only truly Conservative organism would be a dead one. But Conservatives, of course, do not mean anything so silly. They believe that a living society can only change healthily when it changes naturally – that is, in accordance with its acquired and inherited character, and at a given rate. . . .

Reformers who put the revolution first and do not make due concessions to tradition, to the living nature of society which requires changes to be made gently, at a gradual speed, inevitably involve themselves in the use of dictatorial methods, and usually end by producing a reaction which defeats the very objects which they mean to serve.

Moreover, Conservatives also draw the moral that there is an advantage, even from the point of view of those desiring radical change, in preserving the *mystique* of a traditional authority. They believe that much of the bloodshed attached to revolution can be avoided when both sides can be persuaded to play the rules of the Constitutional game. They point to the happy history of our own country since 1660. They observe the contrast between Britain with her traditional monarchy and France based on a revolutionary republic. They think the credit for this lies more with Clarendon than with Cromwell, more with the Tories than the Whigs, more with Disraeli than Gladstone. They admit that the times involve us in one radical change after another. But they consider it proved by experience that such change can only be safely effected within the framework provided by a constitution sanctified by traditional authority and institutions, that it must be effected in a manner conformable to the traditional methods of procedure, and that if confidence is not to be ruptured it had best be effected by a group of men known to be devoted to the traditions of their country in an atmosphere where the people are confident of the ability of the constitutional procedure to achieve reform and in the willingness of all classes to accept it when fairly enacted. These views Conservatives do not claim to be the monopoly of Conservatives to-day, but they do claim that the fact that they are held, and so widely held, can be directly attributed to the influence of the devoted lives of Conservative statesmen in the past, acting in the belief that the traditional is the best corrective yet discovered for the unbalanced and emphemeral influence of the fashion of the moment.

1.3 BENJAMIN DISRAELI: THE DEFENCE OF NATIONAL TRADITIONS

The young Disraeli (1804–81) was a profoundly romantic man of letters. His *Vindication* is a particularly derivative tract, owing much to Burke and possibly even more to his nostalgic view of English history. Disraeli's *Vindication* provides a synthesis of Conservative ideas which in many ways contrasts with that of Peel. The work also provides an early indication of the kind of Conservative rhetoric which was to be so closely identified with him. The extract is remarkable for its defence of historical tradition in an age of unparalleled social change and its indifference to the problems of industrial civilisation. From Benjamin Disraeli: *Vindication of the English Constitution* (1835), pp. 45–9.

This respect for Precedent, this clinging to Prescription, this reverence for Antiquity, which are so often ridiculed by conceited and superficial minds, and move the especial contempt of the gentlemen who admire abstract principles, appear to me to have their origin in a profound knowledge of human nature, and in a fine observation of public affairs, and satisfactorily to account for the permanent character of our liberties. Those great men, who have periodically risen to guide the helm of our government in times of tumultuous and stormy exigency, knew that a State is a complicated creation of refined art, and they handled it with all the delicacy a piece of exquisite machinery requires. They knew that if once they admitted the abstract rights of subjects, they must inevitably advance to the abstract rights of men, and then that the very foundations of their civil polity would sink beneath them. They held this to be too dear a price for the barren fruition of a first principle. They knew that the foundation of civil policy is Convention, and that every thing and every person that springs from that foundation, must partake of that primary character. They held themselves bound by the contracts of their forefathers, because they wished their posterity to observe their own agreements. They did not comprehend how the perpetuity of a State could be otherwise preserved. They looked upon the nation as a family, and upon the country as a landed inheritance. Generation after generation were to succeed to it, with all its convenient buildings, and all its choice cultivation, its parks and gardens, as well as its fields and meads, its libraries and its collections of art, all its wealth, but all its incumbrances. Holding society to be as much an artificial creation as the fields and cities amid which they dwelt, they were of opinion that every subject was bound to respect the established constitution of his country, because, independent of all other advantages, to that constitution he was indebted even for his life. Had not the State been created, the subject would not have existed. Man with them, therefore, was the child of the State, and born with filial duties. To disobey the State, therefore, was a crime; to rebel against it, treason; to overturn it, parricide. Our ancestors could not comprehend how this high spirit of loyalty could be more efficiently fostered and maintained, than by providing that the rights, privileges and possessions, of all should rest on no better foundation than the State itself. They would permit no antagonist principle in their body politic. They would not tolerate nature struggling with art, or theory with habit. Hence their reverence for prescription, which they placed above law, and held superior to reason. It is to this deference to what Lord Coke finely styles, 'reverend antiquity', that I ascribe the duration of our commonwealth, and it is this spirit which has prevented even our revolutions from being destructive.

I do not see . . . that this reverence for antiquity has checked the progress of knowledge, or stunted the growth of liberty, in this island. We are universally held to be the freest people in Europe, and to have enjoyed our degree of freedom for a longer period than any existing state. I am not aware that any nation can fairly assert its claims to superior learning or superior wisdom; to a more renowned skill in arts or arms; to a profounder scientific spirit; to a more refined or comprehensive civilisation. I know that a year or two back the newspapers that are in the interest of the new sect of statesmen, were wont to twit and taunt us with the superior freedom of our neighbours. 'The fact can no longer be concealed,' announced the prime organ of the party, 'the people of France are freer than the people of England. The consciousness of this fact will be the last blow to the oligarchy.' Profound publicist! The formation of a free government on an extensive scale, while it is assuredly one of the most interesting problems of humanity, is certainly the greatest achievement of human wit. Perhaps I should rather term it a super-human achievement; for it requires such refined prudence, such comprehensive knowledge, and such perspicacious sagacity, united with such almost illimitable powers of combination, that it is nearly in vain to hope for qualities so rare to be congregated in a solitary mind. Assuredly this *summum bonum* is not to be found ensconced behind a revolutionary barricade, or floating in the bloody gutters of an incendiary metropolis. It cannot be scribbled down – this great invention – in a morning on the envelope of a letter by some charter-concocting monarch, or sketched with ludicrous facility in the conceited commonplace book of an Utilitarian sage. With us it has been the growth of ages, and brooding centuries have watched over and tended its perilous birth and feeble infancy. The noble offspring of liberty and law now flourishes in the full and lusty vigour of its proud and perfect manhood. Long may it flourish! Long be its life, venerable its age, and distant its beatified euthanasia! I offer this prayer for the sake of human nature, as much as for my country; not more for Britain, than for the world, of which it is the ornament and honour.

1.4 EDMUND BURKE: CHANGE AND CONSERVATION

Burke was fond of declaring that the best means of conserving a State or an institution was to effect timely reforms. In this, Burke was profoundly conscious of what he called 'the great law of change'. For Burke, the intelligent political action was one which sought to co-operate with this eternal principle of social life. He did not believe in attempts to put the clock back nor did he think in terms of blind restoration. In apprehending the reality of inevitable social change, Burke recognised the duty of statesmen as minimising the impact and slowing the rate of such change.

Only thus could the constitution and institutions of the country be preserved.

The two short extracts that follow are famous passages in which Burke pronounces upon the virtues of conservation through accepting social change. The first is from the *Reflections on the Revolution in France* (1790) (Pelican edition, 1968, ed. Conor Cruise O'Brien), p. 106. The second is from *A Letter to Sir Hercules Langrishe* (1792) (*The Works of Edmund Burke*, 2 Vols. 1834, vol. 2, p. 559)

A state without the means of some change is without the means of its conservation. Without such means it might even risque the loss of that part of the constitution which it wished the most religiously to preserve. The two principles of conservation and correction operated strongly at the two critical periods of the Restoration and Revolution, when England found itself without a king. At both those periods the nation had lost the bond of union in their antient edifice; they did not, however, dissolve the whole fabric. On the contrary, in both cases they regenerated the deficient part of the old constitution through the parts which were not impaired. They kept these old parts exactly as they were, that the part recovered might be suited to them. They acted by the ancient organized states in the shape of their old organization, and not by the organic *moleculae* of a disbanded people. At no time, perhaps, did the sovereign legislature manifest a more tender regard to that fundamental principle of British constitutional policy, than at the time of the Revolution, when it deviated from the direct line of hereditary succession. The crown was carried somewhat out of the line in which it had before moved; but the new line was derived from the same stock. It was still a line of hereditary descent; still an hereditary descent in the same blood, though an hereditary descent qualified with protestantism. When the legislature altered the direction, but kept the principle, they shewed that they held it inviolable.

★ ★ ★

We must all obey the great law of change. It is the most powerful law of nature, and the means perhaps of its conservation. All we can do, and that human wisdom can do, is to provide that the change shall proceed by insensible degrees. This has all the benefits which may be in change, without any of the inconveniences of mutation. Every thing is provided for as it arrives. This mode will, on the one hand, prevent the *unfixing old interests at once*; a thing which is apt to breed a black and sullen discontent in those who are at once dispossessed of all their influence and consideration. This gradual course, on the other side, will prevent men, long under depression, from being intoxicated with a large draught of new power, which they always abuse with a licentious insolence. But wishing, as I do, the change to be gradual and cautious, I would, in my first steps, lean rather to the side of enlargement than restriction.

1.5 EDMUND BURKE: ENTITLEMENT TO POLITICAL POWER

In one of the most important passages not only in his *Reflections* but in the entire corpus of modern British Conservatism, Burke considers the claims of merit, blood, property, and election as titles to political power. His repudiation of the rights of election caused an outcry among his radical contemporaries. His affirmation of the power of the landed interest, no doubt, did much to secure the book's, and the author's, enormous popularity in that quarter. From *Reflections on the Revolution in France* (Pelican edition, 1968, ed. Conor Cruise O'Brien, pp. 139–41).

You do not imagine, that I wish to confine power, authority, and distinction to blood, and names, and titles. No, Sir. There is no qualification for government, but virtue and wisdom, actual or presumptive. Wherever they are actually found, they have, in whatever state, condition, profession or trade, the passport of Heaven to human place and honour. Woe to the country which would madly and impiously reject the service of the talents and virtues, civil, military, or religious, that are given to grace and to serve it; and would condemn to obscurity every thing formed to diffuse lustre and glory around a state. Woe to that country too, that passing into the opposite extreme, considers a low education, a mean contracted view of things, a sordid mercenary occupation, as a preferable title to command. Every thing ought to be open; but not indifferently to every man. No rotation; no appointment by lot; no mode of election operating in the spirit of sortition or rotation, can be generally good in a government conversant in extensive objects. Because they have no tendency, direct or indirect, to select the man with a view to the duty, or to accommodate the one to the other, I do not hesitate to say, that the road to eminence and power, from obscure condition, ought not to be made too easy, nor a thing too much of course. If rare merit be the rarest of all rare things, it ought to pass through some sort of probation. The temple of honour ought to be seated on an eminence. If it be open through virtue, let it be remembered too, that virtue is never tried but by some difficulty, and some struggle.

Nothing is a due and adequate representation of a state, that does not represent its ability, as well as its property. But as ability is a vigorous and active principle, and as property sluggish, inert, and timid, it never can be safe from the invasions of ability, unless it be, out of all proportion, predominant in the representation. It must be represented too in great masses of accumulation, or it is not rightly protected. The characteristic essence of property, formed out of the combined principles of its acquisition and conservation, is to be unequal. The great masses therefore which excite envy, and tempt rapacity, must be put out of the possibility of danger. Then they form a natural rampart about the lesser properties in all their gradations. The same quantity of property, which is by the natural course of things divided among many, has not the same operation. Its defensive power is weakened as it is diffused. In this diffusion each man's portion is less than what, in the eagerness of his desires, he may flatter himself to obtain by dissipating the accumulations of others. The plunder of the few would indeed give but a share inconceivably small in the distribution to the many. But the many are not capable of making this calculation; and those who lead them to rapine, never intend this distribution. The power of perpetuating our property in our families is one of the most valuable and interesting circumstances belonging to it, and that which tends the most to the perpetuation of society itself. It makes our weakness subservient to our virtue; it grafts benevolence even upon avarice. The possessors of family wealth, and of the distinction which attends hereditary possession (as most concerned in it) are the natural securities for this transmission. With us, the house of peers is formed upon this principle. It is wholly composed of hereditary property and hereditary distinction; and made therefore the third of the legislature; and in the last event, the sole judge of all property in all its subdivisions. The house of commons too, though not necessarily, yet in fact, is always so composed in the far greater part. Let those large proprietors be what they will, and they have their chance of being amongst the best, they are at the very worst, the ballast in the vessel of the commonwealth. For though hereditary wealth, and the rank which goes with it, are too much idolized by creeping sycophants, and the blind abject admirers of power, they are too rashly slighted in shallow speculations of the petulant, assuming, short-sighted coxcombs of philosophy. Some decent regulated pre-eminence, some preference (not exclusive appropriation) given to birth, is neither unnatural, nor unjust, nor impolitic.

It is said, that twenty-four millions ought to prevail over two hundred thousand. True; if the constitution of a kingdom be a problem of arithmetic. This sort of discourse does well enough with the lamp-post for its second: to men who may reason calmly, it is ridiculous. The will of the many, and their interest, must very often differ; and great will be the difference when they make an evil choice. A government of five hundred country attornies and obscure curates is not good for twenty-four millions of men, though it were chosen by eight and forty millions; nor is it the better for being guided by a dozen persons of quality, who have betrayed their trust in order to obtain that power.

Part Two
THE WORLD OF CONSERVATIVE POLITICS

2.1 QUINTIN HOGG: THE PLACE OF POLITICS

One of the most famous affirmations of the limited role occupied by politics in the Conservative universe was written by Quintin Hogg (Lord Hailsham) in the early pages of *The Case for Conservatism* (1947) pp. 10–1). Even in Hogg there may be found some reflections of the affected anti-intellectualism of many Conservatives. ('The simplest among them prefer fox-hunting – the wisest religion.') Whoever their opponents – whether Jacobins, Utilitarians, Radicals, Liberals, Socialists – the pattern of Conservative argument has been the same: over-politicised and heated missionaries need to be kept in their place and their schemes exposed by the leaders of the Conservative party, who enjoy unrestricted access to the traditions of wisdom accumulated over the centuries.

For Conservatives do not believe that political struggle is the most important thing in life. In this they differ from Communists, Socialist, Nazis, Fascists, Social Creditors and most members of the British Labour Party. The simplest among them prefer fox-hunting – the wisest religion. To the great majority of Conservatives, religion, art, study, family, country, friends, music, fun, duty, all the joy and riches of existence of which the poor no less than the rich are the indefeasible freeholders, all these are higher in the scale than their handmaiden, the political struggle. This makes them easy to defeat – at first. But, once defeated, they will hold to this belief with the fanaticism of a Crusader and the doggedness of an Englishman. One of the earliest English Conservatives, the author of Hudibras, expressed in a single savage couplet his contempt for those

'Who think religion was intended
For nothing else than to be mended'.

This sentiment still animates the Conservative when he faces the political bigots of our time. It will win in the end. Whatever the fanatics may think, in this at least Conservatives have the vast majority on their side. The man who puts politics first is not fit to be called a civilised being, let alone a Christian.

Conservatives do not believe that the whole art and science of government can be summed up in some convenient phrase or catchword like 'Socialism' any more than the whole art of medicine is contained in an advertising slogan like 'night starvation'. They believe that there is an art or science of politics. They believe that disregard of its principles leads to untold suffering and inconvenience; their correct application to modest, but noteworthy advantages. An attempt will be made in this book to state some of these principles and their application. Moreover Conservatives believe that this store of wisdom is not something fixed and unalterable which we have received from our ancestors but a treasury to which it is the duty of each generation to make its characteristic contribution. But it follows from this that Conservatives reject any of the various 'Copernican' or revolutionary theories of politics which are current in our time. They do not believe that each generation in turn should start from scratch, abandoning all the wisdom of the past; on the contrary they consider that progress consists in each generation beginning at the point where their fathers left off. If we acted as if progress consisted in scrapping the achievements of the past, Conservatives do not think we should get very far.

The Conservative does not believe that the power of politics to put things right in this world is unlimited. This is partly because there are inherent limitations on what may be achieved by political means, but partly because man is an imperfect creature with a streak of evil as well as good in his inmost nature. By bitter experience Conservatives know that there are almost no limits to the misery or degradation to which bad governments may sink and depress their victims. But while others extol the virtues of the particular brand of Utopia they propose to create, the Conservative disbelieves them all, and, despite all temptations, offers in their place no Utopia at all but something quite modestly better than the present. He may, and should, have a programme. He certainly has, as will be shown, a policy. But of catchwords, slogans, visions, ideal states of society, classless societies, new orders, of all the tinsel and finery with which modern political charlatans charm their jewels from the modern political savage, the Conservative has nothing to offer. He would rather die than sell such trash, and consequently it is said wrongly by those who have something of this sort on their trays that he has no policy, and still more wrongly by those who value success above honour that he ought to find one. But if he is to be true to the light that is in him, the Conservative must maintain that the stuff of all such visions political is either illusion (in which case they are to be pitied) or chicanery (in which case they are to be condemned). The aim of politics, as of all else, is the good life. But the good life is something which cannot be comprehended in some phrase or formula about any political or social order, and even if it could be so comprehended it could not be brought about, in the main, by political means. The Conservative contends that the most a politician can do is to ensure that some, and these by no means the most important, conditions in which the good life can exist are present, and, more important still, to prevent fools or knaves from setting up conditions which make any approach to the good life impossible except for solitaries or authorites. A depressing creed? A negative creed? No! A Holy Gospel! All the great evils of our time have come from men who mocked and exploited human misery by pretending that good government, that is government according to their way of thinking, could offer Utopia.

The Conservative thinks that in political life it is every bit as important to combat evil as to create good. Unlike the seven new tenants of the house, he holds to the Old Faith that man, apart from the grace of God, is not perfectible. Conservatives read with impatience *Men like Gods* and prefer *The Time Machine*. Both are fantasies, but the one is a false myth, the other more like the truth. Conservatives have observed that H. G. Wells, who despite *The Time Machine* was an ardent perfectionist, died in ultimate and irretrievable despair about the future of Homo Sapiens. Conservatives, where they are not Christians, which the wisest of them are, would agree with him, but cannot make out why so intelligent a man took more than seventy years to discover what they regard as an obvious truth. Accordingly Conservatives do not expect to found a society wherein a perfected human nature will function contentedly, requiring no more attention than a well-oiled machine. They are not careful to use theological terms, but, whatever the theological implications, they are convinced that nothing is more clearly taught by all human history and experience than the fact in human nature which our forefathers simply described as original sin. They believe that persistently in human life, in our own nature no less than in others, is an active positive principle of evil, and that part of the constant duty of the statesman is to combat its operation. Perhaps our Liberal forefathers meant much the same when they said: 'The price of Liberty is eternal vigilance'.

Unlike their opponents, the last thing Conservatives believe is that they have the monopoly of the truth. They do not even claim the monopoly of Conservatism. Modern Conservatives believe in the Liberal democratic state as it has gradually developed according to the British tradition. This means that, despite the dangers which they see in their opponents' policy, they do not believe that the good of Britain would be attained if the Conservatives held a monopoly of power. On the contrary, the whole essence of the type of democracy in which they put their trust is that the public good is attained by the interplay of rival forces, of which they recognise themselves to be but one.

2.2 WILLIAM WORDSWORTH: NATIONAL SENTIMENT

Wordsworth's (1770–1850) *Tract on the Convention of Cintra* (1809) was an attack on the Cintra agreement by which French forces in Portugal were allowed to return to France in spite of the fact that they faced near certain defeat. The Convention provoked an outcry in Britain. Wordsworth's *Tract* argued that Napoleon could not be defeated by the traditional military methods but only by unleashing the forces of patriotism and nationalism which were just beginning to awake. The following lines, then, assert the inadequacy of the politics of oligarchy and endorse natural loyalties to country and fatherland. Wordsworth is referring to one of the most common of political delusions. From *Tract on the Convention of Cintra*, lines 3419–3512.

It is this: that practical Statesmen assume too much credit to themselves for their ability to see into the motives and manage the selfish passions of their immediate agents and dependents; and for the skill with which they baffle or resist the aims of their opponents. A promptness in looking through the most superficial part of the characters of those men – who, by the very circumstance of their contending ambitiously for the rewards and honours of government, are separated from the mass of the society to which they belong – is mistaken for a knowledge of human kind. Hence, where higher knowledge is a prime requisite, they not only are unfurnished; but, being unconscious that they are so, they look down contemptuously upon those who endeavour to supply (in some degree) their want. The instincts of natural and social man; the deeper emotions; the simpler feelings; the spacious range of the disinterested imagination; the pride in country for country's sake, when to serve has not been a formal profession – and the mind is therefore left in a state of dignity only to be surpassed by having served nobly and generously; the instantaneous accomplishment in which they start up who, upon a searching call, stir for the land which they love – not from personal motives, but for a reward which is undefined and cannot be missed; the solemn fraternity which a great nation composes – gathered together, in a stormy season, under the shade of ancestral feeling; the delicacy of moral honour which pervades the minds of a people, when despair has been suddenly thrown off and expectations are lofty; the apprehensiveness to a touch unkindly or irreverent, where sympathy is at once extracted as a tribute and welcomed as a gift; the power of injustice and inordinate calamity to transmute, to invigorate, and to govern – to sweep away the barriers of opinion – to reduce under submission passions purely evil – to exalt the nature of indifferent qualities, and to render them fit companions for the absolute virtues with which they are summoned to associate – to consecrate passions which, if not bad in themselves, are of such temper that, in the calm of ordinary life, they are rightly deemed so – to correct and embody these passions – and, without weakening them (nay, with tenfold addition to their strength), to make them worthy of taking their place as the advanced guard of hope, when a sublime movement of deliverance is to be originated; – these arrangements and resources of nature, these ways and means of society, have so little connection with those others upon which a ruling minister of a long-established government is accustomed to depend; these – elements as it were of a universe, functions of a living body – are so opposite, in their mode of action, to the formal machine which it has been his pride to manage; – that he has but a faint perception of their immediate efficacy; knows not the facility with which they assimilate with other powers; nor the property by which such of them – as, from necessity of nature, must change or pass away – will, under wise and fearless management, surely generate lawful successors to fill their place when their appropriate work is performed. Nay, of the majority of men, who are usually found in high stations under old governments, it may without injustice be said; that, when they look about them in times (alas! too rare) which present the glorious product of such agency to their eyes, they have not a right to say – with a dejected man in the midst of the woods, the rivers, the mountains, the sunshine, and shadows of some transcendant landscape – 'I see, not feel, how beautiful they are:' These spectators neither see nor feel. And it is from the blindness and insensibility of these, and the train whom they draw along with them, that the throes of nations have been so ill recompensed by the births which have followed; and that revolutions, after passing from crime to crime and from sorrow to sorrow, have often ended in throwing back such heavy reproaches of delusiveness upon their first promises.

I am satisfied that no enlightened Patriot will impute to me a wish to disparage the characters of men high in authority, or to detract from the estimation which is fairly due to them. My purpose is to guard against unreasonable expectations. That specific knowledge – the paramount importance of which, in the present condition of Europe, I am insisting upon, – they, who usually fill places of high trust in old governments, neither do – nor, for the most part can – possess: nor is it necessary, for the administration of affairs in ordinary circumstances, that they should. The progress of their own country, and of the other nations of the world, in civilization, in true refinement, in science, in religion, in morals, and in all the real wealth of humanity, might indeed be quicker, and might correspond more happily with the wishes of the benevolent, – if Governors better understood the rudiments of nature as studied in the walks of common life; if they were men who had themselves felt every strong emotion 'inspired by nature and by fortune taught;' and could calculate upon the force of the grander passions. Yet, at the same time there is temptation in this. To know may seduce; and to have been agitated may compel. Arduous cares are attractive for their own sakes. Great talents are naturally driven towards hazard and difficulty; as it is there that they are most sure to find their exercise, and their evidence, and joy in anticipated triumph – the liveliest of all sensations. Moreover; magnificent desires, when least under the bias of personal feeling, dispose the mind – more than itself is conscious of – to regard commotion with complacency, and to watch the aggravations of distress with welcoming; from an immediate confidence that, when the appointed day shall come, it will be in the power of intellect to relieve. There is danger in being a zealot in any cause – not expecting that of humanity. Nor is it to be forgotten that the incapacity and ignorance of the regular agents of long-established governments do not prevent some progress in the dearest concerns of men; and that society may owe to these very deficiencies, and to the tame and unenterprizing course which they necessitate, much security and tranquil enjoyment.

2.3 STANLEY BALDWIN: THE VIRTUES OF EMPIRE

The imperial ideology of Disraeli and of Chamberlain will be discussed later. At its most mature state, Conservative imperalism may be savoured

in the unpretentious, unphilosophical speeches of Stanley Baldwin.
(1864–1947) The first of the following extracts is taken from his speech at
the Albert Hall on 4 December 1924 (printed in Baldwin's: *On England*
(1926), pp. 71–2). The second is taken from a broadcast speech from 10
Downing Street on 24 May 1929 (printed in Baldwin's *Our Inheritance*
(1928), pp. 67–9).

When we speak of Empire, it is in no spirit of flag-wagging. What we
feel, I think, is this: we feel that in this great inheritance of ours,
separated as it is by the seas, we have yet one home and one people,
and we want the realization of that to be so vivid to our own people
that men may ask themselves, as they come to manhood 'Where in
this great inherited estate can I do best for myself? Where have I a
better opportunity of bringing up my family? Where can I do best
for the Empire?' When the answer given is 'overseas', let us do
everything we can do to see that the path is made easy for those who
desire it, that we may help to spread the peoples of our Empire, the
ideals of our Empire, the trade of our Empire from one side of the
world to the other. After all, great as the material benefits are, we do
not look primarily to them. I think deep down in all our hearts we
look to the Empire as the means by which we may hope to see that
increase of our race which we believe to be of such inestimable
benefit to the world at large; the spread abroad of people to whom
freedom and justice are as the breath of their nostrils, of people
distinguished, as we would fain hope and believe, above all things,
by an abiding sense of duty. If ever the day should come when an
appeal to that sense of duty falls on deaf ears among our own kin,
that day indeed would be the end of our country and of our Empire,
to which you and I have dedicated our very lives.

*   *   *

Let us consider for a moment what we mean by heritage. We have
been born into a community settled in a small island, dependent for
our food supplies on the produce of countries overseas, and that food
we pay for by exporting goods. In these circumstances there
inevitably come times when the opportunities of many of our people
are restricted, but for us alone are still opportunities denied to other
nations. It is open to us to settle and work in any climate we may
choose and in almost any part of the world, and find ourselves
amongst people who speak our tongue, who obey our laws, who
cherish the same ideals, and worship according to the rites familiar
to us, who are subjects of the same Sovereign; and to this we must
devote our best energies in the years to come – Tory, Liberal, and

Labour alike – to make our unity such a reality that men and women regard the Empire as one, and that it may become possible for them to move within its bounds to New Zealand, to Australia, to South Africa, to Canada, as easily and as freely as from Glasgow to London or Bristol to Newcastle.

2.4 SIR ARTHUR BRYANT: THE VALUE OF THE MONARCHY

Sir Arthur Bryant was one of the most popular, and prolific, of Tory historians of the twentieth century. He saw the history of Britain as the heroic assertion of the spirit of Britain against its enemies. His book *The Spirit of Conservatism* (1929) summarised in a somewhat melodramatic and unctuous manner the essentials of his Tory creed. That is what he has to say about the monarchy (pp. 66–9).

The King offers something to which the loyalty of a nation, its noblest attribute, may attach. In his person he appeals to the imagination of his subjects; he represents for them all they mean by the sacred word of country, the land of their fathers, their homes, their laws, their liberties. A Parliament, a Council, a Committee, however sensibly and well constituted, can never raise the same passionate and unthinking sentiment of love and devotion as can a King. If a nation is to live, its citizens must be ready to sacrifice all in its service. But for every ten men who would die for their County Council, there are ten thousand who would offer their lives for their King. 'I cannot contain myself within my door,' wrote Sir Bevil Grenville, 'when the King of England's standard waves in the field upon so just occasion – the cause being such as must make all those who die in it little inferior to martyrs. And, for my own, I desire to acquire an honest name or an honourable grave.' It is this spirit which the State must desire to see in all its citizens; the throne, the sceptre and the crown, can alone inspire it.

The King stands for that continuity in human affairs which men, in the pathetic transience of their own lives, so earnestly desire. For, though the life of the King as an individual is as fugitive as any man's, the life of the King as an institution is enduring. The holder of the title dies: a new King is that very instant of time takes his place. 'The King is dead,' the herald cries, 'God save the King'. The prayer that God may save the King – 'Long may he reign' – is not for the living King alone, but for all the Kings of England, for that long line which for over a thousand years has given to all things English unbroken continuity, has preserved our laws and liberties and given to loyalty a watchword and a rallying point – an English institution, as old and undying as the nation itself. Death comes alike to the bearer of the Crown as to the subject:

> This is a sleep
> That from this golden rigol hath divorced
> So many English Kings: –

but in the monarchy itself, the wisdom of our forefathers has left us something 'which is not for time's throwing', and which, in a world of things transient, perpetuates its benefits from generation to generation.

Even in the brief limits of human life, each King affords to his subjects some measure of continuity. The King to-day does not direct the State, but he is the permanent mentor of those who do. They change from Parliament to Parliament, almost from year to year. He alone, during life, does not change. A sovereign, like Queen Victoria, during sixty-four years on the throne, in active and daily touch with every great affair of State and every great man, acquired an unrivalled knowledge of public business. At the end of her reign she was giving to her Ministers the benefit of her vast knowledge and shrewd judgement, gained from her association with the great men of a previous day who had ruled England before the former were born. In a democratic country where the human agents of Government change so frequently, it is something to have ever at their shoulder the wise and experienced advice of a permanent sovereign.

That the crown is hereditary is sometimes held a disadvantage. But since the crown is necessary as a permanent pivot for the forces of government, much would be lost and nothing gained by an elective throne. As it is the King is selected on the same principle as each one of us is selected for his part and place in life – that of birth. He does not have to struggle and push to attain his position and, therefore, does not sustain that loss of natural dignity and generosity, which is too often the price of struggling for place. His position raises no envy and consequently no rift in the Commonwealth, for no one is envious of what can never by any conceivable chance be his. He is above faction and above class; and ambition, 'that last infirmity of noble mind', cannot touch him, for, though he has much to lose, he has no worldly rank or honour to gain. Through lack of any other, his main interest and ambition must lie in the well-being of his subjects and his position in their eyes. From infancy he is trained, as one set apart for a high calling, for the unusual and exacting duties of his great position.

'The wisdom of your forefathers,' wrote Disraeli, 'placed the prize of supreme power without the sphere of human passions. Whatever the struggle of parties, whatever the strife of factions . . . there has always been something in this country round which all classes and parties could rally, representing the majesty of the law, and administration of justice, and involving . . . the security of every man's right and the fountain of honour.'

The King is the representative of the whole nation. By birth he represents his countrymen as Adam represents the human race. He belongs to no class and no Party, and the preferment of any one section of his subjects can avail him nothing. His interest is bound up with that of the nation as a whole; he is greatest when all his people are contented, free and noble. He represents the patriot in us all, that part which responds to the claims of common soil, common blood and common laws. With our self-seeking aims, struggling for the preferment of ourselves, our class, our faction, he has no part or interest, for he is placed by his birth and position beyond the need for pettiness. He, the patriot King, is the true democrat – the representative, not of the majority of the people, but of the people themselves.

2.5 BENJAMIN DISRAELI: THE DEFENCE OF CHURCH ESTABLISHMENTS

Disraeli launched a public exposition of his own brand of Conservatism in two great speeches delivered within a few weeks of each other: the first at Manchester on 3 April 1872, the second at the Crystal Palace on 24 June 1872. The central theme of both speeches was the definition of the vocation of the Conservative party as the defence of national institutions. Prominent among these, of course, was the defence of the Anglican Church. Almost certainly in retaliation to a speech by Sir Charles Dilke at Newcastle in November 1871 which had criticised the cost of the monarchy, Disraeli was at pains in both of his 1872 speeches to redefine the Conservative party's commitment to the defence of the Anglican Church. The most detailed statement of his position is to be found in the Manchester speech. From T. Kebbel (Ed.): *Speeches of the Earl of Beaconsfield* (2 vols, 1882), II, pp. 502–5.

The wisest Sovereigns and statesmen have ever been anxious to connect authority with religion – some to increase their power, some, perhaps, to mitigate its exercise. But the same difficulty has been experienced in effecting this union which has been experienced in forming a Second Chamber – either the spiritual power has usurped upon the civil and established a sacerdotal society, or the civil power has invaded successfully the rights of the spiritual, and the ministers of religion have been degraded into stipendiaries of the State and instruments of the Government. In England we accomplish this great result by an alliance between Church and State, between two originally independent powers. I will not go into the history of that alliance, which is rather a question for those archaeological societies which occasionally amuse and instruct the people of this city. Enough for me that this union was made and has contributed for centuries to the civilisation of this country. Gentlemen, there is the same assault against the Church of England and the union between the State and the Church as there is against the Monarchy and against the House of Lords. It is said that the existence of Nonconformity proves that the Church is a failure. I draw from these premises an exactly contrary conclusion; and I maintain that to have secured a national profession of faith with the unlimited enjoyment of private judgement in matters spiritual is the solution of the most difficult problem, and one of the triumphs, of civilisation.

It is said that the existence of parties in the Church also proves its incompetence. On that matter, too, I entertain a contrary opinion. Parties have always existed in the Church; and some have appealed to them as arguments in favour of its Divine institution, because, in the services and doctrines of the Church have been found representatives of every mood in the human mind. Those who are influenced by ceremonies find consolation in forms which secure to them 'the beauty of holiness.' Those who are not satisfied except with enthusiasm find in its ministrations the exaltation they require, while others who believe that 'the anchor of faith' can never be safely moored except in the dry sands of reason find a religion within the pale of the Church which can boast of its irrefragable logic and its irresistible evidence.

Gentlemen, I am inclined sometimes to believe that those who advocate the abolition of the union between Church and State have not carefully considered the consequences of such a course. The Church is a powerful corporation of many millions of Her Majesty's subjects, with a consummate organisation and wealth which in its aggregate is vast. Restricted and controlled by the State, so powerful a corporation may be only fruitful of public advantage, but it becomes a great question what might be the consequence of the severance of the controlling tie between these two bodies. The State would be enfeebled, but the Church would probably be strengthened. Whether that is a result to be desired is a grave question for all men. For my own part, I am bound to say that I doubt whether it would be favourable to the cause of civil and religious liberty. I know that there is a common idea that if the union between Church and State was severed, the wealth of the Church would revert to the State; but it would be well to remember that the great proportion of ecclesiastical property is the property of individuals. Take, for example, the fact that the great mass of Church patronage is patronage in the hands of private persons. That you could not touch without compensation to the patrons. You have established that principle in your late Irish Bill, where there was very little patronage. And in the present state of the public mind on the subject, there is very little doubt that there would be scarcely a patron in England – irrespective of other aid the Church would receive – who would not dedicate his compensation to the spiritual wants of his neighbours.

It was computed some years ago that the property of the Church, in this manner if the union was terminated, would not be less than between £80,000,000, and £90,000,000; and since that period the amount of private property dedicated to the purposes of the Church has very largely increased. I therefore trust that when the occasion offers for the country to speak out, it will speak out in an unmistakable manner on this subject; and, recognising the inestimable services of the Church, that it will call upon the Government to maintain its union with the State. Upon this subject there is one remark I would make. Nothing is more surprising to me than the plea on which the present outcry is made against the Church of England. I could not believe that in the nineteenth century the charge against the Church of England should be that Churchmen, and especially the clergy, had educated the people. If I were to fix upon one circumstance more than another which redounded to the honour of Churchmen, it is, that they should fulfil this noble office; and, next to being 'the stewards of Divine mysteries,' I think the greatest distinction of the clergy is the admirable manner in which they have devoted their lives and their fortunes to this greatest of national objects.

Gentlemen, you are well acquainted in this city with this controversy. It was in this city – I don't know whether it was not in this hall – that that remarkable meeting was held of the Nonconformists to effect important alterations in the Education Act, and you are acquainted with the discussion in Parliament which arose in consequence of that meeting. Gentlemen, I have due and great respect for the Nonconformist body. I acknowledge their services to their country, and though I believe that the political reasons which mainly called them into existence have entirely ceased, it is impossible not to treat with consideration a body which has been eminent for its conscience, its learning, and its patriotism; but I must express my mortification that, from a feeling of envy or of pique, the Nonconformist body, rather than assist the Church in their great enterprise, should absolutely have become the partisans of a merely secular education. I believe myself, gentlemen, that without the recognition of a superintending Province in the affairs of this world all national education will be disastrous, and I feel confident that it is impossible to stop at that mere recognition. Religious education is demanded by the nation generally and by the instincts of human nature. I should like to see the Church and the Nonconformists work together; but I trust, whatever may be the result, the country will stand by the Church in its efforts to maintain the religious education of the people. Gentlemen, I foresee yet trials for the Church of England; but I am confident in its nature. I am confident in its future because I believe there is now a very general feeling that to be national it must be comprehensive. I will not use the word 'broad', because it is an epithet applied to a system with which I have no sympathy. But I would wish Churchmen, and especially the clergy, always to remember that in our 'Father's Home there are many mansions,' and I believe that comprehensive spirit is perfectly consistent with the maintenance of formularies and the belief in dogmas without which I hold no practical religion can exist.

3.1   EDMUND BURKE: THE PHILOSOPHY OF REFORM

Burke spent most of his political life in opposition, as a leading member of the party of the Marquis of Rockingham. As one of the party's leading propagandists and writers, Burke frequently denounced the system of government which consigned his party to years of almost uninterrupted opposition. In 1780 Burke developed a plan of Economic (i.e. Administrative) Reform which he advocated as a cure for the corruption and inefficiency of government. Such timely reform would equally protect the independence of Parliament from the executive and restore it to its true functions: of acting as a control upon both king and people. In his great speech to the House of Commons when introducing his plan (11 February 1780) Burke outlined his thinking on the virtues of moderate, timely reform. From *Speech on Economical Reform*, 11 February 1780, *Works of Edmund Burke* (2 vols, 1834), vol. I, p. 232.

I do most seriously put it to administration, to consider the wisdom of a timely reform. Early reformations are amicable arrangements with a friend in power; late reformations are terms imposed upon a conquered enemy: reformations are made in cool blood; late reformations are made under a state of inflammation. In that state of things the people behold in government nothing that is respectable. They see the abuse, and they will see nothing else – They fall into the temper of a furious populace provoked at the disorder of a house of ill fame; they never attempt to correct or regulate; they go to work by the shortest way – They abate the nuisance, they pull down the house.

This is my opinion with regard to the true interest of government. But as it is the interest of government that reformation should be early, it is the interest of the people that it should be temperate. It is their interest, because a temperate reform is permanent; and because it has a principle of growth. Whenever we improve, it is right to leave room for a further improvement. It is right to consider, to look about us, to examine the effect of what we have done. – Then we can proceed with confidence, because we can proceed with intelligence. Whereas in hot reformations, in what men, more zealous than considerate, call *making clear work*, the whole is generally so crude, so harsh, so indigested; mixed with so much imprudence, and so much injustice; so contrary to the whole course of human nature, and human institutions, that the very people who are most eager for it are among the first to grow disgusted at what they have done. Then some part of the abdicated grievance is recalled from its exile in order to become a corrective of the correction. Then the abuse assumes all the credit and popularity of a reform. The very idea of purity and disinterestedness in politics falls into disrepute, and is considered as a vision of hot and inexperienced men; and thus disorders become incurable, not by the virulence of their own quality, but by the inapt and violent nature of the remedies. A great part, therefore, of my idea of reform is meant to operate gradually; some benefits will come at a nearer, some at a more remote period. We must no more make haste to be rich by parsimony, than by intemperate acquisition.

In my opinion, it is our duty when we have the desires of the people before us, to pursue them, not in the spirit of literal obedience, which may militate with their very principle, much less to treat them with a peevish and contentious litigation, as if we were adverse parties in a suit. It would, Sir, be most dishonourable for a faithful representative of the commons to take advantage of any inartificial expression of the people's wishes, in order to frustrate their attainment of what they have an undoubted right to expect. We are under indefinite obligations to our constituents, who have raised us to so distinguished a trust, and have imparted such a degree of sanctity to common characters. We ought to walk before them with purity, plainness, and integrity of heart; with filial love, and not with slavish fear, which is always a low and tricking thing. For my own part, in what I have meditated upon that subject, I cannot indeed take upon me to say I have the honour to *follow* the sense of the people. The truth is, *I met it on the way*, while I was pursuing their interest according to my own ideas. I am happy beyond expression to find that my intentions have so far coincided with theirs, that I have not had cause to be in the least scrupulous to sign their petition, conceiving it to express my own opinions, as nearly as general terms can express the object of particular arrangements.

I am therefore satisfied to act as a fair mediator between government and the people, endeavouring to form a plan which should have both an early and a temperate operation. I mean, that it should be substantial; that it should be systematick. That it should rather strike at the first cause of prodigality and corrupt influence, than attempt to follow them in all their effects.

3.2 EDMUND BURKE: POLITICAL THINKING

Burke was fond of denouncing abstract speculation in both political and social affairs. It was, however, the French Revolution, which, according to Burke, proceeded according to the abstract metaphysical ideals of the Enlightenment, afforded the grossest example of the consequences of bad thinking about politics. In the *Reflections* he has a famous passage in which he attacks the evils of abstract speculation in politics. From Edmund Burke: *Reflections on the Revolution in France* (1790), Pelican Edition, 1968, ed. Conor Cruise O'Brien, pp. 152–3.

The science of constructing a commonwealth, or renovating it, or reforming it, is, like every other experimental science, not to be taught *a priori*. Nor is it a short experience that can instruct us in that practical science; because the real effects of moral causes are not always immediate; but that which in the first instance is prejudicial may be excellent in its remoter operation; and its excellence may arise even from the ill effects it produces in the beginning. The reverse also happens; and very plausible schemes, with very pleasing commencements, have often shameful and lamentable conclusions. In states there are often some obscure and almost latent causes, things which appear at first view of little moment, on which a very great part of its prosperity or adversity may most essentially depend. The science of government being therefore so practical in itself, and intended for such practical purposes, a matter which requires experience, and even more experience than any person can gain in his whole life, however sagacious and observing he may be, it is with infinite caution that any man ought to venture upon pulling down an edifice which has answered in any tolerable degree for ages the common purposes of society, or on building it up again, without having models and patterns of approved utility before his eyes.

These metaphysic rights entering into common life, like rays of light which pierce into a dense medium, are, by the laws of nature, refracted from their straight line. Indeed in the gross and complicated mass of human passions and concerns, the primitive rights of men undergo such a variety of refractions and reflections, that it becomes absurd to talk of them as if they continued in the simplicity of their original direction. The nature of man is intricate; the objects of society are of the greatest possible complexity; and therefore no simple disposition or direction of power can be suitable either to man's nature, or to the quality of his affairs. When I hear the simplicity of contrivance aimed at and boasted of in any new political constitutions, I am at no loss to decide that the artificers are grossly ignorant of their trade, or totally negligent of their duty. The simple governments are fundamentally defective, to say no worse of them. If you were to contemplate society in but one point of view, all these simple modes of polity are infinitely captivating. In effect each would answer its single end much more perfectly than the more complex is able to attain all its complex purposes. But it is better that the whole should be imperfectly and anomalously answered, than that, while some parts are provided for with great exactness, others might be totally neglected, or perhaps materially injured, by the over-care of a favourite member.

The pretended rights of these theorists are all extremes; and in proportion as they are metaphysically true, they are morally and politically false. The rights of men are in a sort of *middle*, incapable of definition, but not impossible to be discerned. The rights of men in governments are their advantages; and these are often in balances between differences of good; in compromises sometimes between good and evil, and sometimes, between evil and evil. Political reason is a computing principle; adding, subtracting, multiplying, and dividing, morally and not metaphysically or mathematically, true moral denominations.

3.3 EDMUND BURKE: THE SOCIAL CONTRACT AND HUMAN OBLIGATION

Burke's contract theory occupies a central place in his political philosophy. His characteristic ideas of the contract distance him from most contemporary thinkers and separate him sharply from the radical philosophy of his time. Many elements of his political philosophy derive directly from his contractual ideas: the duty of obedience, the nature of political leadership, his conception of the rights of the majority. The most extended discussion of these themes occurs in *Appeal from the New to the Old Whigs* (1791). Burke is anxious to confront the radical assumptions about the rights of elective majorities and their right to resist authority. Burke is concerned that these assumptions are spreading in his own party and is at pains to reaffirm and to underline some of the arguments which he had raised in the *Reflections*, a year earlier. From Edmund Burke: *Appeal from the New to the Old Whigs* (1791) in *Works of Edmund Burke*, (1834) 2 vols. Vol. II, pp. 521–3.

The factions, now so busy amongst us, in order to divest men of all love for their country, and to remove from their minds all duty with regard to the state, endeavour to propagate an opinion, that the people, in forming their commonwealth, have by no means parted with their power over it. This is an impregnable citadel, to which these gentlemen retreat whenever they are pushed by the battery of laws and usages, and positive conventions. Indeed it is such and of so great force, that all they have done, in defending their outworks, is so much time and labour thrown away. Discuss any of their schemes – the answer is – It is the act of the *people*, and that is sufficient. Are we to deny to a *majority* of the people the right of altering even the whole frame of their society, if such should be their pleasure? They may change it, say they, from a monarchy to a republick to-day, and tomorrow back again from a republick to a monarchy; and so backward and forward as often as they like. They are masters of the commonwealth; because in substance they are themselves the commonwealth. The French Revolution, say they, was the act of the majority of the people; and if the majority of any other people, the people of England for instance, wish to make the same change, they have the same right.

Just the same undoubtedly. That is, none at all. Neither the few nor the many have a right to act merely by their will, in any matter connected with duty, trust, engagement, or obligation. The Constitution of a country being once settled upon some compact, tacit or expressed, there is no power existing of force to alter it, without the breach of the covenant, or the consent of all the parties. Such is the nature of a contract. And the votes of a majority of the people, whatever their infamous flatterers may teach in order to corrupt their minds, cannot alter the moral any more than they can alter the physical essence of things. The people are not to be taught to think lightly of their engagements to their governours; else they teach governours to think lightly of their engagements towards them. In that kind of game in the end the people are sure to be losers. To flatter them into a contempt of faith, truth, and justice, is to ruin them; for in these virtues consist their whole safety. To flatter any man, or any part of mankind, in any description, by asserting, that in engagements he or they are free whilst any other human creature is bound, is ultimately to vest the rule of morality in the pleasure of those who ought to be rigidly submitted to it; to subject the sovereign reason of the world to the caprices of weak and giddy men.

But, as no one of us men can dispense with publick or private faith, or with any other tie of moral obligation, so neither can any number of us. The number engaged in crimes, instead of turning them into laudable acts, only augments the quantity and intensity of the guilt. I am well aware, that men love to hear of their power, but have an extreme disrelish to be told of their duty. This is of course because every duty is a limitation of some power. Indeed arbitrary power is so much to the depraved taste of the vulgar, of the vulgar of every description, that almost all the dissensions, which lacerate the commonwealth, are not concerning the manner in which it is to be exercised, but concerning the hands in which it is to be placed. Somewhere they are resolved to have it. Whether they desire it to be vested in the many or the few, depends with most men upon the chance which they imagine they themselves may have of partaking in the exercise of that arbitrary sway, in the one mode or in the other.

It is not necessary to teach men to thirst after power. But it is very expedient that by moral instruction, they should be taught, and by their civil constitutions they should be compelled, to put many restrictions upon the immoderate exercise of it, and the inordinate desire. The best method of obtaining these two great points forms the important, but at the same time the difficult, problem to the true statesman. He thinks of the place in which political power is to be lodged, with no other attention, than as it may render the more or the less practicable, its salutary restraint, and its prudent direction. For this reason no legislator, at any period of the world, has willingly placed the seat of active power in the hands of the multitude: because there it admits of no controul, no regulation, no steady direction whatsoever. The people are the natural controul on authority; but to exercise and to controul together is contradictory and impossible.

As the exorbitant exercise of power cannot, under popular sway, be effectually restrained, the other great object of political arrangement, the means of abating an excessive desire of it, is in such a state still worse provided for. The democratick commonwealth is the foodful nurse of ambition. Under the other forms it meets with many restraints. Whenever, in states which have had a democratick basis, the legislators have endeavoured to put restraints upon ambition, their methods were as violent, as in the end they were ineffectual: as violent indeed as any of the most jealous despotism could invent. The ostracism could not very long save itself, and much less the state which it was meant to guard, from the attempts of ambition, one of the natural, inbred, incurable distempers of a powerful democracy.

But to return from this short digression, which however is not wholly foreign to the question of the effect of the will of the majority upon the form or the existence of their society. I cannot too often recommend it to the serious consideration of all men, who think civil society to be within the province of moral jurisdiction, that if we owe to it any duty, it is not subject to our will. Duties are not voluntary. Duty and will are even contradictory terms. Now though civil society might be at first a voluntary act, (which in many cases it undoubtedly was,) its continuance is under a permanent, standing covenant, co-existing with the society; and it attaches upon every individual of that society, without any formal act of his own. This is warranted by the general practice, arising out of the general sense of mankind. Men without their choice derive benefits from that association; without their choice they are subjected to duties in consequence of these benefits; and without their choice they enter into a virtual obligation as binding as any that is actual. Look through the whole of life and the whole system of duties. Much the strongest moral obligations are such as were never the results of our option. I allow, that if no supreme ruler exists, wise to form, and potent to enforce, the moral law, there is no sanction to any contract, virtual or even actual, against the will of prevalent power. On that hypothesis, let any set of men be strong enough to set their duties at defiance, and they cease to be duties any longer. We have but this one appeal against irresistible power –

Si genus humanum et mortalia temnitis arma,
At sperate deos memores fandi atque nefandi

Taking it for granted that I do not write to the disciples of the Parisian philosophy, I may assume, that the awful Author of our being is the Author of our place in the order of existence; and that having disposed and marshalled us by a divine tactick, not according to our will, but according to his, he has, in and by that disposition, virtually subjected us to act the part which belongs to the place assigned us. We have obligations to mankind at large, which are not in consequence of any special voluntary pact. They arise from the relation of man to man, and the relation of man to God, which relations are not matters of choice. On the contrary, the force of all the pacts which we enter into with any particular person, or number of persons amongst mankind, depends upon those prior obligations. In some cases the subordinate relations are voluntary, in others they are necessary – but the duties are all compulsive. When we marry, the choice is voluntary, but the duties are not matter of choice. They are dictated by the nature of the situation. Dark and inscrutable are the ways by which we come into the world. The instincts which give rise to this mysterious process of nature are not of our making. But out of physical causes, unknown to us, perhaps unknowable, arise moral duties, which, as we are able perfectly to comprehend, we are bound indispensably to perform. Parents may not be consenting to their moral relation; but consenting or not, they are bound to a long train of burthensome duties towards those with whom they have never made a convention of any sort. Children are not consenting to their relation, but their relation, without their actual consent, binds them to its duties; or rather it implies their consent, because the presumed consent of every rational creature is in unison with the predisposed order of things. Men come in that manner into a community with the social state of their parents, endowed with all the benefits, loaded with all the duties, of their situation. If the social ties and ligaments, spun out of those physical relations which are the elements of the commonwealth, in most cases begin, and always continue, independently of our will, so, without any stipulation on our own part, are we bound by that relation called our country, which comprehends (as it has been well said) 'all the charities of all.' Nor are we left without powerful instincts to make this duty as dear and grateful to us, as it is awful and coercive. Our country is not a thing of mere physical locality. It consists, in a great measure, in the ancient order into which we are born. We may have the same geographical situation, but another country; as we may have the same country in another soil. The place that determines our duty to our country is a social, civil relation.

These are the opinions of the author whose cause I defend. I lay them down not to enforce them upon others by disputation, but as an account of his proceedings. On them he acts; and from them he is convinced that neither, he, nor any man, or number of men, have a right (except what necessity, which is out of and above all rule, rather imposes than bestows) to free themselves from that primary engagement into which every man born into a community as much contracts by his being born into it, as he contracts an obligation to certain parents by his having been derived from their bodies. The place of every man determines his duty.

3.4   EDMUND BURKE: THE PROTECTION OF PROPERTY

Burke was prepared to entertain no interference with the ownership of property. To interfere with the ownership of property threatened the principle of prescription and the very stability of society. To threaten prescription was to threaten titles to property and titles to political power. To weaken one was to weaken the other.

Perhaps Burke's most direct statement of his belief in the unhindered possession of property occurs in his letter to Captain Thomas Mercer (26 February 1790, *Correspondence of Edmund Burke* (vol. VI, 1967, ed. A. Cobban and E.A. Smith), pp. 93–95.)

As far as my share of a public trust goes, I am in *trust* religiously to maintain the rights and properties of all descriptions of people in the *possession* which legally they hold; and in the *rule* by which alone they can be secure in any possession. I do not find myself at liberty, either as a man, or as a trustee for men, to take a *vested* property from one man, and to give it to another, because *I* think that the portion of one is too great, and that of another too small. From my first juvenile rudiments of speculative study to the grey hairs of my present experience, I have never learned any thing else. I can never be taught any thing else by *reason*; and when *force* comes, I shall consider whether I am to submit to it, or how I am to resist it. This I am very sure of, that an early guard against the manifest tendency of a contrary doctrine is the only way by which those who love order can be prepared to resist such force.

The calling men by the names of 'pampered and luxurious prelates', &c, is in you no more than a mark of your dislike to intemperance and idle expence; but in others it is used for other purposes. It is often used to extinguish the sense of justice in our minds, and the natural feelings of humanity in our bosoms. Such language does not mitigate the cruel effects of reducing men of opulent condition, and their innumerable dependents, to the last distress. If I were to adopt the plan of a spoliatory reformation, I should probably employ such language; but it would aggravate instead of extenuating my guilt in overturning the sacred principles of property.

Sir, I say that church and state, and human society too, for which church and state are made, are subverted by such doctrines, joined to such practices, as leave no foundation for property in *long possessions*. My dear Captain Mercer, it is not my calling the use you make of your plate in your house, either of dwelling or of prayer, 'pageantry and hypocrisy', that can justify me in taking from you your own property, and your own liberty to use your own property according to your own ideas of ornament. When you find me attempting to break into your house to take your plate, under any pretence whatsoever, but most of all under pretence of purity of religion and Christian charity, shoot me for a robber and an hypocrite, as in that case I shall certainly be. The 'true Christian religion' never taught me any such practices, nor did the religion of my nature, nor any religion, nor any law.

Let those who never abstained from a full meal, and as much wine as they could swallow, for a single day of their whole lives, satirize 'luxurious and pampered prelates', if they will. Let them abuse such prelates, and such lords, and such squires, provided it be only to correct their vices. I care not much about the language of this moral satire, if they go no further than satire. But there are occasions when the language of Falstaff, reproaching the Londoners, whom he robbed in their way to Canterbury, with their gorbellies, and their city luxury, is not so becoming.

It is not calling the landed estates, possessed by old *prescriptive rights*, the 'accumulations of ignorance and superstition', that can support me in shaking that grand title, which supersedes all other title, and which all my studies of general jurisprudence have taught me to consider as one principal cause of the formation of states; I mean the ascertaining and securing *prescription*. But these are donations made in 'ages of ignorance and superstition'. Be it so. It proves that these donations were made long ago; and this is *prescription*; and this gives right and title. It is possible that many estates about you were originally obtained by arms, that is, by violence, a thing almost as bad as superstition, and not much short of ignorance: but it is old violence; and that which might be wrong in the beginning, is consecrated by time, and becomes lawful. This may be superstition in me, and ignorance; but I had rather remain in ignorance and superstition than be enlightened and purified out of the first principles of law and natural justice. I never will suffer you, if I can help it, to be deprived of the well-earned fruits of your industry, because others may want your fortune more than you do, and may have laboured, and do now labour, in vain, to acquire even a subsistence. Nor on the contrary, if success had less smiled on your endeavours, and you had come home insolvent, would I take from any 'pampered and luxurious lord' in your neighbourhood one acre of his land, or one spoon from his sideboard, to compensate your losses, though incurred (as they would have been incurred) in the course of a well-spent, virtuous, and industrious life. God is the distributor of his own blessings. I will not impiously attempt to usurp his throne, but will keep according to the subordinate place and trust in which he has stationed me, to secure the order of property which I find established in my country.

3.5 EDMUND BURKE: PRESCRIPTION AND THE CONSTITUTION

For Burke the most valid title to authority was prescription, i.e. the existence of an institution time out of mind. Prescription and its attendant features of hereditary transmission and constant adjustment afforded continuity, stability and legitimacy to institutions, powers and practices. Thus the British constitution was a prescriptive constitution and was thus immune from the criticisms of reformers and radicals who might complain about its defective electoral procedures. In his bitter *Letter to a Noble Lord* (1796) Burke attacks the radical Duke of Bedford for his careless and cavalier attitudes towards his inheritance. The finger-wagging lecture on the virtues of prescription which Burke administers to the young aristocrat is rightly regarded as one of the most characteristic, yet most beautiful, passages of Burke's writings. Nevertheless, the most detailed defence of the prescriptive basis of the constitution occurred in Burke's speech of 7 May 1782 when he was opposing William Pitt the Younger's motion for a committee to enquire into the state of the representation. Burke's sense of history, his instinctive feeling that institutions should be made for men and moulded to their needs, and his idealisation of the existing constitution are graphically illustrated in the second of these extracts. From *Letter to a Noble Lord* (1796), Works of Edmund Burke (2 vols, 1834), ii, p. 268; *Speech on a Committee to enquire into the State of the Representation of the Commons in Parliament* (7 May 1782), *ibid*. I, pp. 487–8.

But let him take care how he endangers the safety of that constitution which secures his own utility or his own insignificance; or how he discourages those, who take up, even puny arms, to defend an order of things, which, like the sun of heaven, shines alike on the useful and the worthless. His grants are engrafted on the public law of Europe, covered with the awful hoar of innumerable ages. They are guarded by the sacred rules of prescription, found in that full treasury of jurisprudence from which the jejuneness and penury of our municipal law has, by degrees, been enriched and strengthened. This prescription I had my share (a very full share) in bringing to its perfection. The Duke of Bedford will stand as long as prescriptive law endures: as long as the great stable laws of property, common to us with all civilised nations, are kept in their integrity, and without the smallest intermixture of laws, maxims, principles, or precedents of the grand Revolution. They are secure against all changes but one. The whole revolutionary system, institutes, digest, code, novels, text, gloss, comment, are, not only not the same, but they are the very reverse, and the reverse fundamentally, of all the laws, on which civil life has hitherto been upheld in all the governments of the world. The learned professors of the rights of man regard prescription, not as a title to bar all claim, set up against all possession – but they look on prescription as itself a bar against the possessor and proprietor. They hold an immemorial possession to be no more than a long continued, and therefore an aggravated injustice.

Such are *their* ideas; such *their* religion, and such *their* law. But as to *our* country and *our* race, as long as the well compacted structure of our church and state, the sanctuary, the holy of holies of that ancient law, defended by reverence, defended by power, a fortress at once and a temple, shall stand inviolate on the brow of the British Sion – as long as the British monarchy, not more limited than fenced by the orders of the state, shall, like the proud Keep of Windsor, rising in the majesty of proportion, and girt with the double belt of its kindred and coeval towers, as long as this awful structure shall oversee and guard the subjected land – so long the mounds and dykes of the low, fat, Bedford level will have nothing to fear from all the pickaxes of all the levellers of France.

*　　　　*　　　　*

Our constitution is a prescriptive constitution; it is a constitution, whose sole authority is, that it has existed time out of mind. It is settled in these *two* portions against one, legislatively; and in the whole of the judicature, the whole of the federal capacity, of the executive, the prudential, and the financial administration, in one alone. Nor was your house of lords and the prerogatives of the Crown settled on any adjudication in favour of natural rights, for they could never be so partitioned. Your king, your lords, your judges, your juries, grand and little, all are prescriptive; and what proves it is, the disputes not yet concluded, and never near becoming so, when any of them first originated. Prescription is the most solid of all titles, not only to property, but, which is to secure that property, to government. They harmonize with each other, and give mutual aid to one another. It is accompanied with another ground of authority in the constitution of the human mind, presumption. It is a presumption in favour of any settled scheme of government against any untried project, that a nation has long existed and flourished under it. It is a better presumption even of the *choice* of a nation, far better than any sudden and temporary arrangement by actual election. Because a nation is not an idea only of local extent, and individual momentary aggregation, but it is an idea of continuity, which extends in time as well as in numbers and in space. And this is a choice not of one day, or one set of people, not a tumultuary and giddy choice; it is a deliberate election of ages and of generations; it is a constitution made by what is ten thousand times better than choice, it is made by the peculiar circumstances, occasions, tempers, dispositions, and moral, civil, and social habitudes of the people, which disclose themselves only in a long space of time. It is a vestment, which accommodates itself to the body. Nor is prescription of government formed upon blind unmeaning prejudices – for man is a most unwise, and a most wise, being. The individual is foolish. The multitude, for the moment, is foolish, when they act without deliberation; but the species is wise, and when time is given to it, as a species, it almost always acts right.

The reason for the Crown as it is, for the lords as they are, is my reason for the commons as they are, the electors as they are. Now if the Crown, and the lords, and the judicatures, are all prescriptive, so is the house of commons of the very same origin, and of no other. We and our electors have their powers and privileges both made and circumscribed by prescription, as much to the full as the other parts; and as such we have always claimed them, and on no other title. The house of commons is a legislative body corporate by prescription, not made upon any given theory, but existing prescriptively – just like the rest. This prescription had made it essentially what it is, an aggregate collection of three parts, knights, citizens, burgesses. The question is, whether this has been always so, since the house of commons has taken its present shape and circumstances, and has been an essential operative part of the constitution; which I take it, it has been for at least five hundred years.

This I resolve to myself in the affirmative: and then another question arises, whether this house stands firm upon its ancient foundations, and is not, by time and accidents, so declined from its perpendicular, as to want the hand of the wise and experienced architects of the day to set it upright again, and to prop and buttress it up for duration; – whether it continues true to the principles, upon which it has hitherto stood; – whether this be *de facto* the constitution of the house of commons, as it has been since the time that the house of commons has, without dispute, become a necessary and an efficient part of the British constitution? To ask whether a thing, which has always been the same, stands to its usual principle, seems to me to be perfectly absurd; for how do you know the principles but from the construction? and if that remains the same, the principles remain the same. It is true, that to say your constitution is what it has been, is no sufficient defence for those, who say it is a bad constitution. It is an answer to those, who say, that it is a degenerate constitution. To those, who say it is a bad one, I answer, look to its effects. In all moral machinery, the moral results are its test.

On what ground do we go, to restore our constitution to what it has been at some given period, or to reform and re-construct it upon principles more conformable to a sound theory of government? A prescriptive government, such as ours, never was the work of any legislator, never was made upon any foregone theory. It seems to me a preposterous way of reasoning, and a perfect confusion of ideas, to take the theories, which learned and speculative men have made from that government, and then supposing it made on those theories, which were made from it, to acuse the government as not corresponding with them. I do not vilify theory and speculation – no, because that would be to vilify reason itself. *Neque decipitur ratio, neque decipit unquam.* No; whenever I speak against theory, I mean always a weak, erroneous, fallacious, unfounded, or imperfect theory; and one of the ways of discovering, that it is a false theory, is by comparing it with practice. This is the true touchstone of all theories, which regard man and the affairs of men – does it suit his nature in general? – does it suit his nature as modified by his habits?

3.6 EDMUND BURKE: THE ORGANIC THEORY OF SOCIETY

Perhaps the best illustration of Burke's thought in this area is to be found in the *Reflections* when, generalising from the experience of Britain, he develops the idea of inheritance as 'a sure principle of conservation, and a sure principle of transmission'. Inheritance enables a society to secure what it receives but to build upon that foundation. Nevertheless, the growth and development of society over the centuries occurs according to no fixed plan known to man. There appears to be an instinct in nature which enables societies to grow and develop in this manner. This is the closest Burke comes to articulating an organic theory of society. From

Edmund Burke: *Reflections on the Revolution in France* (1790) (Pelican edition, 1968, ed. Conor Cruise O'Brien), pp. 119–21.

You will observe, that from Magna Charta to the Declaration of Right, it has been the uniform policy of our constitution to claim and assert our liberties, as an *entailed inheritance* derived to us from our forefathers, and to be transmitted to our posterity; as an estate specially belonging to the people of this kingdom without any reference whatever to any other more general or prior right. By this means our constitution preserves an unity in so great a diversity of its parts. We have an inheritable crown; an inheritable peerage; and an house of commons and a people inheriting privileges, franchises, and liberties, from a long line of ancestors.

This policy appears to me to be the result of profound reflection; or rather the happy effect of following nature, which is wisdom without reflection, and above it. A spirit of innovation is generally the result of a selfish temper and confined views. People will not look forward to posterity, who never look backward to their ancestors. Besides, the people of England well know, that the idea of inheritance furnishes a sure principle of conservation, and a sure principle of transmission; without at all excluding a principle of improvement. It leaves acquisition free; but it secures what it acquires. Whatever advantages are obtained by a state proceeding on these maxims, are locked fast as in a sort of family settlement; grasped as in a kind of mortmain for ever. By a constitutional policy, working after the pattern of nature, we receive, we hold, we transmit our government and our privileges, in the same manner in which we enjoy and transmit our property and our lives. The institutions of policy, the goods of fortune, the gifts of Providence, are handed down, to use and from us, in the same course and order. Our political system is placed in a just correspondence and symmetry with the order of the world, and with the mode of existence decreed to a permanent body composed of transitory parts; wherein, by the disposition of a stupendous wisdom, moulding together the great mysterious incorporation of the human race, the whole, at one time, is never old, or middle-aged, or young, but in a condition of unchangeable constancy, moves on through the varied tenour of perpetual decay, fall, renovation, and progression. Thus, by preserving the method of nature in the conduct of the state, in what we improve we are never wholly new; in what we retain we are never wholly obsolete. By adhering in this manner and on those principles to our forefathers, we are guided not by the superstition of antiquarians, but by the spirit of philosphic analogy. In this choice of inheritance we have given to our frame of polity the image of a relation in blood; binding up the constitution of our country with our dearest domestic ties; adopting our fundamental laws into the bosom of our family affections; keeping inseparable, and cherishing with the warmth of all their combined and mutually reflected charities, our state, our hearths, our sepulchres, and our altars.

Through the same plan of a conformity to nature in our artificial institutions, and by calling in the aid of her unerring and powerful instincts, to fortify the fallible and feeble contrivances of our reason, we have derived several other, and those no small benefits, from considering our liberties in the light of an inheritance. Always acting as if in the presence of canonized forefathers, the spirit of freedom, leading in itself to misrule and excess, is tempered with an awful gravity. This idea of a liberal descent inspires us with a sense of habitual native dignity, which prevents that upstart insolence almost inevitably adhering to and disgracing those who are the first acquirers of any distinction. By this means our liberty becomes a noble freedom. It carries an imposing and majestic aspect. It has a pedigree and illustrating ancestors.

3.7 EDMUND BURKE: THE TYRANNY OF THE MAJORITY

Burke's most forceful denunciations of the tyranny of the majority occur during the period of the French Revolution. Even at an early stage he was horrified at what he took to be the impact of popular tyranny upon France. In this extract he passes a very early judgement upon this aspect of the French Revolution. From Burke to Captain Mercer, 26 February 1790. *Correspondence of Edmund Burke*, vol. VI, 1967, ed. A. Cobban and E.A. Smith, pp. 96–7.

I am that determined foe to tyranny, or I greatly deceive myself in my character: and I am sure I am an ideot in my conduct. It is because I am, and mean to continue so, that I abominate the example of France for this country. I know that tyranny seldom attacks the poor, never in the first instance. They are not its proper prey. It falls on the wealthy and the great, whom by rendering objects of envy, and otherwise obnoxious to the multitude, they may more easily destroy; and, when they are destroyed, that multitude which was led to that ill work by the arts of bad men, is itself undone for ever.

I hate tyranny, at least I think so; but I hate it most of all where most are concerned in it. The tyranny of a multitude is a multiplied tyranny. If, as society is constituted in these large countries of

France and England, full of unequal property, I must make my choice (which God avert!) between the despotism of a single person, or of the many, my election is made. As much injustice and tyranny has been practised in a few months by a French democracy, as in all the arbitrary monarchies in Europe in the forty years of my observation. I speak of publick glaring acts of tyranny; I say nothing of the common effects of old abusive governments, because I do not know that as bad may not be found in the new. This democracy begins very ill; and I feel no security; that what has been rapacious and bloody in its commencement, will be mild and protecting in its final settlement. They cannot, indeed, in future, rob so much, because they have left little that can be taken. I go to the full length of my principle. I should think the government of the deposed King of France, or of the late King of Prussia, or the present Emperor, or the present Czarina, none of them, perhaps, perfectly good people, to be far better than the government of twenty-four millions of men, all as good as you; and I do not know any body better; supposing that those twenty-four millions would be subject, as infallibly they would, to the same unrestrained, though virtuous, impulses; because it is plain, that their majority would think every thing justified by their warm good intentions – they would heat one another by their common zeal – counsel and advice would be lost on them – they would not listen to temperate individuals, and they would be less capable, infinitely, of moderation, than the most heady of those princes.

3.8 EDMUND BURKE: THE ROLE OF THE STATE IN SOCIAL AND ECONOMIC LIFE

Few areas of Burke's thought have drawn so much criticism as his belief that the State ought not to interfere in social and economic life. The *Thoughts and Details on Scarcity* (November 1795) have been seen by later critics and commentators as cruel indifference to the fate of the indigent masses. His indifference to their economic plight is regarded as the counterpart to his indifference to their political sentiments. Indeed, Burke regarded the economy as a self-regulating mechanism which it would be dangerous to tamper with. Government regulation might raise wages but in so doing would raise prices, lower profits, inhibit production, create unemployment and thus worsen the lot of the poor. In the same way, then, that the State should not embark upon utopian schemes of political reform so it was not in the interests of producers or consumers for the state to embark upon experiments in economic intervention. From Edmund Burke: *Thoughts and Details on Scarcity* (1795): *The Works of Edmund Burke* (2 vols, 1834), vol. II, p. 247.

Of all things, an indiscreet tampering with the trade of provisions is the most dangerous, and it is always worst in the time when men are the most disposed to it: that is, in the time of scarcity. Because there is nothing on which the passions of men are so violent, and their judgment so weak, and on which there exists such a multitude of ill-founded, popular prejudices.

The great use of government is as a restraint; and there is no restraint which it ought to put upon others, and upon itself too, rather than that which is imposed on the fury of speculating under circumstances of irritation. The number of idle tales, spread about by the industry of faction, and by the zeal of foolish good-intention, and greedily devoured by the malignant credulity of mankind, tends infinitely to aggravate prejudices, which, in themselves, are more than sufficiently strong. In that state of affairs, and of the publick with relation to them, the first thing that government owes to us, the people, is *information*; the next is timely coercion:– The one to guide our judgment; the other to regulate our tempers.

To provide for us in our necessities is not in the power of government. It would be a vain presumption in statesmen to think they can do it. The people maintain them, and not they the people. It is the power of government to prevent much evil; it can do very little positive good in this, or perhaps in any thing else. It is not only so of the state and statesman, but of all the classes and descriptions of the rich – they are the pensions of the poor, and are maintained by their superfluity. They are under an absolute, hereditary, and indefeasible dependence on those who labour, and are miscalled the poor.

The labouring people are only poor, because they are numerous. Numbers in their nature imply poverty. In a fair distribution among a vast multitude none can have much. That class of dependent pensions called the rich is so extremely small, that if all their throats were cut, and a distribution made of all they consume in a year, it would not give a bit of bread and cheese for one night's supper to those who labour, and who in reality feed both one night's supper to themselves.

But the throats of the rich ought not to -be cut, nor their magazines plundered; because in their persons they are trustees for those who labour, and their hoards are the banking-houses of these latter. Whether they mean it or not, they do, in effect, execute their trust – some with more, some with less, fidelity and judgement. But, on the whole, the duty is performed, and every thing returns, deducting some very trifling commission and discount, to the place from whence it arose. When the poor rise to destroy the rich, they act as wisely for their own purposes, as when they burn mills, and throw corn into the river, to make bread cheap.

4.1 WILLIAM WORDSWORTH: THE LOWER CLASSES AND THE SPIRIT OF NATIONAL INDEPENDENCE

In his *Tract on the Convention of Cintra* (1809) Wordsworth argued that the humble peasant is the most likely recipient of sentiments of nationalism than the upper classes, who tend to cut themselves off from the life of the nation. Wordsworth comes close to idealising the peasant as the latent vehicle for nationalist feelings, especially when oppressed by economic burdens. Clearly, Wordsworth's vision of post-Napoleonic Europe embraces a number of independent nation states in which the people are permitted to express their traditions and their love of their country. From *Tract on the Convention of Cintra*, lines 4251–4355.

The progress of these arts also, by furnishing such attractive stores of outward accommodation, has misled the higher orders of society in their more disinterested exertions for the service of the lower. Animal comforts have been rejoiced over, as if they were the end of being. A neater and more fertile garden; a greener field; implements and utensils more apt; a dwelling more commodious and better furnished; – let these be attained, say the actively benevolent, and we are sure not only of being in the right road, but of having successfully terminated our journey. Now a country may advance, for some time, in this course with apparent profit: these accommodations, by zealous encouragement, may be attained, and still the Peasant or Artisan, their master, be a slave in mind; a slave rendered even more abject by the very tenure under which these possessions are held: and – if they veil from us this fact, or reconcile us to it – they are worse than worthless. The springs of emotion may be relaxed or destroyed within him; he may have little thought of the past, and less interest in the future. The great end and difficulty of life for men of all classes, and especially difficult for those who live by manual labour, is a union of peace with innocent and laudable animation. Not by bread alone is the life of Man sustained; not by raiment alone is he warmed; – but by the genial and vernal inmate of the breast, which at once pushes forth and cherishes; by self-support and self sufficing endeavours; by anticipations, apprehensions, and active remembrances; by elasticity under insult, and firm resistance to injury; by joy, and by love; by pride which his imagination gathers in from afar; by patience, because life wants not promises; by admiration; by gratitude which – debasing him not when his fellow-being is its object – habitually expands itself, for his elevation, in complacency towards his Creator.

Now, to the existence of these blessings, national independence is indispensible; and many of them it will itself produce and maintain. For it is some consolation to those who look back upon the history of the world to know – that, even without civil liberty, society may possess – diffused through its inner recesses in the minds even of its humblest members – something of dignified enjoyment. But, without national independence, this is impossible. The difference, between inbred oppression and that which is from without, is *essential*; inasmuch as the former does not exclude, from the minds of a people, the feeling of being self-governed; does not imply (as the latter does, when patiently submitted to) an abandonment of the first duty imposed by the faculty of reason. In reality: where this feeling has no place, a people are not a society, but a herd; man being indeed distinguished among them from the brute; but only to his disgrace. I am aware that there are too many who think that, to the bulk of the community, this independence is of no value; that it is a refinement with which they feel they have no concern; inasmuch as, under the best frame of Government, there is an inevitable dependence of the poor upon the rich – of the many upon the few – so unrelenting and imperious as to reduce this other, by comparison, into a force which has small influence, and is entitled to no regard. Superadd civil liberty to national independence; and this position is overthrown at once: for there is no more certain mark of a sound frame of polity than this; that, in all individual instances (and it is upon these generalized that this position is laid down), the dependence is in reality far more strict on the side of the wealthy; and the labouring man leans less upon others than any man in the community. But the case before us is of a country not internally free, yet supposed capable of repelling an external enemy who attempts its subjugation. If a country has put on chains of its own forging; in the name of virtue, let it be conscious that to itself it is accountable: let it not have cause to look beyond its own limits for reproof: and, – in the name of humanity, – if it be self-depressed, let it have its pride and some hope within itself. The poorest Peasant, in an unsubdued land, feels this pride. I do not appeal to the example of Britain or of Switzerland, for the one is free, and the other lately was free (and, I trust, will ere long be so again): but talk with the Swede; and you will see the joy he finds in these sensations. With him animal courage (the substitute for many and the friend of all the manly virtues) has space to move in; and is at once elevated by his imagination, and softened by his affections: it is invigorated also; for the whole courage of his Country is in his breast.

In fact: the Peasant, and he who lives by the fair reward of his manual labour, has ordinarily a larger proportion of his gratifications dependent upon these thoughts – than, for the most part, men in other classes have. For he is in his person attached, by stronger roots, to the soil of which he is the growth: his intellectual notices are generally confined within narrower bounds: in him no partial or anti-patriotic interests counteract the force of those nobler sympathies and antipathies which he has in right of his Country; and lastly the belt or girdle of his mind has never been stretched to utter relaxation by false philosophy, under a conceit of making it sit more easily and gracefully. These sensations are a social inheritance to him; more important, as he is precluded from luxurious – and those which are usually called refined – enjoyments.

Love and admiration must push themselves out towards some quarter: otherwise the moral man is killed. Collaterally they advance with great vigor to a certain extent – and they are checked: in that direction, limits hard to pass are perpetually encountered: but upwards and downwards, to ancestry and to posterity, they meet with gladsome help and no obstacles; the tract is interminable. Perdition to the Tyrant who would wantonly cut off an independent Nation from its inheritance in past ages; turning the tombs and burial-places of the Forefathers into dreaded objects of sorrow, or of shame and reproach, for the Children! Look upon Scotland and Wales: though, by the union of these with England under the same Government (which was effected without conquest in one instance), ferocious and desolating wars, and more injurious intrigues, and sapping and disgraceful corruptions, have been prevented; and tranquillity, security, and prosperity, and a thousand interchanges of amity, not otherwise attainable, have followed; yet the flashing eye, and the agitated voice, and all the tender recollections, with which the names of Prince Llewellin and William Wallace are to this day pronounced by the fire-side and on the public road, attest that these substantial blessings have not been purchased without the relinquishment of something most salutary to the moral nature of Man: else the remembrances would not cleave so faithfully to their abiding-place in the human heart.

4.2 WILLIAM COBBETT: THE DECLINE OF PATERNALISM

William Cobbett (1763–1835) spent his life attacking the political and economic system of his day. As an old-fashioned Tory Radical, Cobbett looked back nostalgically to the pre-industrial era when landowners fulfilled their paternalist obligations and the poor and the weak were protected. The industrial revolution had dispossessed the old landowning class and replaced it with a new class of rapacious fundholders. (The first excerpt is taken from *The Political Register*, September 1804.) As a consequence, the lower orders were reduced to penury, poverty and the poor house. (The second excerpt is taken from *The Political Register*, December 1830.)

In speaking of this monied interest, I do not mean to apply the phrase, as it was applied formerly, that is to say, to distinguish the possessors of personal property, more especially property in the funds, from persons possessing lands; the division of the proprietors into a monied interest, and a landed interest, is not applicable to the present times, all the people who have any thing, having now become in a greater or less degree, stock-holders . . . .

It was a body very much like this, which may with great propriety, I think, be denominated the *Paper Aristocracy*, that produced the revolution in France. Burke evidently had our monied interest, as well as that of France, in his view; but, when, in another passage of his celebrated work, he was showing the extreme injustice of seizing upon the property of the Church to satisfy the demands of the paper aristocracy of France, he little imagined that an act of similar injustice would so soon be thought of, and even proposed, in England, where clergyman and pauper are become terms almost synonymous. He had been an attentive observer of the rise and progress of the change that was taking place in France. and he thought it necessary to warn his own country, in time, against the influence of a description of persons, who, aided by a financiering minister, who gave into all their views, had begun the destruction of the French monarchy. Our paper-aristocracy, who arose with the schemes of Mr. Pitt, have proceeded with very bold strides; theirs was the proposition for commuting the tithes; theirs the law for the redemption of the land-tax; theirs the numerous laws and regulations which have been made of late years in favour of jobbing and speculation, till at last they obtained a law compelling men to take their paper in payment of just debts, while they themselves were exempted, by the same law, from paying any part of the enormous debts which they had contracted, though they had given promissory notes for the amount! Their project for commuting the tithes was of this sort. All the tithes, small as well as great, *belonging to the Clergy*, were to be sold to the owners of the houses and land subject to such tithes; or, if the owners did not choose to purchase them, they were to be sold to other persons, as fast as such persons could be found . . . .

The country gentleman, who wishes and endeavours to live independently upon his estate, is obliged to pay to the government, for the support of the funding system, so great a portion of the revenue of that estate, that he has not enough left to live upon in the style in which his ancestors lived; and, in order to support that style, he sells part of his patrimony; once broken into, it goes piece by piece; his sons become merchants' clerks or East India cadets; his daughters become companions or lady's women to the wives of those in whose service the sons are embarked; the father, seeing his end approach, secures a life annuity for his widow; some speculator purchases the tottering old mansion; and thus the funding system swallows up the effects in every part of the country, the cause is not so distinctly seen as to render illustration unnecessary. What one loses another gains: the land all remains, belong to whom it will: howsoever much some classes may lose, there is no loss upon the whole; and there is room for contending, that birth, honour, and virtue gain as much wealth in some places as they lose in others. But, the instance of the Church sets this question at rest: from the Church part of the real property has been taken; not part of its revenues: not part of its annual income: but, part of its house and its land has been taken away, sold, and the money applied to the payment of those who have made loans to, and other bargains with, the government: and the Church possesses less than it did by so much, and it never will regain that which it has thus lost, or any portion of it. The same may be said with regard to the alienation, which, at the same time, took place, of the real property of the collegiate establishment, not excepting hospitals and other charitable foundations, part of the property of some of which was thus alienated for the purpose of supporting the funds, while the persons living within the walls of such hospitals and colleges were compelled to have recourse to the parish rates in aid of their income, which, by the depreciating effects of the paper-system, had already been reduced to a pittance, in many instances too small to afford them bread.

*   *   *

The working people of England were, in all former times, better off, better fed, clothed, and lodged, than any other working people in the world. Their rights and their happiness seem to have been the chief effect of the laws of England in all former times. During the predominance of the Roman Catholic religion, the municipal laws so far interferred with the property of the Church as to make it conducive to the relief of the indigent. When that religion was put down, and the property of the Church grasped by the aristocracy, a law was passed to cause provision to be made for all indigent persons. This famous law, passed in the 43rd year of the reign of Queen Elizabeth, appointed officers for each parish, to impose a tax on land and house, and thus to raise *without limit*, whatever money might be wanted for the relief and support of persons unable to provide a sufficiency for themselves. So that there can, if this law be duly enforced, *be no person in England to suffer for want*. This law is called the POOR-LAW; and I beg you to bear in mind the inscription that I have given of it.

The working people, especially the country working people, lived in the happiest state that can be imagined, *until the reign of George III*. His war against our brethren in America, which *added greatly to the taxes of the nation*, made a change for the worse; it made the people *poorer* than they had ever been before, but still they lived tolerably well; much better than the working people of any other country in Europe. It was the long and expensive war against the republic of France that brought them down to real poverty. Before the American war began, it was *a rare thing* that any one, even amongst the aged and the widows, had occasion to apply for aid from the *poor-taxes*; that war made this mark of wretchedness less rare: but *now* the rare thing is to know of a working man, single or married, who is not compelled to resort to the *poor-taxes* to keep himself from perishing with hunger.

4.3 SIR WALTER SCOTT: THE DEFENCE OF A PROPERTIED FRANCISE

Scott (1771–1832) was a novelist and not a philosopher or politician. Nevertheless, his political cast of mind can be reconstructed through attentive reading of his fictional works. He published one piece, however, in which he embarked upon a sustained defence of the economic and political order of early nineteenth century England. It is not a particularly profound essay but it brings together many of the attitudes which were common in Tory circles at this times. From Sir Walter Scott: *The Visionary* (1819), ed. Peter Garside, 1984, University College, Cardiff Press, pp. 11–15.

Capital is the superfluity of the wealthy, but it is the very sustenance of the poor, who live by the various modes in which it is employed; nor can the selfishness of the capitalist devise any mode of disposing it, by which, in his own despite, (were he wicked enough to nourish a hatred against the human race,) the poor would not be fed, clothed, and supported out of his fortune. Let any man sit down and devise an expenditure of capital in such a manner as that, ultimately, it shall not be distributed among the body of the community, and he will find he has undertaken a task almost impossible. The most useless, perhaps, would be that of hoarding large quantities of what are called the precious metals; yet even the existence of these, though unproductive in themselves, would increase the credit of the state, and the hoards of the miser would augment the general wealth of the country. The plan of those short-sighted and suspicious individuals who would annihilate commerce, learning, and all its professions, together with all the various modes of acquiring wealth, which have so much increased the population and comforts of the country, in order to destroy every means of support, saving that which can be afforded by a barren and ill cultivated soil, must commence with dispeopling the land of three-fifths of its inhabitants, and end by starving the greater part of those who might remain.

The subject of Radical Reform and Universal Suffrage, is only worthy of being treated . . . with scorn and derision. The general principle of the British Constitution devolves the choice of the members of the legislature on men of a certain property. The reason is, that the bulk and mass of the population are rendered incapable of the due exercise of an elective franchise, by their want of education and violence of passions, as well as by their dependent situation, which must place their votes at the command of those who pay them daily wages to buy daily bread. The free nations of antiquity, to whose practice we are so fond of appealing, had a short cut for this; – nine-tenths of their population were slaves, and as such, considered not merely as without franchise, but as the goods and chattels of their masters. With more justice, and more humanity, the law of Britain limits the elective franchise to those possessed of certain property, which is ascertained by various arbitrary rules, as the election is more or less popular, while the Constitution extends to all the subjects alike the benefits and protection of equal law.

Property is chosen as the basis of the elective franchise, because it is the most tangible mark of the capacity necessary to exercise it, as well as the most certain sign of the independence of situation, from which, if possible, it should never be divided. The person of property, if it is inherited, must probably have received education, or, if it is acquired by his own industry, he must probably possess talent of some sort or other. In either event, he cannot plead dependence as an excuse for degrading himself by corruption. And though, undoubtedly, these general rules have many exceptions, yet the criterion, generally speaking, comes much nearer the point desired than could be attained in any other way, more especially by rendering elections more popular, since, to judge from the case of Westminster, nothing can be conceived more immoral, more unfair, more brutally disgusting, than the manner in which the grave and momentous exercise of the elective franchise is there exercised. Let those who saw the hustings at the last contest contradict me if they can. An enlargement of the elective privilege, which should bring the fickle, unthinking, and brutal mob into the field, would be a measure which must speedily terminate in military despotism, to which men have fled, in all ages and countries, as an evil whose terrors were incalculably less than those of a factious and furious democracy.

4.4 SAMUEL TAYLOR COLERIDGE: THE MORAL PURPOSES OF THE STATE

Coleridge (1772–1834) based his political philosophy on the idea of an 'ever originating' social contract in the Burkean sense, repudiating the idea of a historic contract beloved of the radical writers. Nevertheless, Coleridge saw in the history of Britain the idea of a constitution which went beyond historic or legal considerations and one which was permeated by powerful moral elements. His defence of the alliance of Church and State is one of the noblest in the Conservative tradition and, of course, occurred when the threat to that alliance appeared to be at its most dangerous. From Samuel Taylor Coleridge: *On the Constitution of*

Church and State (1830), ed. John Colmer (1976), Princeton University Press, pp. 73–5

Among the primary ends of a STATE, (in that highest sense of the word, in which it is equivalent to the nation, considered as one body politic, and therefore includes the National Church), there are two, of which the National Church (according to its idea), is the especial and constitutional organ and means. The one is, to secure to the subjects of the realm generally, the hope, the chance, of bettering their own or their children's condition. And though during the last three or four centuries, the National Church has found a most powerful surrogate and ally for the affectuation of this great purpose in her former wards and foster-children, i.e. in trade, commerce, free industry, and the arts – yet still the nationality, under all defalcations, continues to feed the higher ranks by drawing up whatever is worthiest from below, and thus maintains the principle of Hope in the humblest families, while it secures the possessions of the rich and noble. This is one of the two ends.

The other is, to develop, in every native of the country, those faculties, and to provide for every native that knowledge and those attainments, which are necessary to qualify him for a member of the state, the free subject of a civilized realm. We do not mean those degrees of moral and intellectual cultivation which distinguish man from man in the same civilized society, much less those that separate the Christian from the this-worldian; but those only that constitute the civilized man in contra-distinction from the barbarian, the savage, and the animal.

I have now brought together all that seemed requisite to put the intelligent reader in full possession of (what I believe to be) the right Idea of the National Clergy, as an estate of the realm. But I cannot think my task finished without an attempt to rectify the too frequent false feeling on this subject, and to remove certain vulgar errors, errors, alas! not confined to those whom the world call the vulgar. 'Ma nel mondo non é se non volgo,'* says Machiavel. I shall make no apology therefore, for interposing between the preceding statements, and the practical conclusion from them, the following paragraph, extracted from a work long out of print, and of such very limited circulation that I might have stolen from myself with little risk of detection, had it not been my wish to shew that the convictions expressed in the preceding pages, are not the offspring of

* 'But in the world there are only the vulgar'.

the moment, brought forth for the present occasion; but an expansion of sentiments and principles publicly avowed in the year 1817.

Among the numerous blessings of the English Constitution, the introduction of an established Church makes an especial claim on the gratitude of scholars and philosophers; in England, at least, where the principles of Protestantism have conspired with the freedom of the government to double all its salutary powers by the removal of its abuses.

That the maxims of a pure morality, and those sublime truths of the divine unity and attributes, which a Plato found hard to learn, and more difficult to reveal; that these should have become the almost hereditary property of childhood and poverty, of the hovel and the workshop; that even to the unlettered they sound as *common place*; this is a phenomenon which must withhold all but minds of the most vulgar cast from undervaluing the services even of the pulpit and the reading desk. Yet he who should *confine* the efficiency of an Established Church to these, can hardly be placed in a much higher rank of intellect. That to every parish throughout the kingdom there is transplanted a germ of civilization; that in the remotest villages there is a nucleus, round which the capabilities of the place may crystallise and brighten; a model sufficiently superior to excite, yet sufficiently near to encourage and facilitate, imitation; *this* unobtrusive, continuous agency of a Protestant Church Establishment, *this* it is, which the patriot, and the philanthropist, who would fain unite the love of peace with the faith in the progressive amelioration of mankind, cannot estimate at too high a price.

Part Five
THE TORY PARTY AND PEELITE CONSERVATISM
(1810–1846)

5.1 GEORGE CANNING: HOSTILITY TO THE REFORM OF PARLIAMENT

Canning (1770–1827) was the finest and most influential speaker on the ministerial side of the House of Commons in the early nineteenth century. His opposition to parliamentary reform was of enormous importance in stiffening the resistance of the parliamentary classes to the cause of reform. In his speech on Brand's motion for reform on 21 May 1810 Canning powerfully summarises the Tory case against reform. His arguments were to be repeated on countless occasions over the next two decades. From William Cobbett, *The Parliamentary History*, XVII, pp. 155–61.

The case of France, he would contend, afforded an equally strong ground of objection to the description of reform sought by designing persons out of doors, as that of America. For what, he would ask, had been the case actually in France? The reformed legislative assembly absolutely set out with the principles of revolution; but even if they had not done so; if their ideas had been purely patriotic, they were, in the wild frenzy of fantastic reformation, so strangely constituted, that it was impossible they could move in a natural orbit; it was impossible they should not run into an irregular and eccentric course, whirling every surrounding object into their dangerous deviation. Would the House follow that rash and awful example? Would they go wavering and perplexed to a Committee, without any adequate means to attain their object, or even without any adequate object to attain – without one fixed idea, except the wise notion that whatever is, is wrong, and the sober expectation that, by some lucky expedient, the right may be hit upon! There was, however, one principle to which those reformers pretended, and which of late, they appeared unusually eager to profess – a veneration for the throne itself, and an high respect for the individual by whom it was filled. But, unfortunately, that House well knew such language had not even the merit of originality. By such pretences it was, the unhappy Louis had been deceived. By such men it was he had been deluded into the notion that he had an interest separate from his people, and a place in the hearts of those who flattered that they might betray him. He hoped sincerely there was not a man in that House, who was not eager to ward off the melancholy omen. Why (said Mr. Canning) why should we embark upon this dangerous voyage? Why should we trust ourselves to this unknown ocean? We have heard that the ancient empires of the earth have been uprooted; that the most solid monarchies have been crushed; that oligarchies the best established have been destroyed, and that England alone stands erect among the ruins! And why have we so stood? because, say the reformers, we have been radically corrupt. Sir, I will not bow to the whimsical deduction; I will rather deduce from some wise distinction the source of our prosperity. Like the nations which have fallen, we have a monarchy. Like the nations which have fallen, we have an aristocracy; but unlike every one of those nations, we possess – an House of Commons. This is our proud distinction; this is the sole palladium of our salvation; and this we are now called upon to regenerate, by the mad cry of unmeaning reformation!

But, (say the discontented) the House of Commons, constituted as it now is, has hurried the nation into extravagant expenditure, and unnecessary wars. It is not the fact. There has not been a war during a century, which was not in its commencement strictly popular. The people it was who goaded the government and the House to hostility – the people it was who forced and goaded even the pacific sir Robert Walpole into the declaration of war. The people it was who at first urged the American war, and at last decried it when it became unfortunate; the people it was who encouraged the war with France, which saved this country from all the miseries entailed on that. What a pity then it was, that the House and the Country at large did not become converts to the opinions of the honourable gentleman and the few by whom he was supported in opposition to that war! What a pity they were not dipped in the well of his political sagacity, that they might meet, rebaptised, all the inevitable mischievous consequences which must have followed. After having thus gone through the history of ages, the friends of reform scrutinized the present times, and passed their unqualified censure on every vote·of that House, and on every member with whom they were dissatisfied.

All with whom they were not pleased, had, it seemed some sinister motive. Now, even allowing this to be the case; even allowing that some extra considerations did enter into the minds of each unpopular representative, how would the reformers remedy it? Would they banish human nature from their reformed House of Commons? No, but they would banish the boroughs. Now, if they would only take the trouble to examine borough members' votes, they would find that just as many voted on the popular as on the unpopular side of the question, so they would neither lose nor gain by their reform. They might in this way alternately subtract from each side, till they had eradicated all. Decimation would be mercy compared to this plan of reform; and, indeed, whether one considered its motive or its consequences, its justice would appear exactly to correspond with its policy.

The accusations of the reformers against that House were exactly those which could be made justly against themselves, for there never yet was a state democratic and powerful, which had not a tendency to war. The compliances which they sought from the House it was impossible they ever could obtain. The House of Commons owed to the people, a manly but not a servile obedience; they should be respectful, but not enslaved; they should not watch the eye, nor bend to the nod, nor crouch to the unspoken will of the multitude, but proceed in the plain path of undeviating independence; they should act to the people as representatives, just as they should act toward their Creator as men, virtuously but freely, founding their hopes of retribution on their consciousness of honesty. He was as ready as the honourable gentleman to lament, that more liberal and solid provisions had not been made for securing the liberty of the subject, at the period of the restoration; but this made directly against the right honourable gentleman's own arguments, for Charles the second was restored chiefly by the spirit and strong impulse of the people. Let it be recollected too that it was the extent of the popular influence, which at the restoration prevented the arrangement of those provisions for the security of popular freedom, which an honourable gentleman, repeating an observation in the celebrated tract of his deceased friend (Mr. Fox,) had expressed his regret did not take place. A just sympathy with the people, and a reasonable attention to their desires, was no doubt, the duty and must ever be the inclination of that House. The people, unquestionably, could reason fairly when they had time; but as, notoriously, their first impulse was feeling, he did not think would be politic, or for the interest of the country, to have that House quite subject to popular control.

Every class of the people he must content was fully represented in that House, and its general conduct since the revolution, excepting the septennial act of the whigs, tended to ameliorate the country. Therefore he saw no necessity which had been drawn from particular votes, he asked what assurance could be offered that similar votes would not take place even after the desired reform? He believed that, while human nature was unchanged, no change in the constitution of that House could guard against some improper decisions; and he could not discern, 'mid all the perils off surrounding nations, a nobler security to English independence than the established House of Commons. Should he then ungratefully now forget those benefits? Should he impoliticly fling aside all hope of future advantage, and trust to the conflicting wisdoms of a reforming committee to strike out some new and speculative system? He saw no necessity for the experiment; the House of Commons was all that the honestly patriotic could desire it.

5.2 BLACKWOOD'S MAGAZINE: THE HYPOCRISY OF REFORMERS

The keeper of the Ultra-Tory conscience on a wide variety of issues in the years immediately before the 1832 Reform Act was *Blackwood's Magazine*. The famous article published by David Robinson on 'The Reform of the House of Commons' in April 1830 was one of the most honest and most interesting essays of its type to appear in these years. Robinson concedes that the Lower House has not acquitted itself particularly well but he proceeds to challenge the (by now) fashionable assumption that the mode of election was at fault. To Robinson the root of the trouble was the ruthless competition between Government and Opposition for place. He concludes that parliamentary reform might be confined to an elite of voters and to an elimination of the worst abuses of the rotten borough system.

It is abundantly obvious to all men that the popular branch of the Legislature does not work well – that, from some reason or other, the intended benefits cannot be drawn from it, and it cannot be kept under the necessary constitutional restrictions. This is universally admitted, and the House of Commons, as it is, has all sides against it. Those who do not call for a radical change in its construction, intimate, by charging it with the want of intellect and integrity, that a radical change of some kind is necessary; and, as to defenders, it has none.

We are here supplied with a question of the very highest moment. In times of the most favourable character, the incompetency of this House could not be other than a mighty national evil; but in the present day, when speculative changes and experiments, which spare nothing in law, system, and institution, are the general rage, it must in the nature of things be the parent of national destruction. While it must prevent beneficial changes and experiments on the one hand, it must on the other produce all conceivable ones of an opposite kind, and give them the most fatal operation. To prove that this is not mere hypothesis, we need only point to the fact, that this House, after making those changes which have plunged the community into such fearful suffering, now almost unanimously refuses to make a single one in the way of remedy.

When the gross incompetency of the House of Commons is matter of such general allegation, and the violent corrective of a radical change in its construction is scarcely opposed in any quarter, it may be wise and profitable to enquire dispassionately into causes. No honest man can defend its late and present conduct, or say that a vital alteration is not imperiously called for; but it by no means follows that this should be the change we have named.

Men who require the most solid grounds to induce them to sanction great and perilous changes, will remember that previously to the last few years this empire was governed with as much virtue and wisdom as perhaps human infirmity will admit of. The House of Commons was then fully competent to the discharge of its duties; if the community fell into distress, it promptly investigated the causes, and applied efficient remedies; it was duly influenced by the public voice, and its general labours were distinguished by sound principle, and salutary effect. Yet this House was then chosen precisely as it is at present, with perhaps this difference – the democracy had somewhat less influence in the choice than it now has. This goes far towards providing that the deplorable change in its character and conduct is not to be ascribed wholly to the manner in which it is chosen.

Abundance of additional proof is furnished by those members of it whose election is not in the least influenced by the aristocracy, but proceeds chiefly from the lower orders. In respect of knowledge and ability, they rank as low as the slaves of the borough-monger. As favourable specimens, we may point to the representatives of London, Westminster, and Southwark. Sir F. Burdett, who is so much lauded by interested partisans, is only a voluble disclaimer, who is never, even by these partisans, cited as an authority on any subject. Who would dream of appealing to his opinion on matters of finance, trade and currency, or on any great question of domestic legislation or foreign policy? Who would expect to find him taking a leading part in promoting by practical knowledge and ability the general interests of the state? We need only say farther, that if the House were composed solely of such members as he, Wood, Hobhouse, Wilson, &c. it would be even below what it is in information and talent. Speaking of parliaments in general, the members for the three divisions of the metropolis rank amidst the most inefficient ones.

Such members stand in the lowest rank in respect of independence. The most violent party men – those who are the most insensible to restraint and shame in sacrificing the empire to party and faction – are always to be found among them. They are not less the slaves of party because they affect hostility to the great constitutional ones of the state; they nevertheless have their party; and in bigotry and fanaticism, they surpass Whig and Tory. If they attach themselves to the Ministry, or the regular Opposition, they are quite as servile as any of the rotten borough representatives.

With regard to creed, such members occupy the very lowest place in Parliament. We must look to them, to find the wild enthusiast, the profligate disturber, the godless revolutionist, the reformer, who seeks to sweep away the institutions of the country without sparing its religion, and the projector, whose schemes contemplate the dissolution of society. If the House of Commons were composed wholly, or principally, of such men as those generally are whose election lies solely with the democracy, the empire would be scourged with every conceivable evil.

Such members are not a whit superior to the rotten borough ones in consistency and integrity. When Mr Canning, the ultra Anti-Reformer, was made the Premier, Sir Francis Burdett, the ultra Reformer, proclaimed himself the servile supporter of his Ministry. The Radical Baronet was not to be found when the Marquis of Blandford made his motion for Reform in the last Session, because his party then idly dreamed of incorporation with the Wellington Cabinet. The dream has ceased, the Whig hopes of office and coronets must now rest on opposition, a new election is approaching, and of course Sir Francis Burdett is once more an enthusiastic reformer. There was in proportion as much apostacy amidst such Members when the Catholic question was carried, as amidst the mercenaries of the borough mongers. They are just as ready to sacrifice every thing to interest, and they can be bought by a

Ministry with as little trouble, and at as cheap a rate, as any other Members.

On the most important points of being duly influenced by the national voice, they form the most deaf, insensible, and intolerable part of the House of Commons. If indeed this voice happen to be in favour of their own opinions and schemes, they insist that it ought to be implicitly obeyed, even to the ruin of the State; they proclaim that the 'Sovereignty of the People' is a despotism which cannot be opposed without the commission of unpardonable iniquity. But if it be against them, they take the lead in treating it with derision; they depose the 'people' forthwith, and substitute for the despotic sceptre the chains of the bondsman. It was unanimously acknowledged that the feeling of the country was decidedly opposed to the Catholic Bill in the last Session, yet the members in question were the most obstinate and shameless in despising it; they even went beyond the rotten borough members in heaping derision and insult on public meetings and petitions. The passing of this Bill, looked at with reference to public feelings, constituted a most grave and dangerous act of tyranny; nevertheless Sir Francis Burdett and similar representatives of the 'people' were amidst the most active in forcing it upon the nation, in utter scorn of constitutional feeling and usage. Their conduct is always the same on like occasions.

At present, when the distress of the great body of the community, and especially of the working classes, is so severe, it might reasonably be expected that these representatives of the 'people' would insist on enquiry, and the application of proper remedies. What is the fact? They are either silent, or they oppose enquiry, and instead of proposing rational measures of relief, labour to pervert the distress into an instrument for promoting their own factious objects. They constantly act in the same manner. They have in late years, when the labouring orders have petitioned the Legislature to extricate them from the horrors of starvation, vied with the most abject slaves of the Treasury in disregarding the petitions and defending the sources of suffering. On every motion for investigation and the granting of relief, they have voted with the mercenaries of the Ministry. At present, and on all occasions, they shew less compassion for public distress, are less obedient to public feeling, are less the guardians of public interests, and are more the menials of party and faction, than many of the rotten borough Members.

It is from all this very clear, that the alleged incompetency of the House of Commons cannot proceed wholly from the mode in which it is chosen, and that the proposed change in this mode would be a very inadequate remedy.

5.3   SIR ROBERT PEEL: CONSERVATISM AND REFORM

The most detailed and satisfying exposition of Peel's (1788–1850) Conservatism appears in a much underestimated speech made at a banquet at Merchant Taylor's Hall on 13 May 1838. In many ways, it is very similar to Disraeli's great speeches of 1872. He develops at some length the nature of his Conservative principles in the post-Reform Act period. For a politician who was not fond of lengthy philosophical discussions the speech is a remarkable testament to his political principles. *The Peel Banquet: Speeches of Sir Robert Peel . . . From Lord Stanley . . . and Sir James Graham* (1838).

My object for some years past, that which I have most earnestly laboured to accomplish, has been to lay the foundation of a great party (cheers), which, existing in the House of Commons, and deriving its strength from the popular will, should diminish the risk and deaden the shock of a collision between the two deliberative branches of the legislature – which should enable us to check the too importunate eagerness of well-intending men, for hasty and precipitate changes in the constitution and laws of the country, and by which we should be enabled to say, with a voice of authority, to the restless spirit of revolutionary change, 'Here are thy bounds, and here shall thy vibrations cease.' Gentlemen, I was deeply impressed with a conviction of the necessity of forming such a party from the period when a great change was made in the representative system of the country; I am confident that those who were the most convinced of the abstract merits of that change, who saw its absolute necessity in the progress of events, and the change of public opinion, would now admit (because I heard them admit it at the time) that although a necessary, still it was a fearful experiment – that there was a danger that the great shock given to prescriptive authority might lead to too hasty prescriptive and irrational future changes – that those who were strongest in good intentions might, in their too sanguine hopes of reaching a species of perfection which could not be attained, forego that degree of perfection which was attainable – that there was a risk – and that those who had become possessed of a new power might think it useless if permitted to remain quiescent, and if not brought into constant and daily exercise. Gentlemen, that conviction led me to the conclusion that it was necessary, by prudence, by patience, by assuming a new position, by the rejection of the old tactics of party, suited to other times, and adapted to other circumstances – that it was desirable at that time to form a party whose bond of connexion should be the maintenance of that particular measure of reform, but a determination to resist further constitutional changes – (cheers) – changes having a tendency to disturb the balance of a mixed government. There were at that time in operation other causes which powerfully and mainly influenced the changes of opinion which so rapidly took place with respect to the necessity of reform. There had lately been exhibited to the empire those events which in France, in three short days, had trampled to the dust an ancient dynasty, and had shown physical power triumphant over constituted authority, and had engaged the sympathies of mankind not in favour of constituted authority, but of those who had resorted to a system of violation of all law and order. Gentlemen, I did not disguise to myself the difficulties attending the formation of such a party. Our own party had been reduced by the Reform Act to little more than one hundred members, at least, I believe that in the session which followed the passing of the Reform Bill, not more than 100 voted with me on any great occasion, but I did not despair – Gentlemen, how could I despair – (cheers) – acting as I was in intimate concert and union with that illustrious man – (loud cheers) – the Duke of Wellington, whose name does not shed a lustre merely upon a party, or upon the country which he has defended, but sheds a lustre upon the age in which he lives? – (loud cheers). Acting in intimate union with that man, who has exhibited through his life a conjunction of qualities, rare in their separate excellence, but which are wonderful in their combination – that man who is not without ambition, but is without the ills that attend it, who would highly but holily aspire, who has shown at different periods of his life, both in military and civil affairs, a combination of the utmost fortitude and valour, with the greatest circumspection and prudence, acting in concert with such a man I could not despair. Gentlemen, I need not speak of the military career of the Duke of Wellington, but I may remind you that it was he who in civil life stood forward to assume, on his own undivided responsibility, the whole functions of government for the purpose of exhibiting an instance of self-denial without a precedent, and who has at other times, when a sense of public duty impelled him, had the real courage to assume and maintain a defensive attitude, and if I may so say, to retire within those moral lines which are fortified by circumspection and prudence.

Aided by his authority and his approbation, I looked forward ultimately to the formation of such a party as now exists. I did believe that the good sense of the country would at length place confidence in a party which did not profess hostility to improvement, but which manifested a determination to abide by the leading principles of the British constitution. Gentlemen, allow me to say that I did look with confidence to the ultimate formation of that happy union which now exists between us and the men to whom we were formerly opposed. I looked forward to it with confidence, because I relied upon their adherence to the principles which they professed – because I heard them say, and I believed them, that they desired that reform should be according to the acknowledged principles of the constitution – because I heard them declare that they would not assent to it if they believed it incompatible with the maintenance of the prerogatives of the crown and the privileges of the other house of Parliament. I looked to it with confidence, because I heard them declare that, in their opinion, reform would add new stability to the settled institutions of the country in church and state. I did think, without personal acquaintance with their views, that the union which must be formed would not be the result of conferences – not the offspring of negotiations – (cheers and laughter) – but a union about which nothing would ever be (as nothing has to this hour ever been) said, but which should originally be brought about by the force of circumstances and by a sense of common danger, and which, having been formed, would afterwards be cemented by mutual co-operation and reciprocal confidence and assent.

Gentlemen, as I said before, without conference, without any other negotiation than that which led to the rejection of office, when they removed from office, that union has been formed, and I think I may say that the anticipations which I had formed – the hopes which I had entertained – that, being once formed, it would gain strength from reciprocal esteem and confidence, are fully justified by the result. Thus, Gentlemen, has this party been brought into existence, and you have this day given this evidence of its strength. It has been submitted twice to the test of public opinion – twice has a dissolution taken place under circumstances calculated to determine whether that party has or has not the public confidence. One dissolution took place when it was in power, and the other when power was in the hands of its opponents. On the first dissolution, which took place when I was at the head of the government of this country, the conservative members were suddenly swollen from about 150 to more than double the number. I believe we divided on the nomination of the speaker 306 members, but it was said, 'you owe your success to the possession of your power – wait till another dissolution takes place – till your opponents are exercising the functions of government, which you were discharging when Parliament was assembled in 1835, and be prepared for a reduction of your numbers more rapid still than this increase.' Gentlemen, to that second test we have been subjected. The dissolution which took place in the course of last year was attended by every circumstance calculated to be favourable to our opponents. There was the accession of a youthful and beloved Queen. There was one universal feeling of personal loyalty and attachment to the Sovereign ascending the throne, with everything calculated to prepossess in her favour. There was a lavish use of her Majesty's name for the purpose of influencing elections – (loud cheers); there was a happy coincidence of fortunate events for the government; we had public despatches, approving of the conduct of public officers, printed and circulated on the eve of a general election – (cheers and laughter); there was no fastidious delicacy in the choice of candidates – (laughter) – for the hustings at Westminster exhibited the spectacle of a secretary of state voting in favour of one who had defended insurrection in Canada, and espoused the cause of the Canadians in their revolt. And yet, notwithstanding all these favourable circumstances – notwithstanding the accession of Her Majesty – notwithstanding the unsparing use of her name – notwithstanding the absence of all squeamishness – still the result exhibited our numbers unbroken, and as we voted in 1835 to the number of 306, having all the advantages of a dissolution during the tenure of government, I think the names attached to the invitation of this evening, the names of 313 members of the House of Commons, will show that, notwithstanding the adverse predictions to the contrary, the public confidence has not permitted our numbers to be broken, notwithstanding the dissolution – (cheers). Gentlemen, my noble friend has truly stated that in the whole course of my public life no event has been so gratifying and so satisfactory to me as the meeting of this day; but there are connected with it some feelings of a more serious and anxious character, which chasten and subdue the disposition to triumph and congratulation. Gentlemen, I do not disguise from myself the power which I possess in consequence of your esteem and confidence; and when I see the number around me – when I recollect that their sentiments are shared by all the great interest of the country – by the clergy, by the magistrates, the yeomanry, the gentry of the country, and by a great proportion also of the trading community of the country – it would be impossible to disguise from ourselves the influence which we possess in the national councils; and amongst the feelings which, as I said before, restrain and subdue those which vanity or personal congratulation would inspire, is one of anxiety, that, as I do possess your confidence, I may exercise the power which it confers in such a manner as shall contribute to the permanent interests of the country, and that by no act or advice of mine may your interest and conduct be compromised – (cheers). The possession of strength, the demonstration of power, naturally brings with it some slight inconvenience. There is an impatience in some quarters, seeing the strength we possess, that it should be called into more frequent action. It is said, and said justly, – for allow me to observe, Gentlemen, that, if I have any well grounded title to your confidence, it is because I have always ventured explicitly to state my opinion and to give you the best advice of which I am capable, although it may not always be precisely in accordance with the prevailing opinion ; but I have boldly taken that course, confident that you would place the proper construction upon my motives; – it is said, with perfect truth, that the opposition is at present conducted upon different principles from those upon which opposition would be conducted to us if we were in power – (cheers and laughter). Nothing can be more perfectly true; but we must bear in mind that the practical course which an opposition must take must partly depend upon the principles of that opposition. Our friends, who are more impatient, must recollect this circumstance, and must recollect that we are the same conservative opposition which formerly constituted and supported a conservative government. We adopt the principles which formerly prevailed in administration. We not only adopt the principles of government, but we perform many of the functions of government; and it must be borne in mind that we cannot, in conformity with our own principles, take that line of action which would be adopted by an opposition acting upon precisely opposite principles. An opposition which professed to think the ancient institutions of the country a grievance, and the whole order of English society a mass of abuse, would have a double ground of resistance to the government; first, personal dissatisfaction with the course pursued by that government; and also no indisposition to inflame popular discontent against the institutions of the country. But we must bear in mind that our duty – the duty prescribed by our principles – is the maintenance of the ancient institutions of the country. We have no desire to exalt the House of Commons above the just prerogative of the crown. We have no desire to undermine the privileges of the House of Lords. On the contrary, it is our duty to maintain those institutions. That instrument of an opposition which seeks to reduce and curtail the establishments of the country is denied to us. We wish to see the naval and military establishments of the country maintained in proper vigour and strength. It is denied to us to inflame popular discontent against existing istitutions – to assist in any attack upon the House of Lords, or to lend an arm to shake the throne. Therefore those who are impatient at our apparent indifference and passiveness must recollect that the principles of an opposition do impose some restraint upon the course which it must pursue. I have said, Gentlemen, with perfect truth, that we discharge some of the functions of government. I prove that the principles and the position of the present government are imperfect. We have all the principles which are generally said to belong to government . . . .

If you ask me what I mean by conservative principles – as we have heard something like a vague and unsatisfactory description of them – I will, in conclusion, briefly state what I mean by conservative principles. By conservative principles I mean, and I believe you mean, the maintenance of the Peerage and the Monarchy – the continuance of the just powers and attributes of King, Lords, and Commons, in this country. By conservative principles I mean, a determination to resist every encroachment that can curtail the just rights and settled privileges of one or other of those three branches of the state. By conservative principles I mean, that co-existent with equality of civil rights and privileges, there shall be an established religion and imperishable faith, and that that established religion shall maintain the doctrines of the Protestant Church. By conservative principles I mean, a steady resistance to every project which would divert church property from strictly spiritual uses. I do not mean to raise an unnecessary cry, to serve a political end, 'that the church is in danger;' but I put it to every reasonable man whether protestantism is not in danger if the intention be carried into effect in Ireland of alienating from the church a certain proportion of its property, in violation of the most solemn assurances, and of devoting it to the purposes of education, expressly excluding instruction in the main principles and precepts of the Protestant Church, concurrently with making the bishops stipendiaries of the state, and dissolving that connexion which was preserved between the church and state by the contributions raised for the maintenance of the fabrics of the church, and applying those funds to relieve property from a burden to it which has been subject, and to a dissolution of that connexion which Lord Althorp declared to be essential to the church and state. I will ask any man whether these measures do not endanger the church establishment? By conservative principles I mean, a determination to meet every threatened danger to the protestant establishment – nay, I mean more, I mean that we are determined upon the infliction – if we can inflict it – of 'a heavy blow and a great discouragement' to those principles which are antagonist to the establishment of the protestant faith. By conservative principles I mean, a maintenance of the settled institutions of church and state, and I mean also the maintenance, defence, and continuation of those laws, those institutions, that society, and those habits and manners which have contributed to mould and form the character of Englishmen, and enabled this country, in her contests and the fearful rivalry of war, to extort the admiration of the world, and in the useful emulation of peaceful industry, commercial enterprize, and social improvement, have endeared the name of England and Englishmen in every country in the world to those who seek the establishment of liberty without oppression, and the enjoyment of a national and pure form of religion, which is at once the consolation of the virtuous man, and is also the best guarantee which human institutions can afford for civil and religious liberty.

5.4   BLACKWOODS MAGAZINE: DUTIES OF THE CONSERVATIVE PARTY

Almost as soon as the Reform Act was on the statute book the debate over the future of the Conservative party began in earnest. One of the earliest examples was published in *Blackwood's* in July 1832. Written by Archibald Alison (1792–1867), 'The Duties of the Conservative Party' listed a number of practical activities which the Conservatives could undertake in order to capitalise upon the fund of goodwill which still existed towards them in the nation. It cannot be shown quite to what extent Sir Robert Peel was influenced by the particular suggestions included in the article. That they bore a distinct resemblance to some of the items in the Tamworth Manifesto, however, may be no mere coincidence.

Notwithstanding all that they have suffered from the mania for innovation, and the mighty interests which they have since sacrificed on the altar of Revolution, the Conservative party, as a body, are not, we fear, sufficiently alive either to the magnitude of the danger which threatens them, or the means of averting it which are yet in their power. They have been so long accustomed to repose under the shadow of the Constitution; they have so long been sheltered by the power of the Aristocracy, from the evils of Anarchy, that they cannot be brought to comprehend that a different order of things can ever prevail . . . .

Taught by dear-bought experience, do not let the Conservative party a *second time*, within fifteen months, fall into the same lamentable error. Had the friends of the Constitution every where come forward at the last election, it is almost certain that the Reform Bill would never have passed . . . .

Low as the franchise has been fixed by the Reform Bill, in order to let in the meanest class of householders, in too many places to overwhelm the suffrages of men of education and property, we feel convinced, that almost every where, except in the large and manufacturing towns, the Conservative party could by proper exertions, still at the next election secure the return. The reason is, that the delusive topic which carried away the people, has now disappeared; – political power has been prodigally bestowed upon the populace, and the *next measures of the Revolutionary party must cut down their interests*. Not only, therefore, have the better classes of the people no interest now to support the movement, but their interest is decidedly the other way. The rural electors cannot be so obtuse as not to see that the abolition of the Corn Laws, for which the manufacturers so loudly clamour, must lower, in the *first instance* at least, the price of every species of grain produce to a great degree; and by exposing them to a permanent inundation of foreign grain, raised in countries where wages are not sixpence a-day, and taxes nothing, for ever depress their exertions . . . .

A large portion of the trading classes still think that the reform they have got is to save them from all calamities, because it has put into their hands the means of defending themselves, and rendered the legislature directly dependant upon the wants and interests of the nation. Whether it has really done so, may well be doubted; but be this as it may, it is this class that the Conservative party must now rally to themselves. The means of doing so exist amply in the *commercial interests*, which they have now to defend. It is no longer a contest for the maintenance of political power in a particular body which is to be kept up; the battle of order against anarchy, of property against spoliation, of industry against rapine, must now be fought in every town and village in England. The middling classes will speedily find, that having cast down the barrier of the aristocracy, which protected all the Conservative interests of the state from the revolutionary tempest, its surges will break upon them, and threaten speedily to overwhelm their fortunes. Whether the whole fabric of society is to be overthrown or not, will just depend upon the question, whether a sufficient number of the middling orders discover their danger in time to return a majority of Conservative members for the next Parliament . . . .

Every thing, therefore, now depends upon the House of Commons, and the House of Commons depends entirely on two things, public opinion, and the vigorous efforts of those who are already arraigned on the Conservative side. To public opinion, the Tory party have not paid sufficient attention, and we call upon them now to redeem their error. The talent of the nation, the property of the nation, is with them – of whom then need they be afraid? Nothing is to be feared but the masses of its *half-instructed* and impassioned manufacturers, – a formidable body, doubtless, if headed by intelligence and ability, but totally powerless if these directors are withdrawn, – or the fatal tendency of revolutionary changes to the lower orders is fully explained. We call, therefore, upon the talent and energy of the nation to come forth, and range itself in support of those principles of order which are eternal, and on which alone a new Constitution can be founded . . . .

Let the Conservative party, then, in every country, town, and village in the empire, immediately assemble, sign a declaration, and publish it in the newspapers, pledging themselves to support only a member of Conservative principles. The effect of this is incredible. It at once shews the friends of order their *real strength*, which is so extremely apt to remain unknown, from the unobtrusive habits and noiseless lives of the immense majority of which that party consists. It damps, and often overthrows the spirit of innovation, by shewing how numerous and respectable its opponents are, and how entirely the noisy and clamorous body of revolutionists are dependant on their wealth and exertions. It encourages men of property and character to come forward as candidates, and often shames revolutionary ambition into obscurity, by dragging into the light the despicable character of its wicked and vociferous supporters.

Let a contest, in the next place, wherever a Conservative candidate can be brought forward, be commenced, and continued from a *joint fund* to the very last extremity . . . .

Finally, let the Conservative party universally and firmly act upon the principle of withdrawing their business from all tradesmen whom they employ who do not support the Conservative candidate. In the manufacturing cities, which depend on the export sale, this measure may not have a very powerful effect; but in the metropolis, in the other great towns, and the small boroughs, it would have an incalculable effect. *If universally and steadily acted upon, it would be decisive of the fate of England.* At least four-fifths, probably nine-tenths, of the purchase of articles of commerce come from the Conservative ranks; if this were confined to men of Conservative principles, there is an end of the Revolutionary progress.

5.5   SIR ROBERT PEEL: THE TAMWORTH MANIFESTO (1834)

The Tamworth Manifesto is a disappointing document. It outlines Peel's acceptance of the 1832 Reform Act, recounts his attitude to certain current measures with brevity and sets out the purposes of his party with almost platitudinous simplicity. It is by no means a comprehensive guide to Peelite Conservatism. It was, of course hastily put together in December 1834 in preparation for the General Election which shortly followed. The circumstances of the election – notably the resignation of Peel's brief minority government – appeared to demand some statement of Conservative principles in the wake of the Reform Act. As a national statement of certain Conservative positions the Tamworth Manifesto occupies an important place in the history of the Conservative party. In the history of Conservative political ideas it is of little account. From H. Hanham *The Nineteenth Century Constitution* (1969) pp. 212–150.

With respect to the Reform Bill itself, I will repeat now the declaration which I made when I entered the House of Commons as a Member of the Reformed Parliament, that I consider the Reform Bill a final and irrevocable settlement of a great Constitutional question – a settlement which no friend to the peace and welfare of this country would attempt to disturb, either by direct or by insidious means.

Then, as to the spirit of the Reform Bill, and the willingness to adopt and enforce it as a rule of government: if, by adopting the spirit of the Reform Bill, it be meant that we are to live in a perpetual vortex of agitation; that public men can only support themselves in public estimation by adopting every popular impression of the day, – by abuse, – by abandoning altogether that great aid of government – more powerful than either law or reason – the respect for ancient rights, and the deference to prescriptive authority; if this be the spirit of the Reform Bill, I will not undertake to adopt it. But if the spirit of the Reform Bill implies merely a careful review of institutions, civil and ecclesiastical, undertaken in a friendly temper, combining, with the firm maintenance of established rights, the correction of proved abuses and the redress of real grievances, – in that case, I can for myself and colleagues undertake to act in such a spirit and with such intentions . . . .

It is unnecessary for my purpose to enter into further details. I have said enough, with respect to general principles and their practical application to public measures, to indicate the spirit in which the King's Government is prepared to act. Our object will be – the maintenance of peace – the scrupulous and honourable fulfilment, without reference to their original policy, of all existing engagements with Foreign Powers, – the support of public credit – the enforcement of strict economy – and the just and impartial consideration of what is due to all interests – agricultural, manufacturing, and commercial.

. . . with a resolution to persevere, which nothing could inspire but the strong impulse of public duty, the consciousness of upright motives, and the firm belief that the people of this country will so far maintain the prerogative of the King, as to give to the ministers of his choice, not an implicit confidence, but a fair trial.

5.6   THOMAS DE QUINCEY: POPERY AND MAYNOOTH (1845)

The grant to the Catholic seminary in Ireland, at Maynooth, was part of Peel's wider policy of conciliating the Irish. It was, in particular, an attempt to lessen the hostility of the Irish clergy. The sums were of trifling significance: a building grant of £30,000 and an increased annual grant from £9,000 to £26,000. Nevertheless, acute British sensibilities about Catholic Ireland had grown even more acute since Catholic Emancipation in 1829. Peel's Maynooth grant plunged public opinion into a torrent of excited criticism. One of the less hysterical reactions was by de Quincey (1785–1859) in the pages of *Blackwood's* in May 1845. He was anxious to refute Peel's argument that the principle of state subsidy for Maynooth went back to 1795 and that its renewal fifty years later should be of little consequence.

As to the motives, these grew out of the perils diffused by the French Revolution. The year 1797, which followed the suggestion of this pecuniary aid to the Irish priests, was the last year of Burke's life. In what light he viewed the contagion from the anti-social frenzy then spreading over Europe, may be seen from the oracular works through which he spoke his mind both in 1796 and 1797. He was profoundly impressed with the disorganizing tendencies of the principles, but still more of the licentious cravings for change, which from the centre of Paris had crept like a mist over the whole face of Europe. France was in a less tumultuous state then than in 1792–3–4; but, as respected Europe generally, the aspect of things was worse; because naturally the explosion of frenzy in Paris during the Reign of Terror, took a space of two or three years to reproduce and train the corresponding sympathies in other great capitals of the Continent. By 1797, the contagion was mature. Thence came the necessity for some *domestic* establishment where Irish priests should be educated . . . .

Now, however, not only is it proposed to make it permanent, which (together with the enlarged amount) totally changes its character, but a greater change still is – that the original reason for any grant at all, the *political* reason, has entirely passed away. The objection to a continental education may be strong as regards the convenience of the Irish; but the inconvenience has no longer any relation to ourselves. No air in Europe can be tainted with a fiercer animosity to England than the air of Ireland. In this respect the students of Maynooth cannot be more perilously situated. Whilst we all know by the Repeal rent and the O'Connell yearly tribute, that the Irish Papists could easily raise three times the money demanded for Maynooth, if they were as willing to be just in a service of national duty as they are to be liberal in a service of conspiracy . . . .

Wherever Mr O'Connell wanted an agent, an intriguer, an instrument for rousing the people, he was sure of one in the parish priest. Now this fact is decisive upon the merits of Maynooth. It matters not what latitude may be allowed to variety of political views; no politics of *any* sort can be regarded as becoming to a village pastor. But allow him to be a politician, how could a priest become a tool without ruin to his spiritual character? Yet this is the Maynooth, training its *alumni* to two duties, the special duty of living *in procinctu* and in harness for every assault upon the Protestant establishment of their country, and for the unlimited duty of taking orders in any direction from Mr O'Connell – this is the Maynooth to which, for such merits, we have been paying nine thousand pounds annually for exactly fifty years, and are now required to pay three times as much for ever . . . .

They cannot disguise the broad distinction between the principle in that question and the principle in the question of Catholic emancipation. There the object was purely negative, viz. to liberate a body of men from certain incapacities. Successive penal laws had stripped the Papist of particular immunities and liberties. These were restored by emancipation. A defect was made good. But no *positive* powers were created by that measure. Now, on the other hand, when a large revenue is granted, (as by the pending Maynooth grant,) this is in effect to furnish artillery for covering advances upon hostile ground. This gives positive powers to Popery for propagating its errors.

5.7 SIR ROBERT PEEL: THE REPEAL OF THE CORN LAWS

Peel defied the powerful Protectionist wing in the Conservative Party by deciding in December 1845 that the Corn Laws would have to be repealed. Unwilling to proceed without the support of his party, it was left to Lord John Russell to form a Liberal ministry and repeal the Corn Laws. His attempt to form a government came to nothing and it was left to Peel to repeal the Corn Laws, whatever his party thought. By February Peel had lost the support of two-thirds of his parliamentary party and relied upon the Liberals and Irish to pass the measure. One of the few attempts at self-justification which he made during these weeks came during the debate of 9 February 1846. (Sir Robert Peel: *Speeches* (1853, 4 vols), IV, pp. 607–8.)

Now, Sir, with respect to the course which I have pursued towards those who so long have given me their support. I admit to them that it is but natural that they should withhold from me their confidence. I admit that the course which I am pursuing is at variance with the principles on which party is ordinarily conducted. But I do ask of them, whether it be probable that I would sacrifice their favourable opinion and their support, unless I was influenced by urgent considerations of public duty – unless I was deeply impressed with the necessity of taking these precautions, and advising these measures. Notwithstanding the asperity with which some have spoken, I will do that party (which has hitherto supported me) the justice they deserve. No person can fill the situation I fill, without being aware of the motives by which a great party is influenced. I must have an opportunity of knowing what are the personal objects of those around me; and this I will say, notwithstanding the threatened forfeiture of their confidence, that I do not believe (speaking generally of the great body of the party) that there ever existed a party influenced by more honourable and disinterested feelings.

While I admit that the natural consequences of the course I have pursued, is to offend, probably to alienate, a great party, I am not the less convinced that any other course would have been ultimately injurious even to party interests. I know what would have conciliated temporary confidence. It would have been to underrate the danger in Ireland, to invite a united combination for the maintenance of the existing Corn-law, to talk about hoisting the flag of protection for native industry, to insist that agricultural protection should be maintained in all its integrity – by such a course I should have been sure to animate and please a party, and to gain for a time their cordial approbation. But the month of May will not arrive without demonstrating that I should thereby have abandoned my duty to my country – to my Sovereign – ay, and to the conservative party. I had, and have, the firm persuasion that the present temper of the public mind – the state of public feeling, and of public opinion, with respect to the Corn-laws – independent of all adventitious circumstances, make the defence of the Corn-laws a very difficult task. But with such a calamity as that which is impending in Ireland, it was utterly irreconcilable with my feelings to urge the landed interest to commit themselves to a conflict for the maintenance inviolate of a law which attaches at the present time a duty of 17s. to the quarter of wheat. What were the facts which came under the cognizance of my right hon. friend the secretary of state for the home department, charged with the responsibility of providing for the public peace, and rescuing millions from the calamity of starvation? We were assured in one part of this empire there are 4,000,000 of the Queen's subjects dependent on a certain article of food for subsistence. We knew that on that article of food no reliance could be placed. It was difficult to say what was the extent of the danger – what would be the progress of the disease, and what the amount of deficiency in the supply of that article of food. But, surely, you will make allowances for those who were charged with the heaviest responsibility, if their worst anticipations should be realized by the event. We saw, in the distance, the gaunt forms of famine, and of disease following in the train of famine. Was it not our duty to the country, ay, our duty to the party that supported us, to avert the odious charge of indifference and neglect of timely precautions? It is absolutely necessary, before you come to a final decision on this question, that you should understand this Irish case. You must do so. The reading of letters may be distasteful to you; but you shall have no ground for imputing it to me that I left you in ignorance of a danger which I believe to be imminent. I may have lost your confidence – I will not try to regain it at the expense of truth. I can conciliate no favour by the expression of regret for the course I have taken. So far from it, I declare, in the face of this House that the day of my public life, which I look back on with the greatest satisfaction and pride, is that 1st of November last, when I offered to take the responsibility of issuing an order in council to open the ports, and to trust to you for approval and indemnity.

5.8 RICHARD OASTLER: THE END OF TORY RADICALISM (1835)

Oastler (1789–1861) was a Tory radical from Yorkshire who had been active in campaigns for an Eight Hour Bill and against the Poor Law of 1834. The failure of these campaigns disillusioned Oastler who began to turn to Chartism as a means of improving the living conditions of the masses. His *Eight Letters to the Duke of Wellington* (1835) pp. 36–9, 50–1, 66–7 include a succinct summary of his social and economic theories, his repudiation of capitalism and, not least, his conviction that party politics cannot solve the questions of the day.

That the *Landed Interest*, and the *Labouring Interest* of this country, are now in a state of great distress, no one will deny. The fact is, that the *Money Interest*, and the *Machinery Interest* of the nation, have lately risen to a most preponderating height; – untaxed, and unobstructed, they have well nigh ruined the labouring classes, and are fast engrossing the territories of the ancient Aristocracy, – undermining the Landed Proprietor, who is bound to pay their taxes, and to be insulted by their sneers.

The natural protectors of the laboring poor, *are the owners of the soil, whose property can only be secure and valuable to them when the labourers are content, and happy*, but those two new interests (money and machinery) have interposed, and to serve their own sordid views, have told the labourers that the Aristocracy were their enemies – their tyrants; and that all their sufferings were to be attributed to their oppressors, *the owners of the soil*. The labourers thus duped, have become restless and dissatisfied; they felt that they were suffering, and believed the tales which were propagated by their real oppressors, – the untaxed *Fund-holder*, and the unrestricted *Machine Proprietor*.

The Aristocracy meanwhile, have apparently been insensible of their true position in society; and, as far as I can judge, have been bewildered with their situation, or sleeping at their posts. They have yielded first one measure, and then another, apparently with the expectation, that there was a possible chance of benefit *in any change*. Their two great opponents, have seemed to guide the wheels of Government, and have taken the advantage of every alteration to themselves . . . .

Machinery, which was intended to be a blessing to the labourer, by *decreasing* the severity of his toil, and *shortening* the hours of his labour, is his greatest curse, – and why? – Because the capitalist has been enabled to erect large mills or factories, – to fill them with untaxed machinery, – and to bring thousands into those mills to work at machines *which are not their own*. They consequently have to labour, not only for themselves, but to pay the interest of the expensive establishments of their masters, and an immense profit to satisfy the avaricious demands of the proprietors. Thus have they to work *longer* hours than when they were employed at home, with less perfect machinery. Nay more, the bodily ease which machinery was intended to give to the working man, has, in tens of thousands of cases, thrown him entirely out of employment, – his children, having to labour from twelve to eighteen hours a day; whilst he subsists, unwillingly, in idleness, on the fruits of their excessive toil.

The immense production too, caused by the *unlimited and unrestricted* use of machinery, causes a glut in every market, which produces a competition amongst the manufacturers themselves, which competition reduces the wages of the labourers, constantly *increases* the length of their labour, and necessarily augments the evil in which it originated, viz. *over-production*. . . .

Our whole system of legislation, seems latterly to have been intended to protect individuals in the acquirement of immense sums of money, to pauperize the labourer, and to ruin the landlord, – tending to create two classes, – the very rich, and the very poor. This state of things cannot long continue. The poor only want bread for their labour, and they deserve it. They are not disloyal, – no man can know their feelings better than myself, They absolutely hate the Whigs; and if the Tories would but act upon true Tory 'live and let live' principles, the people would, I am sure, rally round them, and the country might be saved. . . .

The contention of parties *must* now cease; and Tory, Whig, and Radical must become as names of by-gone ages, or we shall very shortly find ourselves involved in bloody civil strife.

The Tories when in power, forgot that *patriotism* ought to have been their *Polar-star*. The Whigs, who boasted that they were *par-excellence* the patriots of the day, no sooner touched the golden-wand of office, than selfishness froze up the springs of patriotism; and because they were poorer and more needy than their predecessors, they became more clamorous for the golden toys; – and if the Radicals were to be invested with the reins of government to-morrow, so sure as man is man, they would not be backward in imitating the conduct of their predecessors, – they would rejoice in taking the sweets of office from their late opponents and oppressors, the Tories and the Whigs. And so in the nature of things it must be, so long as the government is held by any PARTY.

5.9   WILLIAM PAUL: WORKING CLASS CONSERVATISM

Traditions of working class Toryism go back at least as far as Cobbett.

These were strengthened in the 1830s. The Reform Act failed to give the vote to many sections of the working classes and there was great resentment against the New Poor Law. There was a ready reception, therefore, for the attempts made by Tory agents to organise and register new voters from the working classes. The first of these Conservative Operative Societies opened at Leeds in February 1835. The following excerpt rehearses the principles of the Operative Societies and explains why people from the lower classes should become involved with them. From W. Paul: *A History of the Origin and Progress of Operative Conservative Societies* (2nd edn, Leeds, 1839), pp. 7–8, 14–16.

In the meantime I will ask, Were there none of the humble classes of society in these days of delusion and hypocrisy who were faithful among the faithless found? Were there none who possessed sound and Conservative principles amid the struggle of party and the rage of Whig ambition? Were there none among the operatives who saw the golden but delusive bait, and boldly 'nailed their colours to the mast' of Conservatism? Were their none who cultivated the bold, the honest, but aspiring hope, that though Conservatism appeared to be strangled amid the clash of parties, yet ultimately, like another phoenix, it would rise triumphant from its own ashes. O yes, there were to be found among *the people* those who cultivated sound and Conservative principles; who were attached to an established monarchy, believing it to be a form of Government best adapted, in every point of view, to secure the happiness and liberties of a great and mighty people; who were attached to the independence of the House of Lords, inasmuch as they recogised in that part of the legislature a bulwark and a safeguard to all those great liberties which Englishmen alone inherit and enjoy; who were attached to the lower part of the legislature as an integral part of the British Constitution, believing that while it peculiarly guarded the public freedom, it would uphold the Monarchy and its institutions for their own sake; who were attached to an indissoluble union between Church and State, inasmuch as, in the first place, history proves that that union has not been detrimental to us in a national point of view, but has rather been the grand means of raising us, as a nation, to that summit of greatness which we unquestionably maintain in the scale of empires, – and, secondly, they were attached to that union, because they believed it to be the imperative duty of every Government to provide for the religious wants of those whom they govern, and that when they cease to perform this duty, they are no longer fit to be placed at the helm of public affairs. . . .

It matters not how low or how obscure a person may be in the scale of society, if he be an honest-minded, straightforward Conservative – if he appreciate the ten thousand blessings and innumerable advantages which as a Briton he enjoys – if he reverence all those great and invaluable institutions which are at once our country's pride, its glory, and its boast, and which have been secured to us by the blood of patriots and martyrs; – and, if he deem it his imperative duty to rally round these Institutions, and guard them from falling into the destructive hands of a Popish intolerance on the one hand, or a democratic ascendancy on the other, I say such a man can, in his own local though humble sphere, aid and assist the common friends of the Constitution, in fighting its battles, and struggling against those multiplied storms which are assailing it on every side. What I am now stating is positive fact, because every man in his sphere of society, however humble it may be, possesses a certain degree of influence; and when a number of individuals are joined together in one hallowed confederacy, resolved to act and work together, and to bring all their energies and influences to one grand rallying point, I contend that such a course of proceeding cannot but do good to the Conservative cause, whether as it regards the registrations or the elections in general. . . .

I will state some of the reasons why a poor man may be an Operative Conservative. I am very well aware that a man may be joined to a 'Radical Association,' to the 'Working Man's Association,' and to a 'Political Union,' and all will be right and square; but only let a man be a member of an Operative Conservative Society, why astonishment is at once excited, and the exclamation made, 'I cannot for the world see why a man is to be a Conservative Operative.'

The First reason why a poor man may be a Conservative, is this; that he rightly and properly and justly appreciates all those great blessings and advantages which, as an Englishman, he enjoys, and which have accrued to him from living under that invaluable constitution which is the pride of his country and the glory of all lands.

Secondly. That the attempts which are now making by men of all castes, and of all creeds; by men of all religion, and men of no religion; by men of all principles, and by men of no principle, to root up the Constitution under pretence of improving it, will lead ultimately to anarchy and national confusion, and consequently to the prostration of that beautiful structure.

Thirdly. The members of these Societies, being convinced that, should 'the British Constitution fall, truth and reason and the cause of liberty would fall with it; and they who were buried in its ruins would be happier than those who survived it.' I say, being convinced of this important truth, they feel it to be their paramount duty to rally round the Constitution of their country, and if they can by possibility do any good to its cause, even in the most humble way, they cheerfully offer the sacrifice upon its sacred alter.

Fourthly. They are opposed to all those dogmas which are trumpeted forth by a certain class of political empiries, viz. Vote by Ballot, Household Suffrage, and Annual Parliaments, &c., believing that the adoption of these measures would, so far from tending to produce the real welfare of the country, lead to a train of national evils the most woful and lasting in their consequences.

Fifthly. They believe that the principles of Conservatism are founded upon reason, justice, truth, revelation, and sound loyalty; and that, in their general tendencies and operations, they not only contribute largely to the maintenance and preservation of all our great Institutions, but essentially aid in securing to all classes of society that degree of security and happiness which forms the basis of a great and mighty empire.

6.1 BENJAMIN DISRAELI: THE NATURE OF THE BRITISH CONSTITUTION

Conservative writers have frequently adopted an approach to constitutional questions which goes beyond the legalistic details and institutional structures of the political system. In this brief extract from his *Vindication of the English Constitution* Disraeli acknowledges his awareness of those non-parliamentary institutions which contribute so significantly to constitutional government. And these institutions themselves relate back to the laws, customs and attitudes of the British people themselves. From Benjamin Disraeli: *Vindication of the English Constitution* (1835), pp. 82–4.

My Lord, I do not believe that the House of Commons is the House of the People, or that the members of the House of Commons are the representatives of the People. I do not believe that such ever were the characters, either of the House of Commons or the members of the House of Commons; I am sure that such are not now the characters of that assembly, or of those who constitute it, and I ardently hope that such will never be the characters.

The Commons of England form an Estate of the Realm, and the members of the House of Commons represent that Estate. They represent nothing more. It is a very important estate of the realm; it may be the most important estate. Unquestionably, it has of late years greatly advanced in power; but at this very moment, even with all the accession of influence conferred upon it by the act of Reform, it has not departed from the primary character contemplated in its original formation; it consists of a very limited section of our fellow-subjects, invested, for the general advantage of the commonwealth, with certain high functions and noble privileges. The House of Commons is no more the House of the People than is the House of Lords; and the Commons of England, as well as the Peers of England, are neither more nor less than a privileged class, privileged in both instances for the common good, unequal doubtless in number, yet both, in comparison with the whole nation, forming in a numerical estimation, only an insignificant fraction of the mass.

Throughout these observations, in speaking of the English constitution, I speak of that scheme of legislative and executive government consisting of the King and the two Houses of Parliament; but this is a very partial view of the English constitution, and I use the term rather in deference to established associations, than from being unconscious that the polity of our country consists of other institutions, not less precious and important than those of King, Lords, and Commons. Trial by Jury, Habeas Corpus, the Court of King's Bench, the Court of Quarter Sessions, the compulsory provision for the poor, however tampered with, the franchises of municipal corporations, of late so recklessly regarded by short-sighted statesmen, are all essential portions of the English constitution, and have been among the principal causes of the excellent operation, and the singular durability of our legislative and executive Government. The political institutions of England have sprung from its legal institutions. They have their origin in our laws and customs. These have been the profound and perennial sources of their unexampled vigour and beneficence, and unless it had been fed by these clear and wholesome foundations, our boasted Parliament, like so many of its artificial brethren, would soon have dwindled and dried up, and, like some vast canal, filled merely with epidemic filth, only been looked upon as the fatal folly of a nation.

6.2 BENJAMIN DISRAELI: THE REFORM OF PARLIAMENT

The dramatic story of the Reform Act of 1867 has obscured the extremely interesting – and not always inconsistent – development of Disraeli's views on the reform of Parliament. The Derby–Disraeli government introduced a Reform Bill in 1859, on which occasion Disraeli outlined his criteria for reform. This is the subject of the first extract (28 February 1859, *Hansard*, 3rd Series, vol. CLII, pp. 979–80). Furthermore, in his Crystal Palace speech Disraeli enlarged upon the theme of popular support for the 1867 Reform Act, arguing, no doubt with some benefit of hindsight, that the new electors would make marvellously patriotic and conservative voters (*Speeches of the Earl of Beaconsfield*, 2 vols, ed. T. E. Kebbel, 1882, II, pp. 527–9).

You want in this House every element that obtains the respect and engages the interest of the country. You must have lineage and great territorial property; you must have manufacturing enterprise of the highest character; you must have commercial weight; you must have professional ability in all its forms: but you want something more, – you want a body of men not too intimately connected either with agriculture, or with manufactures, or with commerce; not too much wedded to professional thought and professional habits; you want a body of men representing the vast variety of the English character; men who would arbitrate between the claims of those great predominant interests; who would temper the acerbity of their controversies. You want a body of men to represent that immense portion of the community who cannot be ranked under any of those striking and powerful classes to which I have referred, but who are in their aggregate equally important and valuable, and perhaps as numerous. Hitherto you have been able to effect this object, you have effected it by the existing borough system, which has given you a number of constituencies of various dimensions distributed over the country. No one for a moment pretends that the borough system in England was originally framed to represent all the classes and interests of the country; but it has been kept and cherished because the people found that, although not directly intended for such a purpose, yet indirectly it has accomplished that object; and hence I lay it down as a principle which ought to be adopted, that if you subvert that system, you are bound to substitute for it machinery equally effective. That is all I contend for. I am not wedded to arrangements merely because they are arrangements; but what I hope this House will not sanction is, that we should remove a machinery which performs the office we desire, unless we are certain that we can substitute for it a machinery equally effective.

*   *   *

One of the most distinguishing features of the great change effected in 1832 was that those who brought it about at once abolished all the franchises of the working classes. They were franchises as ancient as those of the Baronage of England; and, while they abolished them, they proposed no substitute. The discontent upon the subject of the representation which has from that time more or less pervaded our society dates from that period, and that discontent, all will admit, has now ceased. It was terminated by the Act of Parliamentary Reform of 1867–8. That Act was founded on a confidence that the great body of the people of this country were 'Conservative.' When I say 'Conservative', I use the word in its purest and loftiest sense. I mean that the people of England, and especially the working classes of England, are proud of belonging to a great country, and wish to maintain its greatness – that they are proud of belonging to an Imperial country, and are resolved to maintain, if they can, their empire – that they believe, on the whole, that the greatness and the empire of England are to be attributed to the ancient institutions of the land.

Gentlemen, I venture to express my opinion, long entertained, and which has never for a moment faltered, that this is the disposition of the great mass of the people; and I am not misled for a moment by wild expressions and eccentric conduct which may occur in the metropolis of this country. There are people who may be, or who at least affect to be, working men, and who, no doubt, have a certain influence with a certain portion of the metropolitan working classes, who talk Jacobinism. But, gentlemen, that is no novelty. That is not the consequence of recent legislation or of any political legislation that has occurred in this century. There always has been a Jacobinical section in the City of London. I don't particularly refer to that most distinguished and affluent portion of the metropolis which is ruled by my right honourable friend the Lord Mayor. Mr. Pitt complained of and suffered by it. There has always been a certain portion of the working class in London who have sympathised – perverse as we may deem the taste – with the Jacobin feelings of Paris. Well, gentlemen, we all know now, after eighty years' experience, in what the Jacobinism of Paris has ended, and I hope I am not too sanguine when I express my conviction that the Jacobinism of London will find a very different result.

I say with confidence that the great body of the working class of England utterly repudiate such sentiments. They have no sympathy with them. They are English to the core. They repudiate cosmopolitan principles. They adhere to national principles. They are for maintaining the greatness of the kingdom and the empire, and they are proud of being subjects of our Sovereign and members of such an Empire. Well, then, as regards the political institutions of this country, the maintenance of which is one of the chief tenets of the Tory party, so far as I can read public opinion, the feeling of the nation is in accordance with the Tory party. It was not always so. There was a time when the institutions of this country were decried. They have passed through a scathing criticism of forty years; they have, generally speaking, been always in opposition. They have been upheld by us when we were unable to exercise any of the lures of power to attract force to us, and the people of this country have arrived at these conclusions from their own thought and their own experience.

6.3   BENJAMIN DISRAELI: THE CONDITION OF THE PEOPLE

Disraeli's concern for the welfare of the masses has long been a subject of controversy. Three things can be stated with some confidence. First, disappointing though the record of the ministry of 1874–80 might have been, it compares extremely well with that of other governments before 1906. Second, as the first excerpt illustrates, few parliamentary politicians treated the Chartists with the sympathy that Disraeli did. His sarcastic attack upon the response of Lord John Russell to the Chartists includes several interesting aspects of Disraeli's more general political philosophy (12 July 1839, *Hansard*, 3rd Series, XLIX, pp. 246–52.) Thirdly, in his Crystal Palace speech Disraeli declared 'the elevation of the people' to be one of the three historic functions of the Conservative party; the other two being the maintenance of established institutions and the upholding of imperial interests. In this context, as the second extract reveals, Disraeli was not content simply to announce the principle. He went further and challenged the Liberals to party competition in this area. (*Speeches of the Earl of Beaconsfield*, 2 vols, ed. T. E. Kebbel, 1882, II, pp. 531–3.)

But if the noble Lord supposed, that in this country he could establish a permanent Government on what was styled nowadays, a monarchy of the middle classes, he would be indulging a great delusion, which, if persisted in, must shake our institutions and endanger the Throne. He believed, such a system was actually foreign to the character of the people of England. He believed, that in this country, the exercise of political power must be associated with great public duties. The English nation would concede any degree of political power to a class making simultaneous advances in the exercise of the great social duties. That was the true principle to adhere to; in proportion as they departed from it, they were wrong; as they kept by it, they would approximate to that happy state of things which had been described as so desirable by the honourable Member for Birmingham. The noble Lord had answered the speech of the honourable Member for Birmingham, but he had not answered the Chartists. The honourable Member for Birmingham had made a very dexterous speech, a skillful evolution in favour of the middle classes. But although he had attempted to dovetail the Charter on the Birmingham Union, all that had recently taken place on the appearance of the Chartists before the leaders of the union newly-created magistrates, and the speeches by members of the Convention within the last few days, led to a very different conclusion. There he found the greatest hostility to the middle classes. They complained only of the government by the middle classes. They made no attack on the aristocracy – none on the Corn laws – but upon the newly-enfranchised constituency, not on the old – upon that peculiar constituency which was the basis of the noble Lord's Government. He was aware this subject was distasteful to both of the parties in that House. He regretted it.

He was not ashamed to say, however much he disapproved of the Charter, he sympathised with the Chartists. They formed a great body of his countrymen; nobody could doubt they laboured under great grievances, and it would indeed have been a matter of surprise and little to the credit of the House, if Parliament had been prorogued without any notice being taken of what must always be considered a very remarkable social movement. They had now sat five months; their time had not been particularly well occupied, and he would just call to the attention of the House some of the circumstances which had occurred with reference to this subject. Early in the Session they had heard of lords-lieutenant of counties, noblemen and gentlemen of great influence, leaving the metropolis, travelling by railroads, putting themselves at the head of the yeomanry, capturing and relieving towns, and returning just in time to vote on some important division; and certainly he should have expected that some notice, at least, would have been taken of the occurrence by the noble Lord, the Secretary of State for the Home Department. A short time afterwards, the petition called the 'National Petition', was brought forward by the honourable Gentleman. He called it the National Petition by courtesy. The noble Lord had been critical upon it – he said, it was not national; the noble Lord also said, he was at the head of the reform Government, which some ventured to think was not a reform Government. They should take titles as they found them; but it had a very good title to be called 'national' when it was signed by a large portion of the nation. By a sort of chilling courtesy, the honourable Member was allowed to state the contents of the petition, but the noble Lord said nothing – he gave no sign, and it was only by an accident, he believed, they had been favoured with his remarks that evening – remarks which showed great confidence in the state of the country, in the temper and virtue of the labouring classes – great confidence in himself and in his Government. He hoped the noble Lord had good and efficient reasons for the tone of confidence which he had assumed, and the air, he would not say of contumely, but of captiousness with which he had met this motion. The observations of the noble Lord would go forth to the world, and if the inference he drew from them were wrong, prompt justice would, no doubt, be done him. The noble Lord might despise the Chartists; he might despise 1,280,000 of his fellow-subjects because they were discontented; but if he were a Minister of the Crown, he should not so treat them, even if he thought them unreasonable. The noble Lord had his colonies in a condition so satisfactory – the war in the East seemed drawing to a close – his monetary system was in so healthy a state – that he could afford to treat with such nonchalance a social insurrection at his very threshold. Perhaps it was in vain to expect, whatever might be the state of the country, much attention from her Majesty's Government. Their time was so absorbed, so monopolized, in trying to make Peers, and promising to make Baronets, that but little time could now be given by them to such a subject as this; but probably in the recess, when cabinet councils would be held more frequently, they would give it some consideration. He believed that if they did not, and that if they treated it as a mere temporary ebullition, which was rather the result of a plethoric vein than of any other cause, they would be grievously mistaken; for the seeds were sown, which would grow up to the trouble and dishonour of the realm. He was convinced that if they persisted in their present system of cheap and centralized government, they would endanger not only the national character but also the national throne.

*　　　　*　　　　*

Gentlemen, another great object of the Tory party, and one not inferior to the maintenance of the Empire, or the upholding of our institutions, is the elevation of the condition of the people. Let us see in this great struggle between Toryism and Liberalism that has prevailed in this country during the last forty years what are the salient features. It must be obvious to all who consider the condition of the multitude with a desire to improve and elevate it, that no important step can be gained unless you can effect some reduction of their hours of labour and humanise their toil. The great problem is to be able to achieve such results without violating those principles of economic truth upon which the prosperity of all States depends. You recollect well that many years ago the Tory party believed that these two results might be obtained – that you might elevate the condition of the people by the reduction of their toil and the mitigation of their labour, and at the same time inflict no injury on the wealth of the nation. You know how that effort was encountered – how these views and principles were met by the triumphant statesmen of Liberalism. They told you that the inevitable consequence of your policy was to diminish capital, that this, again, would lead to the lowering of wages, to a great diminution of the employment of the people, and ultimately to the impoverishment of the kingdom.

These were not merely the opinions of Ministers of State, but those of the most blatant and loud-mouthed leaders of the Liberal party. And what has been the result? Those measures were carried, but carried, as I can bear witness, with great difficulty and after much labour and a long struggle. Yet they were carried; and what do we now find? That capital was never accumulated so quickly, that wages were never higher, that the employment of the people was never greater, and the country never wealthier. I ventured to say a short time ago, speaking in one of the great cities of this country, that the health of the people was the most important question for a statesman. It is, gentlemen, a large subject. It has many branches. It involves the state of the dwellings of the people, the moral consequences of which are not less considerable than the physical. It involves their enjoyment of some of the chief elements of nature – air, light, and water. It involves the regulation of their industry, the inspection of their toil. It involves the purity of their provisions, and it touches upon all the means by which you may wean them from habits of excess and of brutality. Now, what is the feeling upon these subjects of the Liberal party – that Liberal party who opposed the Tory party when, even in their weakness, they advocated a diminution of the toil of the people, and introduced and supported those Factory Laws, the principles of which they extended, in the brief period when they possessed power, to every other trade in the country? What is the opinion of the great Liberal party – the party that seeks to substitute cosmopolitan for national principles in the government of this country – on this subject? Why, the views which I expressed in the great capital of the county of Lancaster have been held up to derision by the Liberal Press. A leading member – a very rising member, at least, among the new Liberal members – denounced them the other day as the 'policy of sewage'.

Well, it may be the 'policy of sewage' to a Liberal member of Parliament. But to one of the labouring multitude of England, who has found fever always to be one of the inmates of his household – who has, year after year, seen stricken down the children of his loins, on whose sympathy and material support he has looked with hope and confidence, it is not a 'policy of sewage,' but a question of life and death. And I can tell you this, gentlemen, from personal conversation with some of the most intelligent of the labouring class – and I think there are many of them in this room who can bear witness to what I say – that the policy of the Tory party – the hereditary, the traditionary policy of the Tory party, that would improve the condition of the people – is more appreciated by the people than the ineffable mysteries and all the pains and penalties of the Ballot Bill. Gentlemen, is that wonderful? Consider the condition of the great body of the working classes of this country. They are in possession of personal privileges – of personal rights and liberties – which are not enjoyed by the aristocracies of other countries. Recently they have obtained – and wisely obtained – a great extension of political rights; and when the people of England see that under the constitution of this country, by means of the constitutional cause which my right honourable friend the Lord Mayor has proposed, they possess every personal right of freedom, and, according to the conviction of the whole country, also an adequate concession of political rights, is it at all wonderful that they should wish to elevate and improve their condition, and is it unreasonable that they should ask the Legislature to assist them in that behest as far as it is consistent with the general welfare of the realm?

Why, the people of England would be greater idiots than the Jacobinical leaders of London even suppose, if, with their experience and acuteness, they should not long have seen that the time had arrived when social, and not political improvement is the object which they ought to pursue.

6.4 BENJAMIN DISRAELI: THE IMPERIAL VISION

Disraeli had occasionally expressed some little interest in the value of the empire to Britain but in private his attitude was one of indifference, if not of scorn, to imperial concerns. There can be little doubt that his inclusion of the famous paragraphs about the empire in the Crystal Palace speech were intended to be the opening shots in the next general election campaign. Disraeli grossly exaggerated Liberal neglect of the empire and wrongly attributed to them the principles of the Manchester School. Furthermore, what Disraeli actually said had been to a considerable degree anticipated a year earlier (by J. A. Froude, *Short Studies on Great Subjects*, vol. III, pp. 279–80). Nevertheless, these passages have their place in any account of Disraelian Conservatism. (*Speeches of the Earl of Beaconsfield*, 2 vols, ed. T. E. Kebbel, II, pp. 529–31.)

Gentlemen, there is another and second great object of the Tory party. If the first is to maintain the institutions of the country, the second is, in my opinion, to uphold the Empire of England. If you look to the history of this country since the advent of Liberalism – forty years ago – you will find that there has been no effort so continuous, so subtle, supported by so much energy, and carried on with so much ability and acumen, as the attempts of Liberalism to effect the disintegration of the Empire of England.

And, gentlemen, of all its efforts, this is the one which has been the nearest to success. Statesmen of the highest character, writers of the most distinguished ability, the most organised and efficient means, have been employed in this endeavour. It has been proved to all of us that we have lost money by our colonies. It has been shown with precise, with mathematical demonstration, that there never was a jewel in the Crown of England that was so truly costly as the possession of India. How often has it been suggested that we should at once emancipate ourselves from this incubus. Well, that result was nearly accomplished. When those subtle views were adopted by the country under the plausible plea of granting self-government to the Colonies, I confess that I myself thought that the tie was broken. Not that I for one object to self-government. I cannot conceive how our distant colonies can have their affairs administered except by self-government. But self-government, in my opinion, when it was conceded, ought to have been conceded as part of a great policy of Imperial consolidation. It ought to have been accompanied by an Imperial tariff, by securities for the people of England for the enjoyment of the unappropriated lands which belonged to the Sovereign as their trustees, and by a military code which should have precisely defined the means and the responsibilities by which the colonies should be defended, and by which, if necessary, this country should call for aid from the colonies themselves. It ought, further, to have been accompanied by the institution of some representative council in the metropolis, which would have brought the Colonies into constant and continuous relations with the Home Government. All this, however was omitted because those who advised that policy – and I believe their convictions were sincere – looked upon the Colonies of England, looked even upon our connection with India, as a burden upon this country, viewing everything in a financial aspect, and totally passing by those moral and political considerations which make nations great, and by the influence of which alone men are distinguished from animals.

Well, what has been the result of this attempt during the reign of

Liberalism for the disintegration of the Empire? It has entirely failed. But how has it failed? Through the sympathy of the Colonies with the Mother Country. They have decided that the Empire shall not be destroyed, and in my opinion no minister in this country will do his duty who neglects any opportunity of reconstructing as much as possible our Colonial Empire, and of responding to those distant sympathies which may become the source of incalculable strength and happiness to this land. Therefore, gentlemen, with respect to the second great object of the Tory party also – the maintenance of the Empire – public opinion appears to be in favour of our principles – that public opinion which, I am bound to say, thirty years ago, was not favourable to our principles, and which, during a long interval of controversy, in the interval had been doubtful.

6.5   BENJAMIN DISRAELI: THE DEFENCE OF NATIONAL INSTITUTIONS

Undoubtedly the least innovative of Disraeli's Conservative objectives was the defence of national institutions. All Conservative writers since the days of Burke had pledged themselves to conserve the institutional legacies of the past against whatever movement, group or party appeared to threaten them. To Disraeli, of course, the threat came from the Liberal party of Gladstone, whose professed objective was to reform the institutions of the country. In fact, Disraeli's defence of national institutions was thin and, evidently, undertaken for propagandist effect. The excerpt is taken from the Crystal Palace speech: *The Speeches of the Earl of Beaconsfield*, 2 vols, ed. T. E. Kebbel, II, pp. 525–9.

Now, I have always been of opinion that the Tory party has three great objects. The first is to maintain the institutions of the country – not from any sentiment of political superstition, but because we believe that they embody the principles upon which a community like England can alone safely rest. The principles of liberty, of order, of law, and of religion ought not to be entrusted to individual opinion or to the caprice and passion of multitudes, but should be embodied in a form of permanence and power. We associate with the Monarchy the ideas which it represents – the majesty of law, the administration of justice, the foundation of mercy and of honour. We know that in the Estates of the Realm and the privileges they enjoy, is the best security for public liberty and good government. We believe that a national profession of faith can only be maintained by an Established Church, and that no society is safe unless there is a public recognition of the Providential government of the world, and of the future responsibility of man. Well, it is a curious circumstance that during all these same forty years of triumphant Liberalism, every one of these institutions has been attacked and assailed – I say, continuously attacked and assailed. And what, gentlemen, has been the result? For the -last forty years the most depreciating comparisons have been instituted between the Sovereignty of England and the Sovereignty of a great Republic. We have been called upon in every way, in Parliament, in the Press, by articles in newspapers, by pamphlets, by every means which can influence opinion, to contrast the simplicity and economy of the Sovereignty of the United States with the cumbrous cost of the Sovereignty of England.

Gentlemen, I need not in this company enter into any vindication of the Sovereignty of England on that head. I have recently enjoyed the opportunity, before a great assemblage of my countrymen, of speaking upon that subject. I have made statements with respect to it which have not been answered either on this side of the Atlantic or the other. Only six months ago the advanced guard of Liberalism, acting in entire unison with that spirit of assault upon the Monarchy which the literature and the political confederacies of Liberalism have for forty years encouraged, flatly announced itself as Republican, and appealed to the people of England on that distinct issue. Gentlemen, what was the answer? I need not dwell upon it. It is fresh in your memories and hearts. The people of England have expressed, in a manner which cannot be mistaken, that they will uphold the ancient Monarchy of England, the Constitutional Monarchy of England, limited by the coordinate authority of the Estates of the Realm, but limited by nothing else. Now, if you consider the state of public opinion with regard to those Estates of the Realm, what do you find? Take the case of the House of Lords. The House of Lords has been assailed during this reign of Liberalism in every manner and unceasingly. Its constitution has been denounced as anomalous, its influence declared pernicious; but what has been the result of this assault and criticism of forty years? Why, the people of England, in my opinion, have discovered that the existence of a second Chamber is necessary to Constitutional Government; and, while necessary to Constitutional Government, is, at the same time, of all political inventions the most difficult. Therefore, the people of this country have congratulated themselves that, by the aid of an ancient and famous history, there has been developed in this country an Assembly which possesses all the virtues which a Senate should possess – independence, great local influence, eloquence, all the accomplishments of political life, and a public training which no theory could supply.

The assault of Liberalism upon the House of Lords has been mainly occasioned by the prejudice of Liberalism against the land laws of this country. But in my opinion, and in the opinion of wiser men than myself, and of men in other countries beside this, the liberty of England depends much upon the landed tenure of England – upon the fact that there is a class which can alike defy despots and mobs, around which the people may always rally, and which must be patriotic from its intimate connection with the soil. Well, gentlemen, so far as these institutions of the country – the Monarchy and the Lords Spiritual and Temporal – are concerned, I think we may fairly say, without exaggeration, that public opinion is in favour of those institutions, the maintenance of which is one of the principal tenets of the Tory party, and the existence of which has been unceasingly criticised for forty years by the Liberal party. . . .

Let me say one word upon another institution, the position of which is most interesting at this time. No institution of England, since the advent of Liberalism, has been so systematically, so continuously assailed as the Established Church. Gentlemen, we were first told that the Church was asleep, and it is very possible, as everybody, civil and spiritual, was asleep forty years ago, that that might have been the case. Now we are told that the Church is too active, and that it will be destroyed by its internal restlessness and energy. I see in all these efforts of the Church to represent every mood of the spiritual mind of man, no evidence that it will fall, no proof that any fatal disruption is at hand. I see in the Church, as I believe I see in England, an immense effort to rise to national feelings and recur to national principles. The Church of England, like all our institutions, feels it must be national, and it knows that, to be national, it must be comprehensive. Gentlemen, I have referred to what I look upon as the first object of the Tory party – namely, to maintain the institutions of the country, and reviewing what has occurred, and referring to the present temper of the times upon these subjects, I think that the Tory party, or, as I will venture to call it, the National party, has everything to encourage it. I think that the nation, tested by many and severe trials, has arrived at the conclusion which we have always maintained, that it is the first duty of England to maintain its institutions, because to them we principally ascribe the power and prosperity of the country.

6.6   BENJAMIN DISRAELI: THE CONSERVATIVE PARTY AS THE NATIONAL PARTY

The great art of Disraeli's rhetoric was to ensure that the basic principles of Conservatism could be applied in any situation. Consequently, his attempts to justify the Reform Act of 1867, to take one very important example, referred back to the national destiny of the Conservative party. In a speech made at Edinburgh in October 1867 Disraeli argued that the opportunities presented by the Act in a new and uncertain situation amounted to a challenge which only a truly national party could meet. (*Speeches of the Earl of Beaconsfield*, 2 vols, Ed. T. E. Kebbel, 1882, II, pp. 487–8.)

Gentlemen, I cannot deny that the great measure which has been passed this year will give in some degree a new character to the Constitution, and introduce some new powers and influences into its play and action. Indeed, to accomplish these ends was the object of those who brought it forward. I am told, at least I hear every day, that in consequence of the change which has been effected one must expect great questions to arise. Well, great questions no doubt will arise, and I shall be very sorry if great questions should not arise. Great questions are a proof that a country is progressing. In a progressive country change is constant; and the great question is, not whether you should resist change which is inevitable, but whether that change should be carried out in deference to the manners, the customs, the laws, and the traditions of a people, or whether it should be carried out in deference to abstract principles, and arbitrary and general doctrines. The one is a national system; the other, to give it an epithet, a noble epithet – which, perhaps, it may deserve – is a philosophic system. Both have great advantages: the national party is supported by the fervour of patriotism; the philosophical party has a singular exemption from the force of prejudice.

Now, my lords and gentlemen, I have always considered that the Tory party was the national party of England. It is not formed of a combination of oligarchs and philosophers who practise on the sectarian prejudices of a portion of the people. It is formed of all classes, from the highest to the most homely, and it upholds a series of institutions that are in theory, and ought to be in practice, an embodiment of the national requirements and the security of the national rights. Whenever the Tory party degenerates into an oligarchy, it becomes unpopular; whenever the national institutions do not fulfil their original intention, the Tory party becomes odious;

but when the people are led by their natural leaders, and when, by their united influence, the national institutions fulfil their original intention, the Tory party is triumphant, and then, under Providence, will secure the prosperity and the power of the country.

Part Seven

LATE VICTORIAN CONSERVATISM TO THE FIRST WORLD WAR

7.1 LORD SALISBURY: EXPERIMENTING WITH DEMOCRACY

Lord Salisbury (1830–1903) (or Lord Cranborne as he then was) was the most outspoken Conservative opponent of the 1867 Reform Act. He believed that it ushered in the day of democratic government and the monopoly of power by the working classes. Salisbury's Conservatism is founded upon his distaste for democratic government. In the first of the following extracts he outlines his ideological objections to democracy. ('The Conservative Surrender', *The Quarterly Review*, 1867; reprinted in Paul Smith, *Lord Salisbury on Politics* (CUP 1972)). In the second he explores the consequences of democracy for the House of Commons (27 April 1866, *Hansard* CLXXXIII, 6–24).

The general tendency among those who were responsible for the measure appeared to be, in public to rely upon the virtues of the working class, in private to draw what consolation they could from a belief in its unbounded pliability.

We do not intend to speculate upon the answer which events will give to this interesting question. No past experience can help us to discuss it. The experiment, stupendous as are the interests it puts in hazard, is yet absolutely new. Great cities have before this been placed, for a brief and troubled period, under the absolute control of the poorest classes of their population. Large empires have been governed, and are governed still, with considerable success, by a democracy of petty rural cultivators. But the idea of placing a great empire under the absolute control of the poorest classes in the town has never until the present year been entertained by any nation. We have nothing, therefore, but *a priori* considerations to guide us in a forecast of our future fate. What we know of the fallibility of human nature, of the proneness of mankind to shape their conduct by their desires, and to devise afterwards the code of morality necessary to defend it, is not reassuring. We still think, as we have always thought, that to give the power of taxation to those from whom no taxes are exacted, the supreme disposal of property to those who have no property of their own, the guidance of this intricate machine of government to the least instructed class in the community, is to adopt in the management of the empire principles which would not be entertained for a moment in any other department of human affairs. But it is futile to argue *a priori* now. The decision of this issue has been remitted to the test of experience. For us its teaching will be valueless; for we have taken a step that can never be recalled. But before another generation has passed away, other nations will have learned by our success or our disasters how far the rule of the poorer urban multitudes is favourable to the freedom of property, or to the maintenance of wise and stable government.

Had this revolution been accomplished in fair fight we should have been content to lay aside the controversy at this point. It is the duty of every Englishman, and of every English party, to accept a political defeat cordially, and to lend their best endeavours to secure the success, or to neutralise the evil, of the principles to which they have been forced to succumb. England has committed many mistakes as a nation in the course of her history; but their mischief has often been more than corrected by the heartiness with which after each great struggle victors and vanquished have forgotten their former battles, and have combined together to lead the new policy to its best results. We have no wish to be unfaithful to so wholesome a tradition. As far, therefore, as our Liberal adversaries are concerned, we shall dismiss the long controversy with the expression of an earnest hope that their sanguine confidence may prove in the result to have been wiser than our fears. . . .

The desperate resistance which our fathers made to the last Reform Bill is blamed, not so much because their views were mistaken, as because it was madness to defend those views against so formidable an assault. It is said, – and men seem to think that condemnation can go no further than such a censure – that they brought us within twenty-four hours of revolution. Their successors boast that their prudence will never go so near to the heels of danger. No one will suspect them of it. But is it in truth so great an evil, when the dearest interests and the most sincere convictions are at stake, to go within twenty-four hours of revolution? Did the great classes whose battle had been so fierce, respect each other less when it was once lost and won? Did Sir Robert Peel, who fought it to the end, lose by his tenacity in the estimation of his countrymen? Did the cause he represented suffer through his temerity? He was indeed beaten down in 1832, vainly struggling for a hopeless cause. But before six years had passed he was at the head of half the House of Commons: and before ten years had gone by he led the most powerful Ministry our century has seen.

We live in other days. It may be doubtful how far the more modern plan of yielding every political citadel on the first summons, in order to avert the possibility of disturbance, really springs from the peace-loving sentiments on which it is sometimes justified. There can be little doubt that it tends to screen timidity or foster self-seeking in politicians according to their temperament; and that they are beginning to look on principles which may be upheld with so little danger, and abandoned with so little shame, as mere counters in the game which they are playing. But there can be no question that this view of political duty is widely held among the classes who have always governed this country, and who until the next election will continue to govern it. They value our institutions, they dislike organic change, they object to a large transfer of power. But it is now well established that whatever these objections may be, they are such as a very moderate display of physical force is quite sufficient to remove. This spirit is so different from that which the governing classes of this country have shown during the long period of its history, that it is not easy to estimate that full consequences of the change. But it must inevitably affect largely not only the working of the ordinary machinery of parliamentary government, but the existence of our institutions themselves. . . .

The Conservative party became famous for its organisation and prompt discipline: and yet that discipline did not seem to be the result of any unusual admiration of its leaders. Its ranks were being gradually recruited from a class eminently fit to exhibit the virtues of parliamentary discipline; men who sought a seat for other than political motives, and were more solicitous for the social rank or commercial influence it conferred than for the success of the cause in whose interest it had been avowedly obtained. Elaborate and successful electioneering became one of the attributes of the party: which can only be developed in average politicians by contagion from the classes who support them out of doors, and led by a chief whose Conservative connections were an accident of his career, when they arrived at the year 1867, having just tasted the first fruits of office after a long and dreary fast, they were not in a condition to withstand any severe temptation. The urgent question which lovers of the constitution have to ask themselves is, whether, unless the balance of fears which acts upon their leaders is materially altered, they are likely to be proof against a second temptation of the same kind.

*   *   *

Now, if there is one claim which the House of Commons has on the respect of the people of this country, it is the great historic fame it enjoys – if it has done anything to establish the present balance of power among all classes of the community, and prevent any single element of the Constitution from overpowering the rest, it is that in presence of all powers, however great and terrible they may have been, the House of Commons has always been free and independent in its language. It never in past times, when Kings were powerful, fawned upon them. It has always resisted their unjust pretences. It always refused to allow any courtierly instincts to suppress in it that solicitude for the freedom of the people of this country which it was instituted to cherish. I should deeply regret, if at a time when it is said we are practically about to change our Sovereign, and when some may think that new powers are about to rule over the country, a different spirit were to influence and inspire the House of Commons. Nothing could be more dangerous to the reputation of the House, nothing more fatal to its authority, than that it should be suspected of sycophancy to any power, either from below or above, that is likely to become predominant in the State.

My own feeling with respect to the working men is simply this – we have heard a great deal too much of them, as if they were different from other Englishmen. I do not understand why the nature of the poor or working men in this country should be different from that of any other Englishman. They spring from the same race. They live under the same climate. They are brought up under the same laws. They aspire after the same historical model which we admire ourselves; and I cannot understand why their nature is to be thought better or worse than that of other classes. I say their nature, but I say nothing about their temptations. If you apply to any class of the community special temptations, you will find that class addicted to special vices. And that is what I fear you are doing now. You are not recognizing the fact that, dealing with the working classes, you are dealing with men who are Englishmen in their nature, and who have every English virtue and vice: you are applying to them a special training, and yet refuse to look forward to the special result, which all who know human nature must inevitably expect.

7.2   SIR HENRY MAINE: THE CASE AGAINST DEMOCRACY

Henry Maine (1822–88) was one of the most influential of a cluster of late nineteenth-century Conservative philosophers who in their different ways compiled a substantial indictment against democracy, reform and progress. For Maine, democracy had to be regarded simply as a form of government, as a means of attaining freedom and justice. It had no intrinsic merit in itself. Progress, innovation and creativity owed everything to the individual and the wide distribution of property constituted the most effective defence of freedom. Maine believed that popular government threatened freedom and progress and, as the extract reveals, doubted whether democratic government could survive. From Sir Henry Maine, *Popular Government* (1886), pp. 41–2, 53–5.

Popular governments can only be worked by a process which incidentally entails the further subdivision of the morsels of political power; and thus the tendency of these governments, as they widen their electoral basis, is towards a dead level of commonplace opinion. which they are forced to adopt as the standard of legislation and policy. The evils likely to be thus produced are rather those vulgarly associated with Ultra-Conservatism than those of Ultra-Radicalism. So far indeed as the human race has experience, it is not by political societies in any way resembling those now called democracies that human improvement has been carried on. . . .

There is not at present sufficient evidence to warrant the common belief, that these governments are likely to be of indefinitely long duration. There is, however, one positive conclusion from which no one can escape who bases a forecast of the prospects of popular government, not on moral preference or *a priori* assumption, but on actual experience as witnessed to by history. If there be any reason for thinking that constitutional freedom will last, it is a reason furnished by a particular set of facts, with which Englishmen ought to be familiar, but of which many of them, under the empire of prevailing ideas, are exceedingly apt to miss the significance. The British Constitution has existed for a considerable length of time, and therefore free institutions generally may continue to exist. . . .

One nation alone, consisting of Englishmen, has practised a modification of it successfully, amidst abounding material plenty. It is not too much to say, that the only evidence worth mentioning for the duration of popular government is to be found in the success of the British Constitution during two centuries under special conditions, and in the success of the American Constitution during one century under conditions still more peculiar and more unlikely to recur. Yet, so far as our own Constitution is concerned, that nice balance of attractions, which caused it to move evenly on its stately path, is perhaps destined to be disturbed. One of the forces governing it may gain dangerously at the expense of the other; and the British political system, with the national greatness and material prosperity attendant on it, may yet be launched into space and find its last affinities in silence and cold.

7.3 SIR JAMES FITZJAMES STEPHEN: DEMOCRACY AND EQUALITY

> Stephen (1829–94) is perhaps the most substantial late nineteenth-century *philosopher* of Conservatism. At least, his careful analysis of interventionist, egalitarian and democratic ideas remains impressive after over a century. Stephen is at pains to show that democratic government does not necessarily lead to more just or more humane government. He then approaches the question whether democratic government leads to greater equality. From James Fitzjames Stephen, *Liberty, Equality, Fraternity* (1873), ed. R. J. White (CUP 1967), pp. 210–11.

I now proceed to the most important of the remaining senses of the word 'equality' – the equal distribution of political power. This is perhaps the most definite sense which can be attached to the vague general word 'equality'. It is undoubtedly true that for several generations a process has been going on all over our own part of the world which may be described, not inaccurately, as the subdivision of political power. The accepted theory of government appears to be that everybody should have a vote, that the Legislature should be elected by these votes, and that it should conduct all the public business of the country through a committee which succeeds for the time in obtaining its confidence. This theory, beyond all question, has gone forth, and is going forth conquering and to conquer. The fact of its triumph is as clear as the sun at noonday, and the probability that its triumphs will continue for a longer time than we need care to think about it as strong as any such probability can well be. The question is, what will a reasonable man think of it? I think he will criticize it like any other existing fact, and with as little partiality on either side as possible; but I am altogether at a loss of understand how it can rouse enthusiastic admiration in any one whatever. It certainly has done so for some reason or other. Nearly every newspaper, and a very large proportion of modern books of political speculation, regard the progress of democracy, the approaching advent of universal suffrage, with something approaching to religious enthusiasm. To this I for one object.

In the first place, it will be well to point out a distinction which, though perfectly clear and of the utmost importance, is continually overlooked. Legislate how you will, establish universal suffrage, if you think proper, as a law which can never be broken. You are still as far as ever from equality. Political power has changed its shape but not its nature. The result of cutting it up into little bits is simply that the man who can sweep the greatest number of them into one heap will govern the rest. The strongest man in some form or other will always rule. If the government is a military one, the qualities which make a man a great soldier will make him a ruler. If the government is a monarchy, the qualities which kings value in counsellors, in generals, in administrators, will give power. In a pure democracy the ruling men will be the wirepullers and their friends; but they will no more be on an equality with the voters than soldiers or Ministers of State are on an equality with the subjects of a monarchy. Changes in the form of a government alter the conditions of superiority much more than its nature. In some ages a powerful character, in others cunning, in others powers of despatching business, in others eloquence, in others a good hold upon current commonplaces and facility in applying them to practical purposes will enable a man to climb on to his neighbours' shoulders and direct them this way or that; but in all ages and under all circumstances the rank and file are directed by leaders of one kind or another who get the command of their collective force. The leading men in a trade union are as much the superiors and rulers of the members of the body at large, and the general body of the members are as much the superiors and rulers of each individual member, as the master of a family or the head of a factory is the ruler and superior of his servants or work-people.

7.4 W. H. LECKY: DEMOCRACY AND THE AUTHORITARIAN STATE

Lecky (1838–1903) is more renowned for his historical works, especially his *History of England in the Eighteenth Century* and his *History of European Morals*, than he is for his works of political philosophy. *Democracy and Liberty*, however, offers a coherent indictment of the political movements of his time. Doubting whether parliamentary government was compatible with democracy, he predicted the fragmentation of executive power and the ensuing bitter conflict between sectional groups for command of power within the State. He lamented the prominent part which the Conservative Party, and Disraeli and the Reform Act of 1867 in particular, had taken in this development. 'It has been discovered that the Church, the Aristocracy and the landed interests, if they descend into the arena, are fully able to hold their own in the competition for popular favour, and that some of the tendencies and doctrines which are especially associated with Conservative traditions are peculiarly fitted to blend with democratic politics' (Introduction, p. xiii). The ultimate consequence, however, could be fatal to free government. From W. H. Lecky, *Democracy and Liberty* (2 vols, 1898), I, pp. 257–60.

In our own day, no fact is more incontestable and conspicuous than the love of democracy for authoritative regulation. The two things that men in middle age have seen most discredited among their contemporaries are probably free contract and free trade. The great majority of the democracies of the world are now frankly protectionist, and even in free-trade countries the multiplication of laws regulating, restricting, and interfering with industry in all its departments is one of the most marked characteristics of our time. Nor are those regulations solely due to sanitary or humanitarian motives. Among large classes of those who advocate them another motive is very perceptible. A school has arisen among popular working-class leaders which no longer desires that superior skill, or industry, or providence should reap extraordinary rewards. Their ideal is to restrict by the strongest trade-union regulations the amount of work and the amount of the produce of work, to introduce the principle of legal compulsion into every branch of industry, to give the trade union an absolute coercive power over its members, to attain a high average, but to permit no superiorities. The industrial organisation to which they aspire approaches far more nearly to that of the Middle Ages or of the Tudors than to the ideal of Jefferson and Cobden. I do not here argue whether this tendency is good or bad. No one at least can suppose that it is in the direction of freedom. It may be permitted to doubt whether liberty in other forms is likely to be very secure if power is mainly placed in the hands of men who, in their own sphere, value it so little.

The expansion of the authority and the multiplication of the functions of the State in other fields, and especially in the field of social regulation, is an equally apparent accompaniment of modern democracy. This increase of State power means a multiplication of restrictions imposed upon the various forms of human action. It means an increase of bureaucracy, or, in other words, of the number and power of State officials. It means also a constant increase of taxation, which is in reality a constant restriction of liberty. One of the first forms of liberty is the right of every man to dispose of his own property and earnings, and every tax is a portion of this money taken from him by the force and authority of the law. Many of these taxes are, no doubt, for purposes in which he has the highest interest. They give him the necessary security of life, property, and industry, and they add in countless ways to his enjoyment. But if taxes are multiplied for carrying out a crowd of objects in which he has no interest, and with many of which he has no sympathy, his liberty is proportionately restricted. His money is more and more taken from him by force for purposes of which he does not approve. The question of taxation is in the highest degree a question of liberty, and taxation under a democracy is likely to take forms that are peculiarly hostile to liberty. I have already pointed out how the old fundamental principle of English freedom, that no one should be taxed except by his consent, is being gradually discarded; and how we are steadily advancing to a state in which one class will impose the taxes, while another class will be mainly compelled to pay them. It is obvious that taxation is more and more employed for objects that are not common interests of the whole community, and that there is a growing tendency to look upon it as a possible means of confiscation; to make use of it to break down the power, influence, and wealth of particular classes; to form a new social type; to obtain the means of class bribery.

There are other ways in which democracy does not harmonise well with liberty. To place the chief power in the most ignorant classes is to place it in the hands of those who naturally care least for political liberty, and who are most likely to follow with an absolute devotion some strong leader. The sentiment of nationality penetrates very deeply into all classes; but in all countries and ages it is the upper and middle classes who have chiefly valued constitutional liberty, and those classes it is the work of democracy to dethrone. At the same time democracy does much to weaken among these also the love of liberty. The instability and insecurity of democratic politics; the spectacle of dishonest and predatory adventurers climbing by popular suffrage into positions of great power in the State; the alarm which attacks on property seldom fails to produce among those who have something to lose, may easily scare to the side of despotism large classes who, under other circumstances, would have been steady supporters of liberty. A despotism which secures order, property, and industry, which leaves the liberty of religion and of private life unimpaired, and which enables quiet and industrious men to pass through life untroubled and unmolested, will always appear to many very preferable to a democratic republic which is constantly menacing, disturbing, or plundering them.

7.5   HUGH ELLIOT: THE CASE AGAINST COLLECTIVISM

The publications of the British Constitution Association reflect the assertive and vigorous entrepreneurial values of the manufacturing classes of the industrial revolution. Individual initiative, free enterprise and the profit motive figure largely in its proceedings.

In this extract, Hugh Elliot attacks the case for State intervention in the economic and social life of the nation. Starting from the assumption that the engine of social progress is the individual's wish for self-improvement, he contrasts the inability of the State – with his mediocre class of bureaucratic officials – to meet the needs of the mass of the people. He instances the provision of a uniform system of state education which, he concludes, has failed the country because of its monolithic uniformity. He then proceeds to the more general case against collectivism. From The British Constitution Association: *Political Socialism* (1908), pp. 164–7.

Another sphere into which the State is extending its activities, is in the taking over of various trading enterprises from private companies. The Central Government has a monopoly of the Post Office, Telegraphs, &c., which it mismanages in the supposed interests of the public; while local governing bodies all through the country are embarking upon undertakings such as electric lighting, tramways and anything else the successful management of which is supposed to be of high public importance. The assumption underlying expenditure such as this, is that the governing body is a more infallible index of the need of the public for a certain commodity than is the demand of the public itself for that commodity. Under ordinary circumstances capital is invested where the interest earned by it is the highest possible; that is to say, where the demand of the public for it is the most urgent. When some visionary local body thinks that some scheme ought to be carried out for the good of the public – as in the establishment of steamboats on the river by the London County Council – the capital used in the undertaking does not suddenly come into existence out of thin air;

but is withdrawn from the various other undertakings in which it would otherwise have been invested. To that extent trade is injured, and a public demand left unsatisfied. It is therefore no palliation of the proceedings to say that the municipal enterprise pays. The question is not whether it pays, but whether it pays better than that same capital would have paid if it had been invested according to the ordinary laws of supply and demand. It is possible that here and there an instance may be pointed out where municipal enterprise *has* been successful even in this rigorous sense; but none can deny that as a rule it is not so, and that hence the net result of municipal trading is to deprive the public of what they want in order to present to them what they want little.

This objection applies to all business projects carried on by governing bodies. All arguments in their favour rest on the false assumption that a government knows better what the people want than the people do themselves. By giving to the lowest section of the population an expensive system of education, which they cannot greatly profit by, the country at large is deprived of a vast amount of capital and labour by which it would be otherwise working for its own improvement.

There is another insuperable objection to municipal trading, and that is the set-back which it gives to private enterprise. This ulterior effect is little considered by that numerous section of the population whose political vision does not extend beyond the end of their noses; but for those who recognise that the fate of the nation in the future depends upon its enterprise in trade, the prospect of unlimited municipal trading is indeed terrifying.

Among the various other contrivances for increasing the number of the inefficients and diminishing the number of the efficients, are old age pensions, lax administration of the poor law, assistance to the unemployed. These all originate purely out of *sentiment*. It is not possible to produce sound arguments in their defence; and in default of reason, it is to sentiment that appeal is made. The inequality of wealth now existing must often cause deep pain to sympathetic minds, but if we give way to sentiment, we must beware of the danger of laying up far greater evils for future generations. There is no exception to the rule that where sentiment and emotion come in, science goes out; and as the aim of social science is to secure the highest welfare of society, an enlightened philanthropy will see to it that no sentiment interferes with our study of social diseases and their remedies.

7.6   LORD SALISBURY: THE DUTIES OF THE STATE

One of the few occasions when Salisbury took a personal interest and, indeed, a personal initiative into State welfare schemes occurred on 22 February 1884 when he introduced a motion for a Royal Commission on the Housing of the Working Classes. Salisbury seems to have been well-informed on the subject and, not least, deeply moved by current revelations about the unhealthy conditions in which the poor were forced to live. His speech is an interesting indication of the extent to which the Conservative party had failed to develop the Disraelian theme of the condition of the people. In moving his motion Salisbury refused to apportion any blame for the state of working-class housing, declared that the property interests of landlords and leaseholders must not be harmed and even removed from the terms of reference of the enquiry the question of reducing compensation to finance rehousing. Indeed, the words of the extract which follow deserve the closest attention. In remedying gross public evils, he declares, the prosperity of industry must not be affected. And although he takes the argument into the moral dimension, the essence of his case is that a prosperous society requires a healthy work-force. (22 February 1884, Hansard, CCLXXXIV, 1679–93.)

I will at once say I do not favour any wild schemes of State interference. I am as earnest as any man in this House that, while we approach great public evils, and desire to remedy them, we should scrupulously observe that honesty which is the condition of continued and abiding prosperity for the industries of this country. But while I will maintain that doctrine as earnestly as my noble Friend, I yet would ask the House to avoid that kind of political cowardice which declines to consider and examine a problem, lest its urgency should afterwards seem to be a temptation to provide unlawful and illegitimate methods for its remedy. The evils that we have to deal with are very serious. After all, even my noble Friend may press as earnestly as he will upon us the necessity of leaving every Englishman to work out his own destiny, and not attempt to aid him at the expense of the State; but, on the other side, he must always bear in mind there are no absolute truths or principles in politics. We must never forget that there is a moral as well as a material contagion, which exists by virtue of the moral and material laws under which we live, and which forbid us to be indifferent, even as a matter of interest, to the well-being in every respect of all the classes who form part of the community. If there be material evil, disease will follow, and the contagion of that disease will not be confined to those amongst whom it arises, but will spread over the rest of the community. And what is true of material evil is true of moral evil too. If there are circumstances which produce great moral injury, the contagion will not be confined to the class of those with whom the moral effects arise, but will spread their evil consequences over the whole of the community to which these classes belong. After all, whatever political arrangements we may adopt, whatever the political constitution of our State may be, the foundation of all its prosperity and welfare must be that the mass of the people shall be honest and manly, and shall have common sense. How are you to expect that these conditions will exist amongst people subjected to the frightful influences which the present overcrowding of our poor produce?

7.7 LORD RANDOLPH CHURCHILL: CONSERVATISM IN A COLLECTIVIST AGE

Lord Randolph Churchill (1849–94) in his bid for the leadership of the Conservative Party after the death of Disraeli was fond of making significant speeches on profound subjects. His political ideas, however, are disappointingly derivative. He dresses up in Disraelian language a good deal of cant about the defence of a balanced and propertied constitution in Church and State. In the first of the following excerpts Churchill sets out his ideas for the organisation of the Conservative party (*Speeches of Lord Randolph Churchill*, ed. Louis J. Jennings, 2 vols, 1889. Speech at Birmingham on 16 April 1884, I, pp. 132–4). In the second, he contemplates the growing political power of Labour and the need for the Conservative party to take heed of it (W. Churchill: *Lord Randolph Churchill*, 1906, Letter to the Liberal-Unionist Candidate for Tyneside, 1892, II, pp. 458–60).

Formerly, the organiser had to deal with classes and with cliques. Now he has to deal with great masses, and, moreover, intelligent, instructed, and independent masses of electors. These masses cannot be dictated to. They cannot be driven. They cannot be wire-pulled. They must be argued with and persuaded. This is the first of the duties which I imagine devolves upon all the members of the Midland Conservative Club. I do not think that there will be any indiscretion if I admit that, as regards party organisation, the Liberals have been a little ahead of the Conservative party. They have been the first to adopt the peculiar form of organisation which is known as the Caucus. I hope you won't be shocked at all if I tell you that I see nothing whatever objectionable in that form of organisation which is known as the Caucus. The Caucus, as a form of political organisation, simply means this – that great masses of people, thinking one way, feel that they are too unwieldy for them to manage their own affairs directly, and they confide the management of their affairs to certain elected persons in whom they have confidence, and these elected persons are responsible to the masses who have elected them. That is the organisation which was known in America as the Caucus; but the Radicals always push things to extreme – and they have pushed the Caucus to an extreme which it was never meant to be put to, and they have used it for ends which are undoubtedly mischievous, and dangerous to the freedom of our political life. The Caucus, as you know it here in Birmingham, has not been content to limit its work to party organisation, but has endeavoured to interfere more or less – and rather more than less – tyrannically in dictating the policy which should be pursued on political questions by our public men. I say that when the Birmingham Caucus assumes to decide public questions of the highest interest and of the greatest difficulty, and to issue its mandates to the other associations in the country, and to issue those mandates even to members of Parliament, I say that the Caucus is altogether transgressing the proper limits of its functions.

The Conservative party, though, perhaps, it does not move so rapidly, moves more surely than the Liberal party. We have our popular organisations – they are known by the name of Conservative Associations; and they, as far as I know, have always confined themselves to the duties of strict party organisation, and have not attempted to follow the evil examples which have been set them by your friends in Birmingham. I look to intelligent and experienced men like yourselves, who form this club, to assist those who are endeavouring to popularise the organisation of the Conservative party. Our object is to have a popular organisation, through the selection by voters of an executive, who shall manage their party affairs. Our object is to obtain, if possible, a representative executive; and our object is to obtain, if possible, an executive who shall hold itself responsible to those who have elected it. In fact, my idea would be – and it is the idea, I am happy to say, of many of my friends – that the Tory party should be, like the English people, a self-governed party. That, I believe, is the only form of organisation by which you can attract great masses of the people to the support of the political opinions which you profess. Now, all of you who belong to this club can undoubtedly render immense service to the Conservative party. Most of you are men well acquainted with business, commerce, and trade, and it is in your power to give most enlightened instruction to the masses of the people on subjects which most intimately concern their welfare. I would especially urge upon you the importance of taking steps for the foundation of political clubs for the artisan classes. Many of you, from the position which you hold, have sufficient time on your hands – which the artisan classes do not have – in which you may be able to devote yourself to that most useful work.

*   *   *

The Labour community is carrying on at the present day a very significant and instructive struggle. It has emancipated itself very largely from the mere mechanism of party politics; it realises that it now possesses political power to such an extent as to make it independent of either party in the State; and the struggle which it is now carrying on is less against the Capital, less one of wages or division of profits, but rather one for the practical utilisation in its own interest of the great political power which it has acquired. The Labour interest is now seeking to do itself what the landed interest and the manufacturing capitalist interest did for themselves when each in turn commanded the disposition of State policy. Our land laws were framed by the landed interest for the advantage of the landed interest, and foreign policy was directed by that interest to the same end. Political power passed very considerably from the landed interest to the manufacturing capital interest; and our whole fiscal system was shaped by this latter power to its own advantage, foreign policy being also made to coincide. We are now come, or are coming fast, to a time when Labour laws will be made by the Labour interest for the advantage of Labour. The regulation of all the conditions of labour by the State, controlled and guided by the Labour vote, appears to be the ideal aimed at; and I think it extremely probable that a foreign policy which sought to extend by tariff over our Colonies and even over other friendly States, the area of profitable barter of produce will strongly commend itself to the mind of the Labour interest. Personally I can discern no cause for alarm in this prospect and I believe that on this point you and I are in perfect agreement. Labour in this modern movement has against it the prejudices of property, the resources of capital, and all the numerous forces – social, professional and journalist – which those prejudices and resources can influence. It is our business as Tory politicians to uphold the Constitution. If under the Constitution as it now exists, and as we wish to see it preserved, the Labour interest finds that it can obtain its objects and secure its own advantage, then that interest will be reconciled to the Constitution, will find faith in it and will maintain it. But if it should unfortunately occur that the Constitutional party, to which you and I belong, are deaf to hear and slow to meet the demands of Labour, are stubborn in opposition to those demands and are persistent in the habit of ranging themselves in unreasoning and short-sighted support of all the present rights of property and capital, the result may be that the Labour interest may identify what it will take to be defects in the Constitutional party with the Constitution itself, and in a moment of indiscriminate impulse may use its power to sweep both away. This view of affairs, I submit, is worthy of attention at a time when it is a matter of life or death to the Constitutional party to enlist in the support of the Parliamentary Union of the United Kingdom a majority of the votes of the masses of Labour.

You tell me that you find the designation 'Tory' a great difficulty to you. I cannot see any good reason for this. After all, since the Revolution the designation 'Tory' has always possessed an essentially popular flavour, in contradistinction to the designation 'Whig'. It has not only a popular but a grand historical origin; it denotes great historical struggles, in many of which the Tory party have been found on the popular side. Lord Beaconsfield – who, if he was anything, was a man of the people and understood the popular significance of names and words – invariably made use of the word 'Tory' to characterise his party; and whatever the Tory party may be deemed to be at particular moments, I have always held, from the commencement of my political life, that, rightly understood and explained, it ought to be, and was intended to be, the party of broad ideas and of a truly liberal policy.

7.8   *THE SPECTATOR*: THE DEFENCE OF THE UNION

The resignation of Gladstone in 1894 did not lessen the anxiety of the Conservative party about the future of the Union. Indeed, although they realised that Gladstone's successor, Lord Rosebery, was not an enthusiast for Irish Home Rule in the sense in which Gladstone was an enthusiast the dangers to the Union were now greater. For Rosebery was cool and rational in his advocacy of Home Rule, able to see both sides of the argument in a way that Gladstone was not, and, in general, more diplomatic and more likely to make compromises to secure his objectives. *The Spectator*, like other Conservative journals, was anxious to arouse its readers into some recognition of the danger in which the Union stood. The following excerpt is taken from the issue of 17 March 1894.

So long as Mr. Gladstone was determined to talk down, or beat down by main force, the resistance of the English people, with the aid of his Irish, Scotch, and Welsh allies, we felt no kind of doubt that he would reap the ordinary fate of those who insist upon dashing their heads against a stone wall. But when it was clearly suggested to us that the Ministry intended to abandon that very hopeless enterprise, to devote itself to bringing forward measures likely to fascinate a large section of the people of England, to divert attention for a time from the Irish problem without in any way abandoning their purpose, to intensify the irritation with which English Liberals and Radicals will regard the disinclination of the House of Lords to accept these measures, and, in a word, to mask their Irish policy under cover of an attack on the Lords, we could not help feeling that this was a policy which, though astute and disingenuous, was dangerous, and might, owing to the slowness and density of the English political brain, expose the Union to more peril than any other manoeuvre. It is the policy of the Unionists to bring this controversy with Ireland to a speedy and separate issue. We have always insisted, as our shrewdest leaders have always insisted, that it ought to be disentangled from all those many problems in which the disputes between the democracy and the aristocracy are involved. Whatever the people of England decide on these questions, they ought not to mix up with them the perfectly distinct and most important question as to the disintegration of the United Kingdom into separate Cantons. Whether we are to carry democracy to extreme lengths or not, we ought at least to decide separately what the democratic unit is to be, and not to allow that most fundamental of all questions to be confounded with fifty others not in the least connected with it, certain to obscure it, and probably to conceal it altogether from the political apprehension of the constituencies.

Fortunately for us, the Irish party have come to our aid. It would have been a hard task for the Unionists, without their assistance, to impress adequately on the constituencies how great the danger is of confounding this Irish question with a number of other questions of a totally different kind, in which the privileges of a popular majority are directly involved. Our contention is, that if this question were separately submitted to the people of the United Kingdom, there would be no doubt at all as to the response; but that if it be mixed up inextricably with a number of other questions of a totally different kind, there may appear to be hesitation or weakness. All our efforts are devoted to preventing this mystification of a great problem of the most overwhelming importance to the very life of the nation.

7.9   LORD SALISBURY: THE FUTURE OF THE EMPIRE

Ringing declarations of imperial sentiment are common place in late-Victorian Conservatism. One of the finest was uttered by Salisbury at a banquet for colonial premiers held during the Diamond Jubilee in 1897. Even when allowance has been made for oratorical excess it is still possible to feel the influence of Burke in the stress upon common feelings, thought and descent. Perhaps, too, in such passages may be discerned the origins of Commonwealth unity. From *The Times*, 19 June 1897.

Sir, I will not detain you longer, but I will remind you that this toast really does include within itself all the aspirations and hopes with which we have assocated ourselves together this evening. (Cheers.) We are representing here the growing Empire of Great Britain. We do not know precisely what future is before us. We are aware that we are the instruments of a great experiment. There have been many emigrations, many colonies, before our time. The relation between mother country and dependency has often been set up, but those empires have never lasted, for either the colonies have been swept away by some superior force, or the mother country, by unjust and imprudent government, has driven the colonies to sever the bond which bound them. The fact has been that such empires have never lasted. We are undertaking the great experiment of trying to sustain such an empire entirely upon the basis of mutual goodwill, sympathy, and affection. (Cheers.) There is talk of fiscal union, there is talk of military union. Both of them to a certain extent may be good things. Perhaps we may not be able to carry them as far as some of us think, but in any case they will not be the basis on which our Empire will rest. Our Empire will rest on the great growth of sympathy, common thought, and feeling between those who are in the main the children of a common race, and who have a common history to look back upon and a common future to look forward to. (Cheers.) It is the triumph of a moral idea in the construction of a great political organization which is the object and the effort in which we have all joined, and of which our meeting together is the symbol and seal; but the success of this effort will depend upon the conduct of these various Legislatures, great and small, because with them at last the government must lie. It depends upon their character and their self-restraint, whether this experiment shall succeed. The high ideal of a legislature is to be the arbiter among conflicting interests and classes. The danger to which in our time all Legislatures are exposed is that they will make themselves the instrument of one class to the loss and peril of the rest. Whether our great experiment of a colonial empire succeeds depends upon whether these Legislatures – to which we wish all success and a brilliant future – are able to exercise self-control and fulfil their high ideal. If they are they will produce an empire which the world has not yet seen, and which will make a powerful advance in the progress of humanity.

7.10 JOSEPH CHAMBERLAIN: THE UNITY OF THE EMPIRE

Chamberlain (1836–1914) had taken to the heart Disraeli's compelling idea of an imperial vocation. As early as 1897 he had argued that 'Our rule over these territories can only be justified if we can show that it adds to the happiness and prosperity of the people'. For Chamberlain, the imperial mission fulfilled the national destiny. In his famous speech of 15 May 1903 Chamberlain brought together various ideas he had toyed with for several years for securing a closer degree of imperial unity. From *The Speeches of Joseph Chamberlain* (2 vols, 1914), Speech at Birmingham on Imperial Union and Tariff Reform, II, pp. 131–3.

But the question of trade and commerce is one of the greatest importance. Unless that is satisfactorily settled, I, for one, do not believe in a continued union of the Empire. I am told – I hear it stated again and again by what I believe to be the representatives of a small minority of the people of this country, whom I describe, because I know no other words for them, as Little Englanders – I hear it stated by them, what is a fact, that our trade with our colonies is less than our trade with foreign countries, and therefore it appears to be their opinion that we should do everything in our power to cultivate that trade with foreigners, and that we can safely disregard the trade with our children. Now, sir that is not my conclusion. My conclusion is exactly the opposite. I say it is the business of British statesmen to do everything they can, even at some present sacrifice, to keep the trade of the colonies with Great Britain; to increase that trade, to promote it, even if in doing so we lessen somewhat the trade with our foreign competitors. Are we doing everything at the present time to direct the patriotic movement not only here, but through all the colonies, in the right channel? Are we, in fact, by our legislation, by our action, making for union, or are we drifting to separation? That is a critical issue. In my opinion, the germs of a Federal Union that will make the British Empire powerful and influential for good beyond the dreams of any one now living are in the soil; but it is a tender and delicate plant, and requires careful handling.

I wish you would look back to our history. Consider what might have been, in order that you may be influenced now to do what is right. Suppose that when self-government was first conceded to these colonies, the statesmen who gave it had had any idea of the possibilities of the future – do you not see that they might have laid, broad and firm, the foundations of an Imperial edifice of which every part would have contributed something to the strength of the whole? But in those days the one idea of statesmen was to get rid of the whole business. They believed that separation must come. What they wanted to do was to make it smooth and easy, and none of these ideas which subsequent experience has put into our minds appear ever to have been suggested to them. By their mistakes and by their neglect our task has been made more difficult – more difficult, but not impossible. There is still time to consolidate the Empire. We also have our chance, and it depends upon what we do now whether this great idea is to find fruition, or whether we must for ever dismiss it from our consideration and accept our fate as one of the dying empires of the world.

Now, what is the meaning of an empire? What does it mean to us? We have had a little experience. We have had a war – a war in which the majority of our children abroad had no apparent direct interest. We had no hold over them, no agreement with them of any kind, and yet, at one time during this war, by their voluntary decision, at least 50,000 colonial soldiers were standing shoulder to shoulder with British troops, displaying a gallantry equal to their own and the keenest intelligence. It is something for a beginning; and if this country were in danger – I mean if we were, as our forefathers were, face to face some day, which Heaven forfend, with some great coalition of hostile nations, when we had, with our backs to the wall, to struggle for our very lives – it is my firm conviction that there is nothing within the power of these self-governing colonies that they would not do to come to our aid. I believe their resources, in men and in money, would be at the disposal of the mother country in such an event. That is something which it is wonderful to have achieved, and which it is worth almost any sacrifice to maintain.

Part Eight
THE INTER-WAR YEARS

8.1 STANLEY BALDWIN: THE LEGACY OF DISRAELI

Stanley Baldwin (1867–1947) was fond of evoking the memory of Disraeli in his speeches, writings and radio broadcasts. This he did in a direct and simple manner which enabled the Conservative Party to lay claim to the themes of imperial greatness, national unity and social harmony. In the first extract, taken from a speech made at Bristol on 5 October 1934 (printed in *The Times*, 6 October 1934), Baldwin acknowledges the legacy of Disraeli. In the second, an address to the Primrose League on 3 May 1935 (printed in *The Times*, 4 May 1935), he enlarges, interestingly, on the theme of religious toleration as an element in the Disraelian inheritance. In the third (Stanley Baldwin: *Looking Ahead* (1924), pp. 24–5) he enlarges upon the theme of national unity. In the fourth, a speech to the Royal Society of St George on 6 May 1924 (printed in Stanley Baldwin: *On England* (1926), pp. 6–8), he evokes a nostalgic style of rural patriotism.

When the first Reform Bill, a little over a century ago, was passed, the bulk of the Tories, as they then called themselves, believed they would be excluded from power for ever, and that the country and the Empire would be destroyed. I am old enough to remember the Reform Bill of 1885 and the giving of the franchise to the agricultural labourer. Sixteen years ago there was universal suffrage, since when the Tory Party has been the greatest numerical party in that combination – and in my view for this reason, that the Tory Party has always been a National Party. I do not mean a class party, I mean a party that acts for all classes.

Disraeli laid our principles down at the Crystal Palace many years ago, and you cannot go wrong if you stick to them. They were: 'the maintenance of our institutions and of our religion; the preservation of our Empire, and the improvement in the condition of our people'.

*   *   *

If there is one other thing which Disraeli stressed – and I think when I joined the Primrose League we all took it very much for granted, and I dare say many of us wondered why he did stress it – it was the maintenance of religion. I do not know how far Disraeli had in his mind the continuation of the establishment of the Church of England, although at that time I daresay it did play a part in what he was thinking, because in those days there were attacks of great weight made against the establishment of the Church of England. But I have always interpreted that word myself in the widest sense. I little thought, as you can have little thought in those days before the War, that we should live to see ministers of the Gospel – and I use that word in its widest sense – suffering for their belief in countries that we had believed to be civilized. I wish to say no more about that this afternoon, but I do not want you to lose sight of certain anti-Christian movements in Europe at the present moment, and to resolve firmly that in this country at least there shall not be one inch of ground that shall even be ceded to those who fight the battle against whatever we may mean by religion.

*   *   *

But all these things of which I have spoken – your Empire, India, your industries at home, your defensive forces – are of no effect without a unity of spirit amongst our people at home.

> *And it is for that reason that I and my colleagues are devoting a great deal of our attention now, while we are still in opposition, to see what means we can suggest and devise to make it more difficult to indulge in the luxury of industrial disputes in this country.*

Something may be done by legislation; but whatever may be proposed and whatever may be effected can never succeed until you can drive out of men's minds that militarist spirit which exists in industry, and can replace it by that spirit of goodwill to their own fellow-countrymen which many of those who talk most of goodwill towards foreigners fail to preach.

We know in our Party, and we are in full sympathy with, the aspirations of our people after the War – we know what lies beneath so much of the unrest.

Disraeli said that you can never achieve success without comprehension of the spirit of the age. The spirit of this age is a spirit restless and dissatisfied, and yet that restlessness and dissatisfaction do not arise wholly from motives otherwise than good. One of the right motives is the desire that the bulk of the men and women of this country should be able to enter into the wonderful heritage that science and knowledge and education have opened in all branches of learning, to all those who can take advantage of it, during the last generation.

It is a hunger for better things, and it will be our duty to do what we can to make it easier for our people to satisfy that most legitimate hunger.

That brotherhood which Conservatives and Unionists have among ourselves, and feel towards every class, will do far more to realise the ideals of our people than that preaching of class hatred which, though we hear little of it in the House of Commons, provides the motive force in many of the constituencies which returned the Labour Party to power.

      ★   ★   ★

To me, England is the country, and the country is England. And when I ask myself what I mean by England, when I think of England when I am abroad, England comes to me through my various senses – through the ear, through the eye, and through certain imperishable scents. I will tell you what they are, and there may be those among you who feel as I do.

The sounds of England, the tinkle of the hammer on the anvil in the country smithy, the corncrake on a dewy morning, the sound of the scythe against the whetstone, and the sight of a plough team coming over the brow of a hill, the sign that has been seen in England since England was a land, and may be seen in England long after the Empire has perished and every works in England has ceased to function, for centuries the one eternal sight of England. The wild anemones in the woods in April, the last load at night of hay being drawn down a lane as the twilight comes on, when you can scarcely distinguish the figures of the horses as they take it home to the farm, and above all, most subtle, most penetrating and most moving, the smell of wood smoke coming up in an autumn evening, or the smell of the scutch fires: that wood smoke that our ancestors, tens of thousands of years ago, must have caught on the air when they were coming home with the result of the day's forage, when they were still nomads, and when they were still roaming the forests and the plains of the continent of Europe. These things strike down into the very depths of our nature, and touch chords that go back to the beginning of time and the human race, but they are chords that with every year of our life sound a deeper note in our innermost being. . . . The love of these things is innate and inherent in our people. It makes for that love of home, one of the strongest features of our race, and it is that that makes our race seek its new home in the Dominions overseas, where they have room to see things like this that they can no more see at home. It is that power of making homes, almost peculiar to our people, and it is one of the sources of their greatness. They go overseas, and they take with them what they learned at home: love of justice, love of truth, and the broad humanity that are so characteristic of English people.

8.2 STANLEY BALDWIN: LEADERSHIP OF THE EMPIRE

There was considerable agreement in Conservative circles in the inter-war period that a looser association of peoples would eventually replace the existing imperial structure. Nevertheless, the unity of the empire and its continued leadership by Great Britain were never seriously questioned. Disraeli's ideal of an imperial mission was gradually being transformed into a Commonwealth ideal but the idea of a world mission for the British island race was one of the most powerful ideological assumptions sustaining British Conservatism in the inter-war years.

In the first excerpt, Baldwin acknowledges the failure of his policy of Imperial Protection at the election of 1923 but his underlying conception of empire remains unaltered (Stanley Baldwin, *Looking Ahead* (1924), pp. 22–4). In the second, Baldwin reflects in 1937 on ideals of imperial trust and imperial leadership (Stanley Baldwin: *Responsibilities of Empire* (1937), pp. 10–13).

Now, why have I spoken to you so much to-day about the Empire:

It is in no spirit of boasting: it is to help our people to realise the responsibilities of our heritage.

> *The unity of the Empire is essential, but not for glory . . . not for painting the map red. It is essential to our life.*

Other countries can concentrate on themselves: they are self-contained. We cannot concentrate on ourselves alone. Englishmen can never be Sinn Feiners. The Empire is one and indivisible. If you could picture it broken up, parts might live, parts would be hurled to destruction, and parts would starve. Some of the Dominions, with their great areas, with their small populations, might live, and in time would thrive. The Indian Empire would go down into a bloody destruction, and we in these islands would starve.

That is why there is no work that should lie nearer to you of the Primrose League than to take your part in educating our democracy as to what our Empire stands for.

We have to see that the heart of the nation here in London, in England, the key to the Empire, the key of India, is sound, and to do that we must educate and educate and educate.

With education we must endeavour by every means to bring out the brains of the country, wherever they exist, to use them for the benefit of our race and of mankind. And we must see to it that our people are taught as part of their daily instruction what Empire means. It is no party education; it is education in the things that touch the very lives of our people, and may touch still more the lives of all their children.

We have to see that, so far as a Government may help, this curse of unemployment, which threatens to sap the spirit of the people at home – that this curse shall be fought and dealt with.

I need hardly say to you what I have said so clearly elsewhere, that we, of the Unionist Party, accept the verdict which the country gave in December, and we do not intend again to put forward proposals for a general tariff, except upon clear evidence that on this matter public opinion is disposed to reconsider its judgment.

We propose to deal, so far as we can, if and when returned to power, with industries suffering from unfair competition arising from depreciated currencies, from lower wages and other standards of life, by some means analogous to that of the Safeguarding of Industries Act, by which special measures may be taken to deal with special cases after due inquiry and consideration.

It may be that in the House of Commons Liberals and Labour may register their protest against any such steps being taken. But I know that in the country at large there are thousands and scores of thousands of electors, Liberal and Labour, who, while they may call themselves Free Traders, while they would not support a general tariff, would support measures of that kind, and would help us with both hands when it comes to a fight.

*　　　　*　　　　*

'Ten troubled years have passed – years in which the world as we then knew it has been strangely altered – years in which shadows have passed over the security and peace of our own and other countries. Yet the British Empire has stood firm. The intervening years, so far from loosening, have only strengthened the bonds which hold it together. If in 1926 it could be said that 'the old order changeth, yielding place to new,' in 1937 it may justly be said that the new order has triumphantly survived every test.

We may then take stock of that inheritance which we hold in trust and which, in the fullness of time, we must hand on to our successors; and it is proper that we should do so at this time, for soon we are to crown our King who is at once the Head of the Empire and the link which binds its several members together. We shall do so with traditional ceremony, but that ceremony will be adapted to the altered relationship of the various members of our Commonwealth. . . .

No one country – no group of countries – is so qualified to provide that leadership as the British Empire, of which it has been well said, 'free institutions are its life-blood, free co-operation is its instrument, peace, security, and progress are among its objects.' And I say this with no idea that we are necessarily better than other people, but because of our experience; for we, the peoples of the Empire, in our relations with one another, have set an example of mutual co-operation in the solution of our problems, such as, I believe, no group of nations has ever before achieved.

We have demonstrated to the world in actual practice that difficulties can be resolved by discussion as they cannot be resolved by force. Our representatives meet in conference, not to ratify pronouncements of policy but to exchange ideas, and by discussing those ideas to arrive at the just measure of mutual agreement. In this we find not weakness, but strength. Tolerance creates confidence; and confidence, harmony.

We have shown the world how a system based on these conceptions can serve not only the domestic needs of countries which compose the Commonwealth, but those of the Commonwealth as a whole. May we not hope even to persuade other nations that the method of co-operation would be serviceable on a still wider scale.

Moreover, there is a fundamental difference between the Commonwealth and other political organizations, which should strengthen its power for good – and that is this. The Commonwealth is founded on the conception that war between its component parts is unthinkable, impossible; a conception as striking as it is new to political theory.

8.3 SIR ERNEST BENN: THE STATE, PATRIOTISM AND CLASS

One of the most prolific and influential of Conservative propagandists was Sir Ernest Benn (1875–1954) who, in a number of works, preached against the evils of State provision of social services and State regulation of the economy. Benn appears to have envisaged a future in which a free enterprise Britain would be able to rebuild her economy after the First World War, achieve higher living standards, the removal of class differences and the revitalisation of the traditions of English patriotism. The failure of Britain to realise Sir Ernest's vision did not prevent him from continuing to issue his admonitions until the 1950s. From Sir Ernest Benn: *The Return to Laisser Faire* (1920), pp. 10–11, 41–3.

There have arisen numerous and recurring attempts usually labelled 'social reform' to make the State provide various forms of sustenance for its citizens. Ever since there was a vote it has been used to 'house the working classes,' to make the miners' life a comfortable one, to provide employment and generally to abolish poverty. This movement, slow at first but constantly increasing in ignorance and strength, has reached it zenith in demagogues like Mr. Lloyd George and Mr. Winston Churchill who openly and unashamed offer benefits in exchange for votes, and have so far been able to gain increasing power by blaming the widespread poverty which their quackery produces upon the remnants of sanity that remain with us.

Democracy is also going through the troubles of infancy and adolescence in other ways. With the popular vote the people imagine themselves to be all powerful, but the use of the vote for economic and other purposes to which it is both unsuitable and ineffective, is rapidly shifting the powers and liberties, won at such cost by the people from the autocratic tyrant, to a new class of oppressor more numerous, more secure and, being impersonal, more objectionable, the bureaucratic tyrant.

We have yet to learn how to apply the Individualism which secured for us liberty and freedom, to the proper and effective use of those blessings. In the meantime we are the victims of a wave of Collectivism which having rolled far up the shore of civilisation is now happily and naturally on the ebb. . . .

Let us believe, as we are entitled to believe, that the Englishman is the best thing civilization has yet produced, and that we can, if we will, as an English race, develop a standard and a life which shall not only be happy and comfortable for ourselves, but which will be available by example to the rest of the world. Other nations are, of course, quite entitled to think better of themselves than they do of us, and if through competition and patriotism they are able to do better than we, they will in their turn render us the service of an example which we could with clear conscience copy. Let us have, in a word, competition and patriotism for good.

The Merrie England of the future will differ from the Merrie

England of the past. There will be nothing feudal about it. It will be entirely free from social snobbery. We are almost rid of the snobbery of what used to be regarded as the governing classes. Our dukes and lords and millionaires are among the most humble people in the land, but we must resist the growth of the new snobbery. Our modern governors the bureaucrats, whether they draw their salaries from rates and taxes or from trade union funds, are in a fair way to establish a new brand of snobbishness, a new class consciousness which is far worse than anything which oppressed us in feudal times.

Class consciousness is preached by people imbued with social snobbery and anxious to reap its rewards. Social snobbery is rapidly dying in the ranks of peers and baronets and bishops and other functionaries, who have after all some historic claim to be snobs, but it is developing fast and furious in other classes of life.

The trade union official is often a frightful snob. Your big trade union snob will talk eloquently about the workers and call them comrades from the platform, but the comradeship in question does not, with some of them at least, extend to the length of a game of bowls on a Sunday afternoon. Merrie England must rid itself of snobbery, and surely the real Englishman can be, if he will, as free from this particular vice as any living creature.

By way of balance, for all things in life require to be balanced, we may have to develop, or rather re-develop, the patriotism of the Englishman, that delightful sense of national pride to which no human being is more entitled than the solid, sure, phlegmatic, typical English philosopher. He must come out of his shell and begin to assert himself again.

8.4 NEVILLE CHAMBERLAIN: THE RETURN TO PROTECTION

The return to protection was announced by Neville Chamberlain (1869–1940) to the House of Commons on 4 February 1932. Baldwin, of course, had earlier been a protectionist and in some ways Neville Chamberlain can be seen to be completing the work of his father. Although the Conservatives had been defeated in two elections because of their support for Protection (those of 1906 and 1923) there can be no doubt that it formed the lynch-pin of their economic policy for the rest of the inter-war period. Chamberlain began his speech by outlining the objectives of Protection but he dealt in some detail with the effects of the measure upon imperial relationships and markets (*Hansard*, 5th Series, vol. 261, pp. 287–94).

First of all, we desire to correct the balance of payments by diminishing our imports and stimulating our exports. Then we desire to fortify the finances of the country by raising fresh revenue by methods which will put no undue burden upon any section of the community. We wish to effect an insurance against a rise in the cost of living which might easily follow upon an unchecked depreciation of our currency. We propose, by a system of moderate Protection, scientifically adjusted to the needs of industry and agriculture, to transfer to our own factories and our own fields work which is now done elsewhere, and thereby decrease unemployment in the only satisfactory way in which it can be diminished.

We hope by the judicious use of this system of Protection to enable and to encourage our people to render their methods of production and distribution more efficient. We mean also to use it for negotiations with foreign countries which have not hitherto paid very much attention to our suggestions, and, at the same time, we think it prudent to arm ourselves with an instrument which shall at least be as effective as those which may be used to discriminate against us in foreign markets. Last, but not least, we are going to take the opportunity of offering advantages to the countries of the Empire in return for the advantages which they now give, or in the near future may be disposed to give, to us. In that summary, under seven heads, we believe that we have framed a policy which will bring new hope and new heart to this country, and will lay the foundations of a new spirit of unity and co-operation throughout the Empire . . . .

The basis of our proposals is what we call a general *ad valorem* duty of 10 per cent upon all imports into this country, with certain exceptions to which I shall allude a little later. The purposes of that general duty are two-fold. We desire to raise by it a substantial contribution to the Revenue, and we desire also to put a general brake upon the total of the imports coming in here.

Of course, if our sole object were the reduction of imports, we might achieve that purpose by a different method. We could take certain particular items and exclude them altogether. That would be a method which would bring about the greatest possible disturbance of trade, and in introducing a fundamental change of this character we naturally desire to do it with as little dislocation of existing arrangements as may be found necessary . . . .

I now come to the position of the Empire countries in connection with this change in our fiscal system. The Committee is aware that next July the Imperial Conference is to be held in Ottawa, when the economic relations of the members of the British Commonwealth will be discussed. His Majesty's Government attach the utmost importance to that Conference, and they intend to approach it with a full determination of promoting arrangements which will lead to a great increase of inter-Imperial trade. I have no doubt that the Dominions would no more question our right to impose duties in our own interests, for the object either of raising revenue or of restricting imports, than we have questioned theirs to do the same, but considerations of that kind have to be weighed against the advantages to be obtained from preferential entry into Dominion markets, even though they should involve some surrender of revenue or some lessening of the reduction of imports; and since, until we meet the Dominion representatives, we shall not be in a position to estimate the advantages or the disadvantages on either side, and since we desire to mark at every stage our wish to approach this Conference in the true spirit of Imperial unity and harmony, we have decided that, so far as the Dominions are concerned – and in this arrangement we shall include India and Southern Rhodesia also – neither the general nor the additional duties shall become operative before the Ottawa Conference has been concluded . . . .

The Colonies, the Protectorates and the Mandated Territories are in a somewhat different position from that of the Dominions. They lie, for the most part, in tropical or semi-tropical latitudes; they have scarcely any manufactures of importance; and their products, which are for the most part fruits and vegetables, seeds and nuts used for expressing oils, and fibres, are not of a kind which compete with the home products of this country. Anyone who has visited those parts of the British Empire will know that they are characterised by an intense loyalty to the British connection. In their times of prosperity they have always been large buyers of British goods, partly by means of voluntary preferences on the part of the inhabitants, partly by means of preferences deliberately arranged in their fiscal systems . . . .

What have we done in return for our Colonies? I am afraid we must say that we have done very little, and that frequently in the past our colonists have had the mortification of seeing that, while they were suffering adversity themselves, their neighbours and competitors were enjoying a prosperity which was given to them because of the preference in the markets of the Mother country. The recent terrific fall in the value of the commodities which they produce has brought many of them to-day into a condition of such dire distress that they have been obliged to come to the British Exchequer and seek for some assistance in their need. . . .

It is obvious that in such circumstances as that it would be useless to ask the Colonies to sacrifice revenue by lowering their tariffs in our favour, but we have here a great opportunity of helping them, because there is hardly any product which they produce which is not covered by these new Duties and upon which we cannot give them here a better and a more secure market than they have had in the past. The preference that we might give to them would not only benefit industries already established there but would encourage the starting of new industries and the growing of new products which are not at present derived from the Colonies, but which might equally well be grown there if only they had the encouragement that we could give them. We propose that all produce from all Colonies, Protectorates and Mandated Territories shall be completely exempt from either the general or the additional Duties. We have confidence that this new departure in British policy will be most warmly welcomed throughout the Empire. I have no doubt it will evoke an immediate response. I attach even greater importance to the stimulation of the prosperity and the increased purchasing power of customers of ours who have shown that they always have the will, if they have not always had the power, to buy the bulk of their requirements from the old country.

8.5 HAROLD MACMILLAN: *THE MIDDLE WAY*

Perhaps the most distinguished of all contributions to Conservative thinking in the inter-war period, *The Middle Way* was nothing less than an attempt to evolve a new type of economic order, alternative to Capitalism or Socialism. Macmillan (1894–   ) did not believe that existing experiments in planning were sufficient: they were piecemeal and partial. For Macmillan it was necessary to carry the idea of planning further. At the same time, he had no wish to drift into a pale imitation of Socialist planning. Macmillan was worried about the threat to personal liberties which might be entailed by an extension of State control. Macmillan envisaged a state-sponsored system of co-operation which would yet enable the theory and practice of free enterprise to produce and distribute 'a wide range of goods and services lying outside the field of minimum human needs', Macmillan wished to avoid conformity and uniformity; he valued prosperity, variety, spontaneity. In his desire to establish a new economic order, however, Macmillan was a true Conservative in wishing to see society not as a simple laboratory but a complex organism, 'as an inheritance of the past and a precursor of the future; as a changing and developing structure which must of necessity be modified and adapted to new circumstances' (*The Middle Way*, p. 109). He denied that theoretically pure 'Capitalism' had ever existed or that a theoretically pure 'Socialism' ever could. His proposal for a pragmatic 'Middle Way', therefore, is characteristically Conservative in intention and in method. From Harold Macmillan, *The Middle Way* (1938), pp. 36–7, 96–7, 102–3, 184, 186.

We have lived through half a century in which the dominant political issues were in essence humanitarian. The social policies that were the subject of controversy could all be paid for out of the expanding revenues of profitable enterprise, or by the newer procedure of contributory schemes which widen the area of taxation. On the basis of the political thinking of the Victorian reformers and their immediate successors we have travelled a long way. But we have now almost exhausted the possibilities of progress on the lines that were suitable to their time. We have reached the end of an era of radical reformism. It has become essential that we should do some fresh thinking for ourselves and try to discover the route of progress in the new circumstances of our time. A new age of radicalism would not be able to rely upon the negative method of meeting social obligations out of the transference of wealth. It must take a firmer hold upon the economic system than that. It must improve economic and social organisation so that the weight of the social burdens will be reduced. And it must achieve an increased production of wealth out of which to support the satisfactory minimum standards that so obviously are essential. Economic reconstruction has today become the only possible or sound basis for social reform. . . .

I reject the old method of humanitarian social reform on the basis of a transference of wealth through taxation, because it has reached almost the limits of what it can achieve. It is an obsolete and inadequate policy in the circumstances of today. I reject the Fascist and the Communist theories of violent change because (a) they are politically impossible, and (b) the revolutionary seizure of power would be, and must be, followed by a political tyranny in which man's cultural freedom (which is the prerequisite of human progress) would be sacrificed. I reject the constitutional Socialist approach because, even if their 'economic totalitarianism' would work without political tyranny, it would sacrifice the beneficial dynamic element that private enterprise can give to society when exercised in its proper sphere, and because it would not provide the scope for human diversity which is essential if men are really to be free. But the most important reason for the rejection of these theories is that they are remote from what is immediately practicable in the circumstances of our time. . . .

But I do not propose to employ this defence of private enterprise in the fields for which it is best suited in order to condone or excuse the poverty and insecurity in the basic necessities of life, which we have today as a legacy of unrestrained competition and uneconomic waste and redundancy. I shall advocate all the more passionately on grounds of morality, of social responsibility, as well as of economic wisdom, a wide extension of social enterprise and control in the sphere of minimum human needs. The satisfaction of those needs is a duty which society owes to its citizens. In carrying out that responsibility it should adopt the most economical methods of large-scale co-operative enterprise. The volume of the supply of these necessities, the prices at which they are sold, and the power of the consumer to buy them should not be left to the determination of the push and pull of competitive effort. We have to evolve a new system by which the supply of those articles which we have classified as being of common need and more or less standardised in character, would be absorbed into an amplified conception of the social services. . . .

At every stage in the development of modern Capitalism there have been industries and services which have arrived at different stages of development. The existence of declining industries today is not a new phenomenon pointing to a decline of the whole system. It merely raises the question whether (1) it is possible to provide a means by which the scaling down of old industries can be conducted in such a way as to avoid detrimental consequences to the general economy and to the life of the people, and (2) whether we can facilitate the development of new industries on a sufficient scale to compensate for the decline of the old. This explanation of the different stages of development of industries is intended also to justify the view that a policy of industrial reconstruction must take these differences into account and should be flexible enough to provide for the variation of treatment that is required. . . .

Britain has been moving along the road towards economic planning for many years now in accordance with the traditional English principles of compromise and adjustment. Unless we can continue this peaceful evolution from a free capitalism to a planned capitalism, or, it may be, a new synthesis of Capitalist and Socialist theory, there will be little hope of preserving the civil, democratic, and cultural freedom which, limited as it may be at the moment by economic inefficiency, is a valuable heritage. It is only by the adoption of this middle course that we can avoid resorting to measures of political discipline and dictatorship. Such methods, whether exercised by the 'right' or by the 'left', are the very opposite of that liberation and freedom which mankind should be striving to achieve.

8.6 QUINTIN HOGG: A TOTALITARIAN LABOUR PARTY

Ever since the 1880s Conservative writers had been quick to associate their British Socialist opponents with the suppression of political freedom. Such polemics remained a standard technique of scaremongering long into the twentieth century. Usually it amounted to nothing more than the assertion that centralised State power would assume overpowering dimensions. In this extract from *The Case for Conservatism*, however, Quintin Hogg argued that the very structure of the Labour party itself facilitated totalitarian tendencies. Although published in 1947, the work epitomises attitudes commonly held earlier. (*The Case for Conservatism*, (1947) pp. 58–9.)

The expression 'the party', which in free and democratic states connotes the main instrument of canalising the popular will and crystallising the popular choice, assumes a new and sinister significance. It is the same institution but has been made to serve purposes fundamentally different. It promulgates policy, formulates issues, conducts public discussions, operates to select and publicise leaders and leadership, combines to overthrow opposition and to resist separatist tendencies. The old institutions, Trade Unions, Co-operatives, great organs of production and distribution go on. Elections are held. Parliaments may assemble and pass decrees. But this is on the surface. An organised minority can always defeat an unorganised majority, and no other party is permitted to exist. From the smallest Trade Union branch to the Parliament itself only party members can effectively make themselves heard. 'The party' is to the citizen what the priesthood is to a corrupt Church, the one means of promotion, the single vehicle of grace, the sole dispenser of truth, tolerating neither heresy nor schism, claiming as its privilege alike the prerogative of Caesar and the infallibility of the Godhead. . . .

The danger is that in its present aims and objects, in its present constitution and in its way of doing business, the British Labour Party shows signs of developing many of the defects of totalitarianism. By their insistence on the authority of the Party Congress and its policy, by their refusal to reply to arguments directed by the opposition to the merits of the case, by their continued insistence on an alleged 'mandate' to carry out their election policy without amendment and despite argument, by their control of the Trade Union and Co-operative movements and their claim that so long as these remain affiliated to the Labour Party and the main contributors to their funds, the little organised minorities who control these movements should enjoy a certain superiority to the law, by their assumption and concentration of power in the hands of a few bosses at the centre in despite of free private enterprise, in despite of public municipal enterprise, in despite of independent charitable enterprise, and lastly by their declared intention of 'exterminating' the Tories, the Labour Party harbours within its own movement the seeds of a genuine form of totalitarianism.

9.1   THE 1945 ELECTION MANIFESTO: PLANNING THE NEW WORLD

The Conservative Party General Election Manifesto of 1945 (officially titled 'Mr Churchill's Declaration of Policy to the Electors') summarises the developments in Conservative thought which had occurred during the war. Not surprisingly, the first quarter of the manifesto deals with foreign, imperial and defence issues. Significantly, however, the last quarter contains a surprisingly anti-regulationist view of the role of the State in economic affairs. Although State control of the coal industry is accepted on a permanent basis, the planning of the transport system would remain under wartime controls only for a time. Indeed, the removal of controls and regulations is the major theme of economic reconstruction. The middle sections of the manifesto, however, strike a different note on welfare policy.

FOUR YEARS' PLAN

More than two years ago I made a broadcast to the nation in which I sketched a four years' plan which would cover five or six large measures of a practical character, which must all have been the subject of prolonged, careful and energetic preparation beforehand, and which fitted together into a general scheme.

This plan has now been shaped, and we present it to the country for their approval. Already a beginning has been made in carrying it out, and the Education Act for which our new Minister of Labour is greatly respected is already the law of the land.

BACK FROM THE WAR

We welcome the opportunity of fulfilling all obligations of Service men and women. The financial engagements, the provision of opportunities for training for careers, and, above all, the plans for treatment and rehabilitation of the disabled will be our duty and our aim.

The broad and properly considered lines of the demobilisation proposals, based on age and length of service, which Mr. Bevin has elaborated with much wisdom, will be adhered to, and release will be made as quickly as the condition of the tormented world permits.

WORK

In the White Paper presented to Parliament by the late administration are sound plans for avoiding the disastrous slumps and booms from which we used to suffer, but which all are united in being determined to avoid in the future.

The Government accepts as one of its primary aims and responsibilities the maintenance of a high and stable level of employment.

Unless there is steady and ample work, there will not be the happiness, the confidence, or the material resources in the country on which we can all build together the kind of Britain that we want to see.

To find plenty of work with individual liberty to choose one's job, free enterprise must be given the chance and the encouragement to plan ahead. Confidence in sound government – mutual co-operation between industry and the State, rather than control by the State – a lightening of the burdens of excessive taxation – these are the first essentials.

HOMES

In the first years of peace, the provision of homes will be the greatest domestic task.

An all-out housing policy will not only make a tremendous contribution to family life, but also to steady employment and to national health. All our energy must be thrown into it. Local authorities and private enterprise must both be given the fullest encouragement to get on with the job.

Prices of materials must be controlled as long as supplies are short. Even so, building costs will be high at first. They must be brought down as rapidly as possible. Subsidies will be necessary for local authorities and for private enterprise alike . . . .

FOOD AND AGRICULTURE

We must produce a great deal more food than we did before the war, because food is scarce in the world to-day, and in any case we shall not be able to buy as much imported food as we did.

A healthy and well-balanced agriculture is an essential element in our national life. British agriculture will be maintained in a condition to enable the efficient producer to obtain a reasonable return on the enterprise and the capital invested, and to enable wages to be paid to the worker sufficient to secure him a proper standard of living.

We must maintain the fertility of the soil; we must be skilful in the use and management of our land for the production of the foodstuffs which it is best fitted to provide, and which are most required to satisfy the nutritional needs of our people.

We need Imperial co-operation, leading to international co-operation, in the orderly production and marketing of food; and within this country we shall have improved systems of marketing of home products and such other arrangements as may be necessary to maintain stability and avoid the evils of recurring scarcity and gluts. For this purpose each product will be treated on its own merits . . . .

NATIONAL INSURANCE

National wellbeing is founded on good employment, good housing and good health. But there always remain those personal hazards of fortune, such as illness, accident or loss of a job, or industrial injury, which may leave the individual and his family unexpectedly in distress. In addition, old age, death and child-birth throw heavy burdens upon the family income.

One of our most important tasks will be to pass into law and bring into action as soon as we can a nation-wide and compulsory scheme of National Insurance based on the plan announced by the Government of all Parties in 1944.

In return for a single consolidated contribution there will be new and increased benefits, amongst which is to be an old age or retirement pension of 20/- for single people and 35/- for married couples. Family allowances are one part of the great scheme, and the arrangements made will ensure that men and women serving in the Forces and those disabled will benefit equally with other classes in the community . . . .

HEALTH

The Health services of the country will be made available to all citizens. Everyone will contribute to the cost, and no one will be denied the attention, the treatment or the appliances he requires because he cannot afford them.

We propose to create a comprehensive health service covering the whole range of medical treatment from the general practitioner to the specialist, and from the hospital to convalescence and rehabilitation; and to introduce legislation for this purpose in the new Parliament.

9.2 CONSERVATIVE PARTY CONFERENCE: A NEW VIEW OF EMPIRE

In retrospect, the transition from an imperial to a commonwealth commitment seems to have been both inevitable and natural. So long as the idea of British leadership of a world-wide union of nations could be sustained then the Conservative leadership had little difficulty in persuading its party activists, at least, to effect that transition in policy. The following statement of policy was, in fact, endorsed at the London Party Conference in 1949 without a single dissentient. (Conservative Party Proceedings)

In this statement of policy we frequently use the term 'British Empire' because it is short and familiar. This does not mean that we fail to recognise the immense changes which have taken place in recent years in the relations between various parts of the Empire. Even before the end of the First World War the full nationhood of Canada, Australia, the Union of South Africa, New Zealand, Newfoundland, and, shortly afterwards, the Irish Free State, was recognised. They had become the equal partners of Great Britain.

During the thirty years which divide us from the first World War, further developments have taken place. Three new Dominions – India, Pakistan and Ceylon – have come into being. Burma has seceded from the Commonwealth, Newfoundland has joined Canada, and Eire (the Irish Free State), which chose neutrality during the Second World War, has severed her connection with our family of nations. Southern Rhodesia was represented at the 1947 Prime Ministers' Conference, and has thus taken a significant step towards Dominion status.

The attainment of Dominion status by three Asiatic countries has radically altered the whole pattern of the Empire. Previously all the self-governing Dominions drew their racial traditions from Europe and, indeed, except South Africa and parts of Canada, from the United Kingdom in particular. Strong mutual ties of kinship, culture and religion existed to strengthen common political and economic interests. In the case of India, Pakistan and Ceylon, the same is not true. Therefore, it cannot be expected that the relations between Great Britain and these new countries will necessarily develop along lines identical with those established between the 'home country' and the other members of the Commonwealth.

While these changes have been taking place in the British Commonwealth the position of the Colonies has not remained static. The mandates over the former German colonial territories, given by the League of Nations to Great Britain after the First World War, have now been placed, on our own initiative, under the Trusteeship Council of the United Nations. Palestine, previously a mandate, has been handed back to the United Nations. Malaya has become a Federation and a Commissioner-General for S.E. Asia has been appointed. Great Britain has temporarily assumed responsibility for certain former Italian colonies in North and East Africa which were occupied by British troops during the Second World War. Steps have been taken towards the establishment of representative government in the Sudan. Malta, G.C., has been given a new constitution, and important developments have taken place in Africa, the West Indies, Gibraltar, Mauritius and elsewhere mainly as a result of the initiative of Mr. Churchill's Coalition Government.

The effect of all these changes, great and small, has been to inaugurate a new phase in the political development of the British Empire. Much of the machinery of common action needs repair and renewal.

The Conservative Policy recognises that the British Empire now as ever can only survive through a process of constant evolution, and aims at advancing the political progress of our peoples in accordance with the best interests of each community and of the Commonwealth as a whole . . . .

No one underestimates the practical difficulties with which the achievement of this great conception abounds. At the same time, we live in a dangerous world and it would be sheer folly to ignore the threat to democratic freedom which Soviet aggression presents. The British Commonwealth has greater resources of political experience than any other nation. Moral leadership in the 'cold war' against the new barbarism must, therefore, devolve largely upon its shoulders. To those who believe that the days of world leadership for the British Empire and Commonwealth are over, we reply 'British leadership is more vital to the future of civilisation now than at any time in history'.

The Conservative Party affirms its faith in the ideals of the United Nations and in the importance of developing regional agreements including the project for Western Union. It will not, however, permit any such agreement to override or conflict with the political, economic or defence obligations falling on Great Britain as a member of the British Empire and Commonwealth of Nations.

It pledges itself to a vigorous policy aimed at restoring the British Empire and Commonwealth to its role as a leader of free peoples against the encroachments of World Communism.

9.3   R. A. BUTLER: *THE INDUSTRIAL CHARTER* (1947)

The Blackpool Conference in 1946 appointed a committee under the chairmanship of Butler to draw up a declaration of economic policy. *The Industrial Charter* was published in May 1947 and endorsed at the Brighton Conference in October of the same year with only three dissentient votes. Regarded in many quarters as the epitome of the New Conservatism, the Charter clearly owed much to the developments in economic thought and policy which had affected the Conservative party in the 1930s. It owes much, too – especially its commitment to full employment and its approval of deficit budgeting – to the Coalition government of 1940–45. As R. A. Butler affirms in the first of the following extracts, the contents of the Charter 'will not seem particularly new or startling' (R. A. Butler: 'The Industrial Charter', published in *Advance*, Vol. I.3, April/June 1947). We should not forget that *The Industrial Charter*, as the second extract, taken from the opening section of the document itself, makes clear, was concerned with the regeneration of a preponderantly capitalist economy through a variety of measures, some of which tend in the direction of planning as a means to an end. Many of the measures envisaged were expressions of wishful thinking. Co-operation between industry and the State was to be on a voluntary basis. There was much talk of plans and national budgets, of relating incomes to productivity and even of reducing wage differentials between different industries. Yet no machinery was suggested for achieving these objectives. The document accepted some, though by no means all, of the elements of war-time collectivism pioneered by the Coalition government.

As the result of a resolution moved at the Blackpool Conference last October, a committee was appointed under my chairmanship to investigate and make a statement upon industrial policy. The report of that committee – 'The Industrial Charter' – has now been published.

The conclusions which we have reached are the fruit not only of intensive research into the industrial position at home but also of due consideration of experiments and practices in the Dominions and foreign countries. Unlike the present Government's much-publicised 'Economic Survey for 1947', moreover, our statement on industry is not merely the result of work behind closed doors in London. During its preparation there has been the widest possible consultation with employers and workers all over the country.

The Charter is not a final party programme, nor is it a series of Working Party reports each laying down a detailed plan for one particular industry. It is a statement of the general Conservative policy towards industry as a whole and it is divided into three distinct parts.

Part one is short-term. It sets out the immediate steps which we consider must be taken to deal with the present crisis.

Maximum productivity must be restored by improved industrial relations, by once more giving a real incentive to all levels in industry, by the drastic reduction of unproductive labour, by making shorter hours dependent on greater output and by ensuring that vital industries are rendered more attractive to the worker.

The basic industries, on which the nation's economic life depends, must have priority over all others and they must also be given an order of priority among themselves to cover cases where their interests clash. We consider that Coal and Power, Transport, Capital Equipment and Housing, Food and Agriculture come under this heading.

Finally, the value of the pound must be stabilised and the inflationary process halted. This can be achieved by cuts in Government expenditure, by slowing down the pursuit of the cheap-money policy and by expanding the output of goods and services. Our answer to the present crisis may, therefore, be summed up in the three words Productivity, Priorities and the Pound.

Part two is long-term and deals with the relationship which should, in our view, be established between Government and Industry. This is the longest and most complex section of the Charter and it sets out our attitude on planning and controls, employment policy, taxation, monopoly, overseas trade, trade unions, the individual trader, and the nationalised industries. It is only possible here to refer to one or two of the most important points.

We believe in planning, but on principles and by methods different from those of the Socialists. There must be strong central control of resources by the Government but co-operation between Government and Industry in the making of plans and decentralisation to industries in their detailed implementation. Burdensome and uneconomic minor controls must be swept away.

We are opposed in principle to nationalisation but we do not therefore intend to sacrifice common sense to ideology and denationalise blindly. We will reintroduce private ownership where it is practicable to do so.

In applying and extending the employment policy evolved by the Coalition Government in 1944 we believe we have the answer to the problem of unemployment.

We are strongly in favour of trade union organisation in industry. Every worker should be free to join the union of his choice. We condemn unofficial strikes and we consider that some sections of the Trades Disputes Act must be restored.

We are opposed to restrictive practices wherever they arise and we suggest that an independent tribunal should be set up to investigate cases of monopoly which are alleged to be against the public interest.

We aim to give enterprise a chance by cutting Government expenditure and reducing taxation on earned income at all levels.

We will protect the individual trader against unfair and subsidised competition.

In overseas trade we stand by Imperial Preference.

Part three – 'The Workers' Charter' – completes the long-term plan and is our prescription for industrial peace. Under the three headings of Security, Incentive and Status we have set out a code of human relations which we would seek to enforce by law but which would be submitted to Parliament for approval and enforced thereafter in the same way as the Fair Wages Clause.

In this code Security is recognised as the fundamental problem. Its solution lies in a positive employment policy and we believe that such a policy can be reinforced by pensions schemes within individual firms or industries to supplement National Insurance, and by contracts of employment favouring long-service personnel.

If security is to be 'a springboard and not a cushion,' however, it must be accompanied by incentive. We therefore strongly favour systems of payment by results, giving extra reward to extra effort and initiative, equal pay for men and women where similar services achieve similar results and full recognition for the principle of promotion by merit at all levels. A comprehensive training system must be developed in industry, stretching uninterrupted from vocational guidance in the schools at one end to courses on management at the other.

Finally, on the subject of status we believe, with Sir George Schuster, that 'every firm must seek to make work a soul-satisfying activity for its employees.' To this end we wish to see a revival and extension of wartime arrangements for joint consultation, so that workers may obtain a clear picture both of the part which they play in their firm and also of the role of the firm in the economic structure of the country. Where the circumstances of an industry are favourable, moreover, the fundamental identity of interest of owners and employees may often be well expressed by schemes of profit-sharing and employee-shareholding.

This then, in brief outline, is 'The Industrial Charter.' To those who are well-versed in Conservative principle and practice the views it expresses will not seem particularly new or startling. To those members of the public, however, who have been deluded by Socialist propaganda into believing that we have no policy, that we are opposed to the whole idea of 'planning,' that we are the enemies of trade unionism, that we have no answer to unemployment and that we think of nationalisation purely in terms of 'unscrambling eggs,' it may come as something of a surprise.

★   ★   ★

Man cannot live by economics alone. Human nature will give of its best only when inspired by a sense of confidence and of hope. We base all our plans on a belief in the unlimited power of the human personality to meet and to overcome difficulties and to rise above them.

We are completely opposed to the imposition of a rigid strait-jacket of doctrinaire political theory, either upon the individual regardless of his individuality or upon the nation regardless of the economic facts of the moment.

Our abiding objective is to free industry from unnecessary controls and restrictions. We wish to substitute for the present paralysis, in which we are experiencing the worst of all worlds, a system of free enterprise, which is on terms with authority, and which reconciles the need for central direction with the encouragement of individual effort. We point to a way of life designed to free private endeavour from the taunt of selfishness or self-interest and public control from the reproach of meddlesome interference. The Government totally misconceive wherein lies the greatness of a free and resourceful nation. They imagine that the men and women who fought and worked together in the war can now be exhorted, controlled and regimented into producing goods, building houses and rendering services in time of peace. The proof of their error lies in the level of production, which was and is disastrously low. The Conservative policy is the opposite: to give the people opportunities.

Opportunities are often lost because there is no incentive to make the extra effort. A man asks himself what is the good of working harder if he is not to receive a just reward for his extra toil or ingenuity. Here the Socialists have carried their passion for equality to lengths which have stifled man's will to do the best of which he is capable. The desire for increased rewards, whether it be expressed in terms of the profit motive or higher wages, animates the great bulk of mankind. We hold that there should be healthy rewards for work done. We shall propose methods to curb monopolies and unfair privileges. We are determined to restore by all reasonable means that great stimulus to personal endeavour – fair incentive.

A restoration of freedom and incentives would not mean, as has been falsely held, an end to security in our social and industrial system. Justice demands that the aim of national policy should be to provide a basic standard of living and security of outlook for all our people. This can be achieved in a variety of ways. Our national system of social services, which we have helped to create, has recently been enlarged to cover better provision for pensioners in their old age, for the sick through the universal health service, for the unemployed, for widows and for parents of large families. But something more than provision for exceptional circumstances is necessary. We set out below our proposals for an employment policy which are designed to remove as far as lies within human power the fearful dread of enforced idleness. The sum of our recommendations is designed to create and ensure that prosperity without which Industry and Agriculture cannot maintain a stable level of wages. But we go further. We describe how each individual must be given the chance to rise above the level of security and to win special rewards. Justice is frustrated by exact equality of reward to all, but it is found where there is equality of opportunity and incentive to win a variety of rewards.

A sense of realism, free opportunity, incentives and justice should inspire all industrial policy, whether it has to meet an economic storm such as is gathering today, or whether it is designed for the calmer years when the tempest has been outridden.

9.4   HAROLD MACMILLAN: ECONOMIC POLICY AND CONSERVATIVE IDEOLOGY

Politics is, no doubt, a pragmatic activity and the precise role of ideas difficult to calculate. Nevertheless, Macmillan appears to have taken seriously *The Industrial Charter* at the ideological level and to have accepted it as a legitimate expression of Tory philosophy. In the following excerpt (*Tides of Fortune*, 1969, pp. 302–6) Macmillan not only discusses the intellectual ancestry of *The Industrial Charter* but credits it with determining the economic policy of his own administration.

The 'Industrial Charter', as it was called, proved our determination to maintain full employment, to sustain and improve the social services, and to continue the strategic control of the economy in the hands of the Government, while preserving wherever possible the tactical function of private enterprise. Our purpose was 'to reconcile the need for central direction with the encouragement of individual effort'. We also accepted as irreversible the nationalisation of coal, the railways, and the Bank of England, and the impossibility of unscrambling these scrambled eggs. The final section comprised the so-called 'Workers' Charter', of which the general object was 'to humanise, not nationalise'; to create security and status for industrial workers with continuity of employment and defined contractual rights.

The principles laid down in this document guided our policies in the future Conservative Governments. Many of the detailed proposals have been translated into law. Monopolies have been dealt with, at least to some degree; price maintenance has been abolished with rare exceptions; many of the provisions for improving the status of the workers have been given legislative effect. Nevertheless the importance of declarations of this kind, especially from parties in Opposition, lies not so much in the detailed proposals as in their general tone and temper. . . .

Broadly, those elements in the party which followed consciously or unconsciously the Whig or the older Liberal tradition were opposed to the new Conservatism. The true Tories accepted it with growing enthusiasm.

Inside the party and in academic and intellectual circles, Butler managed affairs with extraordinary skill. Backed by the highly gifted members of the Research Department, he had been largely responsible or the development of the new policy. He defended it with equal knowledge and subtlety. A great part of the burden of public speaking in favour of the charter and of counter-attacking its opponents, in whatever quarter, fell on my shoulders. I was only too happy to undertake this task because it seemed to me that the policy and character of the party were now almost miraculously developing on the lines that I had preached during those sterile years between the wars. To this end I spoke at meetings all over the country and wrote a number of articles in the Press. This was all the easier for me because it had been my consistent theme in earlier months. For instance, in the previous autumn I had declared our intention to put forward a new industrial and economic policy in the light of modern conditions:

> Whether it is to be called a new policy or not, I do not know. It is certainly in the true tradition and philosophy of Conservatism at its best. The broad division between the Opposition and the Government is now beginning to appear in a precise form. The Socialist Government talks about planning, but it is more and more apparent that they do not understand, and certainly do not apply, its principles. They confuse the roles of the State and the individual. By attempting too much, they risk achieving too little. . . . [Our policy] is based upon the theme of co-operation between Government and industry. It insists on each playing its proper part. It will require a new sense of partnership between ownership, management and labour. The distribution of property is the basis of democracy, not its concentration in fewer and fewer hands – least of all centralised ownership by a semi-totalitarian State. It is by the separation, not the confusion, of functions that we shall find our way through the many dangers which threaten us.
>
> Socialism leads inevitably to Totalitarianism. German Socialism led to Nazism. Russian Socialism led to Communism.
>
> The British tradition, to be found equally in Toryism and Radicalism, rejects the inevitability of the class war and insists upon the essential unity of the nation.

I had also insisted on the need for a new relationship between capital and labour:

> The problem of industry is only partly economic; it is largely moral and psychological. The cure is to be found in a new code – if you like, a new charter – by which capital, management and labour shall work as a team, in healthy and genuine co-operation for a common purpose.
>
> In peace, no less than in war, a house divided against itself cannot stand.

With regard to nationalisation, I had continued to follow the line of the Middle Way:

> Nationalisation of industry does not solve the human problem. A great State monopoly is no better – in some ways it is worse – than private monopoly. We are against monopoly – public or private.
>
> That is not to say that there is no place for the State in industry. Of course there is. But with a few exceptions, when special conditions prevail, that place is at the centre, not the circumference. The Government must settle the broad strategy of policy.

Accordingly I declared:

We believe that the State exists to serve the people; not the people to serve the State. We want to level up, not level down. We do not want to abolish property, but to make it more widely distributed.

We believe in real democracy, political and economic. In every country it is becoming more and more apparent that Socialism and democracy cannot live together. One means tyranny, benevolent or otherwise. The other means the cultivation of Freedom and Progress.

9.5 WINSTON CHURCHILL: THE SOCIALIST ALTERNATIVE

Conservative politicians loved to depict their Labour opponents as totalitarian wolves in the clothing of constitutional sheep. The Attlee government, of course, provided sufficient ammunition to fuel many a speech and pamphlet. During his Woodford campaign at the general election of 1950 Churchill usually inserted a lengthy anti-Socialist tirade. It is difficult to see why he did so. He had lost much political credit by referring to his opponents as the Gestapo during the campaign of 1945 and he knew Attlee and the other Labour leaders well enough to understand that their constitutional credentials were as sound as his. It is also difficult to be sure how serious he was in passages like the following, taken from an election speech, delivered at the Woodford Country School for Girls on 28 January 1950. From R. R. James *Winston S. Churchill: His Complete Speeches*, Chelsea House Publishers, 1974, Vol. 8 pp. 7907–13.

They will of course nationalize the steel industry. Quite apart from the injury to this magnificent feature in our domestic life and export trade, this will give them the power to dominate for their party interests a large group of other industries for whom steel in one or other of its thousand forms is the foundation. They will have immense political power over all these industries and can make or mar them by expediting or delaying vital supplies, about which a tangle of formalities will be created in triplicate. Here, in itself, would be a long step forward to the establishment of the Socialist State. All this is rendered possible by the harmless looking words, 'The steel industry will be responsible to the nation.' It has certainly rendered our country incomparable and irreplaceable service, under the system which has been in practice for so many years of free enterprise, subject to Government supervision on prices and development as in Conservative days.

All this is to be thrown into disorder not because the Government want more steel but because they want more power . . . .

Other prosperous and well-managed industries, like cement and sugar and chemicals, are to be nationalized so that the consumer will have to pay more for their products, as he does for coal and electricity and transport, and so that a new horde of officials can be set up over them with new vistas of patronage opening out to Socialist politicians. Having made a failure of everything they have so far touched, our Socialist planners now feel it necessary to get hold of a few at present prospering industries so as to improve the general picture and the general results. There appears to be no plan or principle in the selection of these industries, except caprice and appetite. It does not matter how well they are now managed, how well they are serving the public, how much they sustain our export trade, how good are the relations between employers and employed. The Socialists just like the look of them, and so they think they will have them. But here you have your vote and your responsibility . . . .

But beware! For we may be at the parting of the ways. The wisdom of our forebears for more than 300 years has sought the division of power in the Constitution. Crown, Lords and Commons have been checks and restraints upon one another. The limitation of the power of absolute monarchy was the cause for which as Liberals used to say, 'Hampden died in the field and Sidney on the scaffold.' The concentration of all power over the daily lives of ordinary men and women in what is called 'the State', exercised by what is virtually single-chamber government, is a reactionary step contrary to the whole trend of British history and to the message we have given to the world. The British race have always abhorred arbitrary and absolute government in every form. The great men who have founded the American Constitution expressed this same separation of authority in the strongest and most durable form. Not only did they divide executive, legislative and judicial functions, but also by instituting a federal system they preserved immense and sovereign rights to local communities and by all these means they have maintained – often at some inconvenience – a system of law and liberty under which they thrived and reached the physical and, at this moment, the moral leadership of the world. The Socialist conception of the all-powerful State entering into the smallest detail of the life and conduct of the individual and claiming to plan and shape his work and its rewards is odious and repellent to every friend of freedom. These absolute powers would make the group of politicians who obtained a majority of seats in Parliament, the masters and not the servants of the people and centralize all government in Whitehall.

So far we are only at the first stage in this evil journey. But already enterprise, daring and initiative are crippled. Property is destroyed by the heaviest taxation in the world. Regulations increasingly take the place of statutes passed by Parliament. These are contained in twenty-eight volumes, which can be purchased by all and sundry for £65. In these you may find that there are thousands of new crimes unknown before the war, now punishable by fine or imprisonment. The right is claimed in full peace by the executive Government to direct a man or woman to labour at any work or in any place a Minister or the officials under him may choose. Here are the words which Mr Isaacs, the Minister of Labour, used in the House of Commons on 3 December 1947, nearly three years after the war had stopped; when defending the Order giving him absolute power over the livelihood and employment of all men and women between the ages of 18 and 50 and 18 and 40 respectively:

> 'If any specific case is brought to our notice of a person claiming conscientious objection to a particular job we will give it our consideration; but we are not prepared to recognize that anyone has a right to conscientious objection to going to work unless that person is prepared at the same time to say that he will not eat.'

This is the old and shameful doctrine of 'Work or starve', which no Government in Britain has ever dared to utter in time of peace for more than a hundred years. It is the greatest affront offered in modern times to the dignity of labour which rests upon a man's right to choose or change his job. I made my protest at the time, but in vain. The Regulation was imposed. It is still imposed. The Socialists have not dared to use it on any large scale, as yet. They are waiting for a renewal of their mandate. Conservatives and National Liberals on the other hand are resolved to expunge this blot from our industrial life.

9.6   ENOCH POWELL: THE ORGANIC THEORY OF THE WELFARE STATE

The 'One Nation' group was particularly fond of asserting its place in the Disraelian tradition of social reform. Iain Macleod was especially apt to acknowledge the inheritance of Disraeli and even that of Lord Randolph Churchill. On one occasion he managed to quote extensively from Disraeli's 1872 speeches *and* from Churchill's *Elijah's Mantle* (Sanitas Sanitatum: The Condition of the People: a lecture delivered at the Conservative Political Centre, 1954, published in Nigel Fisher: *Iain Macleod* (1973), pp. 327–36.) Enoch Powell (1912–   ) was less inclined to vindicate himself by acknowledging heroes long since dead but he was characteristically careful to relate the social philosophy of one nation to the historic tradition of Conservatism. In the extract that follows, Powell argues against the use of the social services as a levelling instrument and defends the principle of minimum provision ('Conservatives and the Social Services', *The Political Quarterly*, April–June, 1953).

TO THE MODERN SOCIALIST the equalising effect of social services supported by high taxation afforded a moral and political justification which took the place of humanitarianism and the nonconformist conscience. For example, Mr. Roy Jenkins in New Fabian Essays (1952), after noting that 'the recent move towards equality can be largely accounted for . . . by the use of heavy taxation upon the rich to finance a gradually extended structure of social services', recognised with regret that 'any further extensions in the social services which take place (defining an extension as an increase in the perceentage of the national income devoted to the service) are unlikely to be redistributive in any broad class sense'. Accordingly, in recent Conservative thought about the social services, we find added to the old motifs a new one, which protests against the concept of the social services as an equalising force and which traces to that use of the social services many of the defects arising in the post-war 'welfare-state'.

To this concept the modern Conservative Party opposed that of a generous and, if possible, rising minimum standard, in all the basic needs of life, guaranteed by the community to all individuals and families. In this formulation several terms are of critical importance. The 'community' is not necessarily the State: it may be for the State to co-ordinate, to complete, or even to do the lion's share, but wherever possible the contribution of local responsibility and initiative is jealously guarded and individual beneficence is not regarded as having played out its role. Secondly, the emphasis is upon minimum – not in the sense of least possible, but as the opposite to average or uniform: the social services are not to be a levelling instrument. Finally, they apply only to the main essentials of decent life: it must remain for the less essential and the infinite range of varying standards to be pursued by individuals and families according to their inclinations and abilities.

The pamphlet One Nation [C.P.C.,1950] – easily the most important pronouncement of the Conservative Party on the social services since the war – was an essay upon this theme. It argued that because the Labour Government had sought in health, in insurance, in education, in housing to supply through the social services an average standard for all, it had thereby in practice failed to meet the requirements of those in greatest need. The health service, by attempting everything at once, had starved some of the most essential branches like dental health and mental treatment; by building council houses only, the nation had obtained fewer houses altogether; by endeavouring to eliminate difference of educational opportunity, the State was threatening the standards of the ablest; the changing age structure of the population had been too little regarded in the planning of national insurance. The machinery of the welfare State was not helping the weak by its repression of the opportunities and independence of the strong.

It was a logical development of the idea of the minimum standard that two of the authors of One Nation in *Needs and Means* [C.P.C., 1952], posed and attempted to answer the question: how, if the social services were designed to meet need, was that need properly to be ascertained; and they arrive incidentally at the conclusion that in the post-war period of inflation the new social services had in point of fact never met the requirements of the poorest.

The expression 'welfare state', which has been used above in relation to the post-war form of the social services, would, correctly speaking, be repudiated by the Conservative Party, though it might frequently be found in use. Attention through the social services to the needs and standard of life of all members of the community is regarded by the Conservative Party as something which ought to flow from the nature and organisation of the community itself. The State in fact is not a machine constructed to produce welfare – as the expression 'welfare state' implies, but an organism, which, if it is sound and healthy, will assure the well-being of its members. This sense of the relationship and proportion of the social services to the capabilities and prosperity of the nation as a whole underlies the characteristic Conservative concern with the financing of the social services. The limit of what the nation can afford to redistribute through these services, though never capable of being precisely defined, is the final expression of that due relationship and proportion.

10.1   FRIEDRICH HAYEK: THE TOTALITARIAN PROSPECT (1944)

The Road to Serfdom appeared in 1944. It was not until 1956, however, that an American edition of the book first appeared. In an Introduction specially written for the occasion, Hayek (1899–   ) reflected upon the reception of his work in England. Looking back upon the history of the Attlee administration, Hayek was convinced that his warnings had been prophetic. He quotes several instances of government authoritarianism, such as the revival of the war-time labour conscription laws. He seizes upon evidence that a docile and regulated population is coming into existence and he reflects upon the manner in which totalitarianism occurs in such a situation. F. Hayek: 'The Road to Serfdom after Twelve Years', printed in F. Hayek: *Studies in Philosophy, Politics and Economics* (1967), pp. 222–6.)

It is true, of course, that in the struggle against the believers in the all-powerful state the true liberal must sometimes make common cause with the conservative, and in some circumstances, as in contemporary Britain, he has hardly any other way of actively working for his ideals. But true liberalism is still distinct from conservativism, and there is danger in the two being confused. Conservativism, though a necessary element in any stable society, is not a social programme; in its paternalistic, nationalistic, and power-adoring tendencies it is often closer to socialism than true liberalism; and with its traditionalistic, anti-intellectual, and often mystical propensities it will never, except in short periods of disillusionment, appeal to the young and all those others who believe that some changes are desirable if this world is to become a better place. A conservative movement, by its very nature, is bound to be a defender of established privilege and to lean on the power of government for the protection of privilege. The essence of the liberal position, however, is the denial of all privilege, if privilege is understood in its proper and original meaning of the state granting and protecting rights to some which are not available on equal terms to others. . . .

Of course, six years of socialist government in England have not produced anything resembling a totalitarian state. But those who argue that this has disproved the thesis of *The Road to Serfdom* have really missed one of its main points: that the most important change which extensive government control produces is a psychological change, an alteration in the character of the people. This is necessarily a slow affair, a process which extends not over a few years but perhaps over one or two generations. The important point is that the political ideals of a people and its attitude towards authority are as much the effect as the cause of the political institutions under which it lives. This means, among other things, that even a strong tradition of political liberty is no safeguard if the danger is precisely that new institutions and policies will gradually undermine and destroy that spirit. The consequences can of course be averted if that spirit reasserts itself in time and the people not only throw out the part which has been leading them further and further in the dangerous direction, but also recognize the nature of the danger and resolutely change their course. There is not yet much ground to believe that the latter has happened in England.

Yet the change undergone by the character of the British people, not merely under its Labour government but in the course of the much longer period during which it has been enjoying the blessings of a paternalistic welfare state, can hardly be mistaken. These changes are not easily demonstrated but are clearly felt if one lives in the country. . . .

What I have argued in this book, and what the British experience convinces me even more to be true, is that the unforeseen but inevitable consequences of socialist planning create a state of affairs in which, if the policy is to be pursued, totalitarian forces will get the upper hand. I explicitly stress that 'socialism can be put into practice only by methods of which most socialists disapprove' and even add that in this 'the old socialist parties were inhibited by their democratic ideals' and that 'they did not possess the ruthlessness required for the performance of their chosen task'. I am afraid the impression one gained under the Labour government was that these inhibitions were, if anything, weaker among the British socialists than they had been among their German fellow-socialists twenty-five years earlier. Certainly the German Social Democrats, in the comparable period of the 1920s under equally or more difficult economic conditions, never approached as closely to totalitarian planning as the British Labour government has done.

10.2 ENOCH POWELL: THE DECLINE OF BRITAIN

The themes of imperial greatness and decline fascinated Powell and they figure largely in his speeches even in the early 1960s. As a Conservative he wished to exorcise some of the myths which clung to the British people and distorted their vision of the world around them – and of themselves. Powell preached that it was a myth to believe that the loss of empire was a sign of imperial decline, a myth to believe that because Britannia no longer ruled the waves that the country was in a state of terminal illness and that because we were no longer the workshop of the world then the economy was in dire straits. In this excerpt from his speech at Trinity College, Dublin on 13 November 1964 Powell enlarges on these arguments. From Enoch Powell: *Freedom and Reality* (ed. John Wood), Batsford, 1969, pp. 246–53.

To get down to business, then, practically all the people of Britain today accept the following two myths. Britain was once a great imperial power, which built up a mighty empire over generations and then, in the lifetime of most of us, lost or gave it up – whether from weakness, benevolence, or some other cause or causes, is an optional 'extra', about which tastes and fashions vary. Item, Britain was once the workshop of the world, superior in industrial efficiency and inventiveness to all other nations, and then allowed herself to sink into a subordinate place in the international 'league table' through losing or disusing the qualities which once gave her the primacy. Taken together, these two great myths add up to a conviction of national decline, the more prevasive for being accepted as self-evident and based upon undisputed fact.

My purpose is to assert that both these myths are to all practical intents and purposes false; that, being false, they entail upon Britain grave psychological damage and errors of judgment; and that accordingly they ought to be destroyed. The Delphic precept, 'know thyself', applies to nations as much as it applies to men. . . .

Until very nearly the Diamond Jubilee of Queen Victoria – when a certain thing happened – if you mentioned 'the Empire' to a man in the street in London, he would think you meant the United Kingdom, with its three capitals (London, Edinburgh, Dublin) and its 'imperial parliament' at Westminster. If you mentioned the colonies, he would think of Canada and New South Wales, which England he supposed had 'colonised' as it earlier colonised the United States. You may search through the literature, the poetry, and the official minutes of the great Victorian era and find no trace of that kind of empire which we have imagined back into it from the standpoint of the 1890s and since.

The exception to the absoluteness of this statement is 'Empire' in the context of India; and that is the exception which proves the rule, indeed goes far to illustrate it. . . .

The same magic lantern which has projected an empire into Britain's Victorian age has also thrown upon that screen the spurious colours of 'splendid isolation' and 'Britannia ruling the waves' – an operatic air, incidentally, of the 1740s! Viewed objectively the period never existed in which a *Pax Britannica* was imposed and maintained by an unchallenged and invincible British Navy. Viewed subjectively, the British only believed in its existence after they supposed it to have ceased to exist, and were looking back upon it as on a Golden Age, legendary like all other golden ages. Search the contemporary records, the speeches, the memoranda of the Victorian years, and you find anything but security and conviction of a recognised supremacy which rendered Britain indifferent to the policies and combinations of other powers. On the contrary, you find yourself in a world of anxiety and fears entirely familiar: you see politicians and public blundering from one entanglement to another, most of them flowing ultimately from the great central entanglement – India. . . .

Even more important than the Victorian sense of proportion about Britain's industrial and commercial situation and prospects, is the fact that all the phenomena which today are supposed to be the symptoms, if not the causes, of Britain's alleged decline from her position as 'workshop of the world' can be traced right back to and beyond the heyday of the first Industrial Revolution. . . .

There was a constant refrain of complaint that inventions made in England remained for decades unadopted or unexploited in manufacture, and that systems eventually adopted from America were often in essence of British design. The British tendency to make capital and durable goods 'to last for ever', as the phrase is, was contrasted with the American readiness to economise on capital on the presumption that a new and superior process would be coming along before long. The British hankering for 'one off' production and high standards of craftsmanship was contrasted with the American readiness to accept a standard product if that facilitated production.

The significance of all this is that the characteristics of British industry which are supposed today to account for loss of ground to other industrial nations were just as evident in the Victorian heyday, when Britain enjoyed the preponderant share of the world trade in manufactured goods. They are not factors which have crept in as a cause or concomitant of supposed decadence; they are not the modern degeneracy of a Britain which once possessed the opposite qualities. If Britain in the 1960s is, as we are informed, slow to embrace automation, so was Britain in the 1860s. . . .

Of course nothing halted, because nothing could halt, the continued decline in the relative size of Britain in the industrial and commercial world; but the longer it continued, the more firmly the British embraced the myth of the world's workshop as a lost Golden Age, and the more they flagellated themselves for the supposed latter-day sins which had earned them expulsion from that economic Garden of Eden. The Americans did not do this; the Dutch and Belgians did not do this; the Germans did not do this; but the British did. It was our own private hell, as the myth of empire was our own private heaven, and under both hallucinations together two generations have laboured.

10.3 *THE RIGHT APPROACH*: A NEW START FOR BRITAIN (1976)

The Right Approach was not an election manifesto, rather a statement of objectives to mark the new leadership. Without a new start, a new set of realistic policies which offend 'neither against common sense nor against the instincts of the majority' then parliamentary democracy in Britain could be threatened. The main theme of the document is the sorry state of decline into which Britain has fallen. The first priority in rescuing Britain is to remedy her economic performance.

Britain faces this new world in a weaker and relatively poorer state than most of our competitors. We have suffered from low productivity and low profits, and therefore low investment and industrial stagnation. Most recently we have endured a wounding bout of inflation, leading to very high unemployment, and we are now heavily in debt.

The priorities of any government should be the reduction of our debt burden and the mastering of inflation, leading to a fall in unemployment and the resumption of soundly based economic expansion. These objectives cannot be achieved without restraint, sacrifice and a change in direction. We should not pretend that oil will provide an easy way out. The tapping of the North Sea's riches is not going to put right structural weaknesses in our home economy.

There are few excuses for our poor economic performance. But how much is due to government? How much is due to the cumulative effect of government policies on attitudes to work, and competence at work, at all levels? How much is due to a conscious decision to give up the benefits of a better economic performance in favour of other things?

There are certainly many failings in our economy for which governments have been directly responsible. We are, as a country, over-taxed. The rewards for additional skill and effort have been heavily cut back in the last two years. The public sector now controls about 60 per cent of the national income, compared with around 50 per cent as recently as 1973. The Government has nationalised great sections of industry, which it has subsequently mismanaged. It has also hemmed in with restrictions and controls those parts of industry left in the free enterprise sector. The standard of living of the whole country – whether measured in terms of the pay packet or of effective social provision – has suffered as a result in comparison with that of our friends and competitors.

Foreigners have often claimed to perceive the roots of our economic failure in industrial attitudes. They argue that the class war dominates British industrial life, and that the trade union movement perpetuates this struggle because of the power it wields in a sophisticated and inter-dependent economy.

Trade unions do exercise great power. But so do other groups in our inter-dependent society. And the question many of them have begun to ask themselves is, 'Why should we act responsibly when no one else seems to do so?'. Yet men and women do not enter their work-places for the first time determined to see how little work they can do, how much disruption they can cause. They want a satisfying job and a fair reward for their hard work.

Two and a half years ago, we fought a General Election in which the central question was the relationship between parliamentary authority and industrial power. Much of what we said then has been borne out by events. Concern about this issue is one of the reasons why an increasing number of people has begun to question the adequacy of existing institutions.

There are many other aspects of our life, some of which we have taken for granted for years, that are being questioned today. After more than fifteen years of debate about the structure of our education system, people have begun to worry about what is actually being taught – or not taught – in the classroom. They wonder whether our National Health Service, which used to be regarded as one of the wonders of the world, can survive in its present form. They are worried about a tax and social security system which, while it does not help the genuinely needy as much as they think would be right, does lead to obvious unfairness and even positively encourages dependence on the State. They ask how it can be sensible to go on building so many council houses of enormous cost to taxpayers and ratepayers when most people want to own their homes. They are deeply concerned about the increase in violence, the erosion of standards, the growth of bureaucracy, and the fact that no one seems to listen to what they have to say, for example on immigration or environmental matters.

Many of these worries have been intensified by our economic problems, the solution of which is the first essential.

10.4   SIR KEITH JOSEPH: THE SOCIAL VALUES OF THE NEW RIGHT

One of the most interesting, and for a time one of the most influential, converts to New Right ideology was Sir Keith Joseph (1918–   ). In a series of speeches in 1974–75 he subjected the politics of consensus to stringent analysis and proclaimed the need for the new politics. He was at pains, however, in a speech to the Economic Research Council on 15 January 1975 to spell out the social objectives of New Right politics. In the following remarkable extract he boldly proclaimed the relevance of bourgeois values to the state of Britain in the mid-1970s. From Sir K. Joseph: *Reversing the Trend* (1975), pp. 55–61.

Our attention is focused at present on solvency, national solvency, and rightly so. But this is not so much an objective as *conditio sine qua non*, for the attainment of any objectives. The objective for our lifetime, as I have come to see it, is *embourgeoisement*.

It is significant that we lack a native English word for *embourgeoisement*   at least to the best of my knowledge. We tend to translate *bourgeois* as middle-class, but the words are not identical. A middle class implies that there must be a class or classes above and below. If one could say 'we are all middle class now', one would strictly be saying that we have a classless society. To say that we are all bourgeois now – provided it were to be made true – would be to proclaim a common value system.

What alternatives are being proposed to *embourgeoisement* as the economic and social basis for advance towards *the* good life at this stage in our social evolution? Class struggle for class struggle's sake? Permanent revolution as a good in itself, a goal to which one segment of the Communists are so compulsively committed? Our idea of the good life, the end product, and of *embourgeoisement* – in the sense of life-style, behaviour pattern and value-structure – has much in common with that traditionally held by Social Democrats, however we may differ about the kind of social economic structure best capable of bringing about and sustaining the state of affairs we desire.

From the mid-Victorian era till a few years ago, we were confident that our society was moving under its own momentum, or as a result of our reforms, towards the goals summed up by the term *embourgeoisement*. The artisan of Victorian days, who read serious literature, supported radical causes, was sober and self-improving, gave hope that the workers would become bourgeois. This confidence was shared even by those who regretted the development, for one or another of several highly disparate reasons. Engels, in later life, complained that the High Victorian middle-class values were conquering the whole of British society, that alongside a bourgeoisie there would be a bourgeois aristocracy and a bourgeois working class in this most bourgeois of all countries; who would then provide the impetus for Socialism? In their inception, the trades unions, co-operative societies and friendly societies reflected bourgeois thought, and aspired to achieve the benefits of bourgeois life for their members, as Lenin, among others, complained.

Has the middle-class life-style and its values spread further and further with the growth in prosperity, and the substantial change in the pattern of income distribution between the social classes, as we were led to expect? It does not seem to have done so; in some senses the opposite has been taking place.

An important element in bourgeois, or what we call middle-class, values is a further time-horizon, a willingness to defer gratification, to work hard for years, study, save, look after the family future. By contrast, workers in this country have traditionally tended to spend their money as it comes. This is not a function of income but of class status and traditions; the peasant and small shopkeeper have traditionally shared this emphasis on the future with the better-off members of the middle class.

Historically, bourgeois values have rested on personal economic independence, whether based on property or independently marketable skills. The peasant or small shopkeeper or independent craftsman exemplified this independence, as did the free professions – 'free' meaning that the profession was self-governing, that any member of the profession could put up his brass plate and earn his living by serving clients, unbeholden to anyone if he did not wish to be.

This was the historical basis of the emergence of bourgeois values, and indeed political democracy. When the middle classes set the tone of society, wage and salary earners' values and life-styles tended to be moulded by this dominant value-system, the more so in periods of rising incomes, mobility, and wider economic security. But will these values survive almost universal proletarianization – or 'salarization'? Will it survive as the self-employed are driven out of their modest castles and forced to seek paid employment, increasingly in the public sector dominated by the political machine? Will it survive the loss of independence based on property ownership – whether property provides an income or just the means of earning an independent living? This is not meant to be a rhetorical question. It is a serious question whether life-styles which emerged in one set of circumstances can survive under another. The question is complicated by the fact that at present it is not only the social and economic base of these values which is under attack, but the values themselves, often in a completely nihilistic way.

In this age of inflation, spend-what-you-have-because-it-is-not-worth-saving, and of pop culture, one can hardly look for *embourgeoisement*, indeed we shall be fortunate if we can stem the tide. The middle classes in this country are beginning to learn what they can from the working class; what they learn is militancy, solidarity, put-your-claim-in-and-spend-what-you-have-while-you-have-it. . . .

Britain never really internalized capitalist values, if the truth be known. For four centuries, since wealthy commercial classes with political standing began to be thrown up following the supercession of feudalism and the selling off of monastic property, the rich man's aim was to get away from the background of trade – later industry – in which he had made his wealth and power. Rich and powerful people founded landed-gentry families; the capitalist's son was educated not in capitalist values but against them, in favour of the older values of army, church, upper civil service, professions, and land-owning. This avoided the class struggles between middle and upper strata familiar from European history – but at what a cost.

If you re-read the original Fabian essays, you will find in them much of the upper middle class professional and service families' disdain for commercial folk, for the businessman, the industrialist. The idea that the government ought to run everything, rather than private individuals or companies, which forms the core of Socialism, is not new at all. It is pre-capitalist, upper-class. In a sense, it meant the militarization of society; for the army is organized as Socialists would organise an economy. It meant that bureaucratization of society, with the civil service running everything instead of just something.

10.5   MARGARET THATCHER: THE POLITICS OF RENEWAL

The political and social values of Thatcherite Conservatism may be observed in embryo in some of her early Conference speeches as party leader. Most of these, perhaps inevitably, were spent attacking the record of the Labour government of James Callaghan. Occasionally, however, she allowed a glimpse of the mentality of the New Right. In her 1977 Conference speech she responded to the charges that she was both extreme and reactionary. From Conference Proceedings, 1977 (Conservative Political Centre), pp. 133–4.

I am *extremely* careful never to be extreme. I am *extremely* aware of the dangerous duplicity of Socialism, and *extremely* determined to turn back the tide before it destroys everything we hold dear. I am *extremely* discinclined to be deceived by the mask of moderation that Labour adopts whenever an Election is in the offing, a mask now being worn, as we saw last week, by all who would 'keep the red flag flying here'. Not if I can help it! The Conservative Party, now and always, flies the flag of one nation – and that flag is the Union Jack. So much for my so-called 'extremism'.

There is another word our opponents like. The word is 'reactionary.' They say that a Thatcher Government – and I must say that I like the sound of that; I like it a little more each time I hear it and they use it quite a lot so they must believe it – they say that a Thatcher Government would be reactionary. If to react against the politics of the last few years, which undermined our way of life and devastated our economy – if that is reactionary – then we are reactionary, and so are the vast majority of the British people.

They believe, as we do, that Government is far too big – indeed, the next generation were telling us so earlier in the week. They believe, as we do, that Government does not know all the answers, that it has downgraded the individual and upgraded the State.

We do not believe that if you cut back what Government does you diminish its authority. On the contrary, a government that did less, and therefore did it better, would strengthen its authority. Our approach was put very simply by a Chinese philosopher centuries ago: 'Govern a great nation,' he counselled, 'as you would cook a small fish. Don't overdo it.'

If you ask whether the next Conservative Government will cut controls and regulations and keep interference in people's lives to a minimum, my answer is 'Yes, that is exactly what we shall do.' The best reply to full-blooded Socialism is not milk and water Socialism, it is genuine Conservatism. . . .

If I have one message above all else it is this: I am not prepared to settle for the second, third or fourth best for Britain. I do not believe that our decline was inevitable any more than I believe that an accident of nature off our coasts has made our recovery automatic. I believe that if we confront – yes, 'confront' is the word I use – if we confront reality, if we pin our trust on the skill, the resource, and the courage of our people, then this country can work out its salvation and regain its prosperity, regain the respect of others and its own self-respect.

Some people regard this as dangerous talk. 'The Tories,' they say, 'want change; they want to challenge the rules and ideas and policies that govern Socialist society.' 'Risky,' they murmur. 'Right, of course, but risky – might upset Arthur Scargill or Jack Jones – better not do it, better not do it.' And there you have the root and heart of the choice facing our nation. What worries Jack Jones is that the leaders of his Party are living too well. What worries us is that ordinary people are not living well enough.

That is why the next election will be so crucial. All elections are crucial, but this time the choice could be decisive for a generation, because this time how the country votes will settle which party is entrusted with the immense benefits of North Sea oil. If it is the Socialists, then the profits of free enterprise will be used to purchase Socialism, and to take more powers for the State. If it is the Conservatives, they will be used to give power back to the people. The choice is the classic choice. Labour will do what it has been doing for the last three years, only more so. We shall do what we have said we will do – set the people free.

10.6   JOHN REDWOOD: THE CONSEQUENCES OF MONETARISM (1976)

Economists of the New Right are often criticised for placing too much weight upon the effectiveness of monetarist techniques. They did envisage that other weapons would have to be used, in addition, and they did recognise that the undertaking would require many years. In one of the earliest, and most articulate, statements of the new financial discipline, John Redwood placed monetarism within its overall *economic* context. His optimism about the prospects for employment are perfectly typical of the mid-1970s when, it was believed, temporary difficulties would be offset by new demands for labour elsewhere in the economy. From John Redwood: 'Managing the Economy', in *The Conservative Opportunity* (1976, Macmillan), pp. 86–8.

It is often objected that financial independence of the nationalised industries entails labour-shedding, that control of the money supply and government expenditure is deflationary, and that a harsher attitude towards declining industries also tends to greater unemployment. There is sufficient truth in all of these propositions to warrant analysis, but like so many politically oriented statements they amount to little more than half-truths. Financial independence of the nationalised industries should entail a more positive attitude towards the development of new markets, new services and products, which can employ the existing labour force in more productive activities, which can generate more income and more profit for society at large. It is the fabric of price control, of large wage increases within the context of a sluggish strategy towards markets and products, that has led to the financial crisis in the nationalised industries which besets us today. Control of the money supply and of government expenditure is not necessarily deflationary. It is a policy which attempts to influence the balance of resources between public and private, and also attempts to ensure that resources are used in the most efficient and productive way. This cannot be deflationary: it can prevent inflation, and as a sensibly pursued package of policies it can ensure a higher rate of growth in the economy as a whole, which will entail more income and wealth for everyone.

One must concede that a harsher attitude towards declining industries is also a policy which may in the short term produce hardship in that people who have been employed in an industry most of their life or all of their life may find that that industry can no longer support them in their occupation. Given sensible policies for early retirement the worst social consequences of allowing the rundown of unproductive and outmoded industries can be overcome, and the economy as a whole can benefit by retraining people for more productive uses in which they will make a greater contribution to the wealth and prosperity of the whole nation.

Government must take every opportunity to foster and support compensatory employment opportunities through creating the right atmosphere in which business can operate, and supporting training programmes within the economy. The broad areas in which employment should increase ought to lie in export industries and services, service activities for the home market, high technology and specialised manufacturing sectors, and new product and growth areas like plastics, pharmaceuticals and chemicals. The strategy of the counter cyclical economy combined with a lower rate of domestic inflation should lead to a shift of resources into exports: in this connection the opportunities for selling management and professional expertise in growth areas in the Middle East, South America and parts of Africa are of great importance.

A strategy of setting industry free, of rewarding entrepreneurship and initiative, of reducing high taxation rates on corporations and individuals alike and marking proper limits to the public deployment of resources could give every incentive to create a better balanced economy, a more invigorating atmosphere to replace the museum economy philosophy which now confronts us. At the moment it seems to be the intention of policy makers to take the existing employment structure as being the ideal one for the economy, and to freeze it at whatever price in subsidisation and call on government resources this might entail. In place of the archival preservation of dead or dying industries we need to put belief in ourselves to create employment, to make products and provide services which the world at large wishes to buy, and which can improve our own standards of life at home. We have now seen that policy of indiscriminate government subsidisation and expenditure leads to inflation, which in its turn leads to a harsh reality of dole queues, despair and frenetic self-questioning. The people of our country are able and well educated, not the material for the dole queue, the declining industry, or the lack of prospects which confront so many of our ablest people through no particular fault of their own. It must be the task of an incoming Government to set the people free, to congratulate the profit makers rather than to tax them and legislate against them, to congratulate those who invest and accumulate and save in order to provide the British economy with the machine power which it requires to compete with the Japanese, the Americans and the Germans. The country which pioneered the first industrial revolution, now needs another revolution in attitude and in the role of government in order to bring its economy back to the first division in the league rather than letting it continue to sink into the mire of economic failure.

The UK economy is a declining economy relative to world output, but it is an internationally oriented economy where we have to plan in an international context. First, commodity producers' power does necessitate home resource control over utilisation. Secondly, developing countries are going to want to control part of the industries growing up in their economies, and the role of the Western nations is a participatory and advisory one rather than ownership. Thirdly, our comparative advantage lies not in mass-produced goods, but in specialist and high-technology goods, and in services. To sustain these advantages the economy must maintain a high standard of education, and must foster initiative and enterprise.

The argument of this Chapter has not centred upon the dismantling of the welfare state, or on the reduction of the high environmental and welfare standards that we have rightly come to expect. The main contention, that government expenditure and the growth of the public sector have to be arrested, is an argument over the control and management of services and industry. Welfare benefits, a health and education service and other transfer benefits are and must remain an integral part of our society.

It is rather the contention of this chapter that more resources can be freed for higher standards of health and welfare service, by curbing the scope of public sector industrial activity, and curbing the marginal services and activities that have proliferated in government. The ending of nationalised industry revenue subsidies and allocating housing and food subsidies to individuals rather than indiscriminately would reduce public expenditure by 10 per cent, whilst Government should, through its fiscal and industrial policies, encourage profitability and new ventures, rather than seek to fossilise the economy by subsidies. The prime aim of our strategy must be to raise the long term rate of growth, thus generating more wealth and income in order to afford better private and public standards.

10.7   *THE RIGHT APPROACH*: THE DECLINE OF THE STATE (1976)

The Right Approach endeavoured to place the new direction which the Conservative party was to take within the historical and philosophical traditions of British Conservatism. Repudiating the claims of Socialists, Liberals and, interestingly, noting 'the failure of the Social Democrats to establish either a convincing philosophy or viable practical policies' within the Labour party, the document proceeds to define the philosophical foundation of the New Right as a recognition of Man as both an individual and a citizen. The role of the State is to act 'as the trustee of the whole community in any economic system, holding the balance between different interests'. Obviously, as the following extract makes clear, closely defined limits need to be set against the power of the State. In the closing lines there is a clear recognition that the role of the State must be reduced.

For answers which are relevant to Britain's real problems, and which are based on a philosophical approach that matches 'the manners, the customers, the laws, the traditions' of the British people, the country will need to turn to the Conservative Party.

Man is both an individual and a social being, and all political philosophies have sought to accommodate these two, often conflicting, elements in human nature. Conservatism has always represented a balance between the two, arguing against Liberal individualists for man's social role and against Socialists for the right of the individual to develop as far and as fast as he can, choosing freely from a wide range of opportunities while recognising his duties towards his fellows.

We have laid particular stress on the individual and his freedom in recent years because Socialism has tipped the balance so far the other way. Moreover, many of the developments of modern industrial society have tended to dehumanise life and threaten the individuality and independence of men and women.

But we do not base our approach solely on the individual, on the view that the only role of society is to provide a framework of laws within which individual opportunities can flourish without becoming self-destructive. If we were to do this, a number of other things in which Conservatives believe – patriotism, loyalty, duty – would be meaningless. Man is an individual answerable to himself. But he is also a citizen, the member of a complex network of small communities which go to make up society – family, neighbourhood, church, voluntary organisation, work-place and so on.

While the network of social ties in the community may have narrowed as the State has assumed more and more social responsibilities, the network of economic ties has constantly widened as our economy has become more sophisticated. But the philosophy of these interdependent economic units – trade unions, pressure groups, industrial and commercial institutions – has become increasingly and stridently individualistic. As one group has discovered and used its strength, so others have come to question whether restraint is wise or necessary or right. What we have to set out, and it is in the main stream of Conservatism for us to do so, is a political philosophy that goes beyond the State and the individual, and begins to express in human terms the complex network of reciprocal rights and duties in an orderly society.

Such a philosophy will recognise that private ownership of property is essential if we are to encourage personal responsibility and the freedom that goes with it. Property diffuses power, increases choice and is an important source of independence. Since some people have more ability and a greater opportunity to acquire property than others, there are bound to be social and economic inequalities. Conservatives are not egalitarians. We believe in levelling up, in enhancing opportunities, not in levelling down, which dries up the springs of enterprise and endeavour and ultimately means that there are fewer resources for helping the disadvantaged. Hostility to success, because success brings inequality, is often indistinguishable from envy and greed, especially when, as Alexander Solzhenitsyn has pointed out, it is dressed up in the language of the 'class struggle'.

We believe that an economic system predominantly based on private enterprise does most to increase resources and opportunities through individual pioneering, effort and skill. Enterprise comes first from individuals, not from 'National Boards'. But this does not make us a laissez-faire party. We have always conceded that the State should have a role as the trustee of the whole community in any economic system, holding the balance between different interests.

The precise limits that should be placed on intervention by the State are reasonably the subject of debate within the Conservative Party, as are the proper boundaries between State and private provision. What no Conservative disputes is that intervention must be strictly limited to defined purposes, justified by particular circumstances rather than by doctrinaire theories.

In holding the balance, in reconciling conflicting groups, the State exercises powers which rest in our society on the twin pillars of parliamentary democracy and the rule of law. We have not in the past needed a written constitution, setting out in precise terms how these powers can be used, because there has been general acceptance that where change is necessary its evolution must respect our traditions. Those who want the State to take on more and more responsibilities have found this an increasingly burdensome constraint, and it is not surprising that largely as a result of their actions, the merits of a written constitution are being canvassed.

In practical terms, our policies aim to achieve a reasonable balance between the use of the nation's resources by the public and private sectors, between the use of the effective weapons available to a government in the abatement of inflation, between what the State takes from its citizens in tax and what they retain, between those who are organised in powerful trade unions and the majority of workers who are not, between the thrust for greater size in most social and economic activities and the growing demand to reduce them to a human scale, between what the nation can afford to spend and a broadly agreed agenda of social priorities, between central and local government, between the improvement of quality and the widening of opportunity in education, between ownership by the State and ownership by the individual.

The balance which we seek has its roots not only in a distinctive, if too rarely articulated, Conservative approach, but also in basic common sense. That has always been one of the great strengths of Conservatism. The facts of life invariably do turn out to be Tory.

10.8 MAURICE COWLING: THE DEFENCE OF THE SOCIAL ORDER.

Elitism and Conservatism have never been very widely separated. In spite of the populist rhetoric of the New Right and the constant appeals to national unity, one of the avowed purposes of the politics of the New Right is to preserve the existing social order. Terrified by the industrial disorder of the early and mid-1970s, alarmed by the threat to national unity posed by the Welsh and Scottish National parties as well as by the continuing difficulties in Ulster and frightened by high rates of inflation, some Conservative writers were prepared to utilise Thatcherite politics in defence of the social order. In the following extract such conservationist objectives are bluntly stated and unavowedly proclaimed. Maurice Cowling is a Cambridge historian who has done much to foster – together with Professor Gash and Lord Blake – a Conservative historiography which emphasises the role of 'high politics' in charting the destiny of the nation. Cowling's position is that the Conservative party ought to aspire to more than economic liberalism. Its role in defending the existing social structure should be both prominent and assertive. Lying behind the

Conservative party's emphasis on individual freedom are quite different considerations. From M. Cowling: *Conservative Essays* (1978), pp. 9–12.

In the Conservative conception of freedom, in other words, there is a great deal of double-talk and many layers of concealed consciousness. Conservatives, if they talk about freedom long enough, begin to believe that that is what they want. But it is not freedom that Conservatives want; what they want is the sort of freedom that will maintain existing inequalities or restore lost ones, so far as political action can do this. And this is wanted not only by those who benefit from inequalities of wealth, rank and education but also by the enormous numbers who, while not partaking in the benefits, recognize that inequalities exist and, in some obscure sense, assume that they ought to. They assume, that is to say, that a nation has to be stratified and that stratification entails privilege; and they assume this not as a matter of principle but because it is something to which they are accustomed. They are accustomed to inequalities; inequalities are things they associate with a properly functioning society and they do not need an ideological proclamation in order to accept them. They assume them pragmatically in the course of identifying themselves socially in a way they would not do if confronted with a principle. Indeed, to present inequality as a principle can even now be damaging politically since the climate of assumption is very different from the climate of explicit thought which continues to accept Mr Hattersley's dictum that Conservative freedom means freedom for Sir Ian Gilmour to send his sons to Eton so long as others send their sons to comprehensive schools elsewhere.

It is in this context that the freedom rhetoric must be understood. It is a way of speaking which resonates somewhat and seems to have resonated effectively in the last three years. But it is not what Conservatives want, even if it *fits in* with what they want. Indeed, it is a way of not saying what they want, a way of attracting sympathy and support for, and attributing principle to, a social structure which they wish to conserve or restore.

They wish to conserve, or restore it, of course, because it is the only one they know. They wish to conserve, or restore it – some of them – because it is one from which they benefit. But they wish to conserve, or restore it, most of all because they believe that it is, or can be made to be, beneficial in itself and more beneficial than any that is in sight.

The 'social structure' is a subject about which it is necessary to speak carefully. For Burke, who inserted it into modern thinking, it meant Monarchy, Aristocracy, Church and People; for us it means something very much more complicated. It means all the gradations of classes that exist in a modern society, including a far larger middle class than Burke had conceived of, a more powerful and less Christian intelligentsia than he thought desirable and a division, which scarcely existed in his mind, between the lower-middle classes and an immense, self-conscious working class beneath them. It includes the conception that taxation should not prevent responsibility being rewarded, provided that that does not entail penalizing those who have wealth without assignable social responsibility. It includes a system of law which makes it possible to maintain a variety of educational systems, to own, accumulate and pass on property, and to enjoy a legally defined freedom to speak, publish and so on.

To put this in terms of inequality is to adopt a socialist analysis. But, since inequality is an unavoidable feature, it is best to meet the analysis head on and agree that the Conservative conception of a social structure not only assumes that marked inequalities are inevitable but also declines to justify them because their inevitability makes justification unnecessary.

To decline justification of the principle is not to say that there cannot be discussion of the content; almost all determination of the form and incidence of taxation and the direction and distribution of state spending involves a discussion of this sort. It is not the principle or the discussion, however, but the balance of operative power that determines the outcome, and it is difficult to see how it could be otherwise when the conservative classes are, quite naturally, by instinct and assumption, as much as anyone else, jacobin or republican royalists who deny legitimacy, get what they can and try to keep what they get, and are Conservative because instinct and self-interest coincide in the judgment that existing arrangements should be preserved.

The Conservative party exists now, as at any other time since 1886, because those who perform the duties or acquire the benefits connected with inequality, do not want democratic arrangements to break down. They judge it better if possible, to get part of what they want by acting effectively through the parliamentary system than to get a bigger proportion under some other sort of regime. They accept the fact that a balancing of costs is involved and that, if the price that is paid for parliamentary government is too high, there will be those who will want parliamentary arrangements superseded.

This volume is written in the hope that parliamentary arrangements will be retained, that most of what is needed can be secured by rhetoric rather than force and that the function of the Conservative party in these circumstances is two-fold – to press the existing elite and its replacements to think and act in a conservative manner, and to give public expression on their behalf to opinions that will help create a public sentiment of national solidarity with them.

Elite is not a word to conjure with among Conservatives. But it is a conception that has to be faced. England today is a suburban country and run by middle-class professionals. So is the Conservative party; it is run by middle-class professionals and will go on being run by them for a long time in the future. If the failing of aristocratic politicians was a tendency to pick up a second-rate intellectual language in the hope of reconciling the thinking classes to them, the failing of middle-class professionals is to think solemnly and speak earnestly as if it were enough merely to say what they mean in order to be understood. In order to be understood and followed in a democratic system (as indeed under any other form of government) it is necessary to do something more. In particular it is necessary to persuade citizens that they belong to a city that is worth belonging to.

One way of doing this is to provide material benefits, in relation to which economic growth on the I.E.A. model provides an intelligible answer to economic growth on a Keynesian model. Growth, however, cannot be guaranteed; even when it is achieved, it does not necessarily determine the reactions of sentiment which constitute the basis of political solidarity. There is no reason to believe that long-term reactions of sentiment yield at all readily to fluctuations in economic prosperity, which are much less important in the determination of political opinion than the creative activity of the intelligentsia.

BIBLIOGRAPHY

BAILYN, B. (1962) 'Political experience and enlightenment ideas in eighteenth-century America', *American Historical Review*, 67.

BARNES, J. (1969) *Baldwin: a Bibliography*. Weidenfeld & Nicolson.

BARNES, J. (1977) *The Age of Balflour and Baldwin*. Weidenfeld & Nicolson.

BEER, S. H. (1957) 'The representation of interests in British government', *American Political Science Review*, 51.

BELLAIRS, C. E. (1977) *Conservative Social and Industrial Reform*.

BENNETT, G. (ed.) (1962) *The Concept of Empire*.

BENNETT, R. J. (1977) 'The Conservative tradition of thought' in N. Nugent and R. King: *The British Right: Conservative and Right Wing Politics in Britain*. Saxon House.

BLAKE, R. (1966) *Disraeli*. Eyre & Spottiswoode.

BLAKE, R. (1970) *The Conservative Party from Peel to Churchill*. Fontana.

BLAKE, R. (1976) *Conservatism in an Age of Revolution*. Macmillan

BLAKE, R. (ed.) (1976) *The Conservative Opportunity*. Conservative Political Centre.

BLOCK, G. D. (1964) *Source Book of Conservatism*. Conservative Political Centre.

BRIGGS, A. (1954) *Victorian People*. Pelican.

BRINTON, C. (1926) *Political Thought of the English Romantics*. Oxford U.P.

BRYANT, SIR A. (1929) *The Spirit of Conservatism*. Methuen.

BURN, W. L. (1959) 'The Conservative tradition and its reformulation', in M. Ginsberg (ed.) *Law and Opinion in the Twentieth Century*. Stevens and Sons.

BUTLER, SIR G. (1957) *The Tory Tradition*. Conservative Political Centre.

BUTLER, M. (1981) *Romantics, Rebels and Reactionaries*. Oxford U.P.

BUTLER, R. (1971) *The Art of the Possible*. Hamilton.

BUTLER, R. (1977) *The Conservatives*. Allen & Unwin.

CANAVAN, F. (1960) *The Political Reason of Edmund Burke*. Durham, North Carolina.

CECIL, LADY G. (1921) *Life of Robert, Marquis of Salisbury* (4 vols.) Hodder & Stoughton.

CECIL, LORD H. (1912) *Conservatism*. Williams & Norgate.

COLLEY, L. (1982) *In Defiance of Oligarchy*. Cambridge U.P.

COSGRAVE, P. (1978) *Margaret Thatcher*. Collins.

COWLING, M. (1978) *Conservative Essays*. Cassell.

CRUICKSHANKS, E. (1979) *Political Untouchables*. Duckworth.

DAVIS, H. W. C. (1929) *The Age of Grey and Peel*. Oxford U.P.

DICKINSON, H. (1976) 'The eighteenth century debate on the Glorious Revolution', *History*, **61**.

DICKINSON, H. (1977) *Liberty and Property: Political Ideology in Eighteenth Century Britain*. Methuen.

DOZIER, R. (1983) *For King, Constitution and Country: the English Loyalists and the French Revolution*. University Press of Kentucky.

DREYER, F. (1979) *Burke's Politics*. Wilfred Laurier U.P., Ontario.

DRIVER, C. (1946) Richard Oastler: Tory Radical. Octagon.

DRUCKER, H. M. (1974) *The Political Uses of Ideology*. Macmillan.

EDDLESHALL, R. (1977) 'English conservatism as ideology', *Political Studies*, **25**.

ELDRIDGE, C. C. (1973) *England's Mission: The Imperial Idea in the Age of Gladstone and Disraeli, 1868–80*. Macmillan.

FABER, R. (1961) *Beaconsfield and Bolingbroke*. Faber & Faber.

FEILING, SIR K. (1924) *A History of the Tory Party, 1640–1714*. Oxford U.P.

FEILING, SIR K. (1930) *Sketches in Nineteenth Century Biography*. Oxford U.P.

FEILING, SIR K. (1938) *The Second Tory Party*. Oxford U.P.

FEILING, SIR K. (1946) *Neville Chamberlain*. Macmillan.

FEUCHTWANGER, E. J. (1968) *Disraeli, Democracy and the Tory Party*. Clarendon Press.

FISHER, N. (1973) *Iain Macleod*. Andre Deutsch.

FORBES, D. (1975) *Hume's Philosophical Politics*. Cambridge U.P.

FOSTER, R. (1981) *Lord Randolph Churchill*. Clarendon Press.

FREEMAN, M. (1977) 'Edmund Burke and the sociology of revolution', *Political Studies*, **25**.

FREEMAN, M. (1978) 'Edmund Burke and the theory of revolution', *Political Theory*, **6**.

FREEMAN, M. (1980) *Edmund Burke and the Critique of Political Radicalism*. Basil Blackwell.

GAMBLE A. (1974) *The Conservative Nation*. Routledge & Kegan Paul.

GARDINER, G. (1975) *Margaret Thatcher*. William Kimber.

GASH, N. (1953–1977) *Politics in the Age of Peel*. Longman.

GASH, N. (1965) *Reaction and Reconstruction in English Politics 1832–52*. Clarendon Press.

GASH, N. (1968) *The Age of Peel*. Edward Arnold.

GASH, N. (1984) *Lord Liverpool*. Weidenfeld & Nicholson.

GILBERT, M. (1981) *Churchill's Political Philosophy*. Oxford U.P.

GILBERT, M. and CHURCHILL, R. (1977) *Winston S. Churchill*. Heinemann.

GILMOUR, I. (1977) *Inside Right*. Hutchinson.

GLICKMAN, H. (1961) 'The Toryness of English Conservatism', *Journal of British Studies*.

GOLDIE, M. (1983) 'Obligations, utopias and their historical context', *Historical Journal*, **26**.

GREENE, J. P. (1969) 'Political mimesis: a consideration of the historical and cultural roots of legislative behavior in the British colonies in the eighteenth century', *American Historical Review*, **75**.

GREENLEAF, W. H. (1975) 'The character of modern British politics', *Parliamentary Affairs*, **28**.

HARRIS, N. (1972) *Competition and Corporate Society: British Conservatism, the State and Industry*. Methuen.

HARRIS, R. W. (1968) *Reason and Nature in the Eighteenth Century*. Blandford.

HARRIS, R. W. (1969) *Romanticism and the Social Order, 1780–1830*. Blandford.

HART, J. (1965) *Bolingbroke: Tory Humanist*. Toronto U.P.

HAYEK, F. (1946) *The Road to serfdom*. Routledge.

HAYEK, F. (1949) *Individualism and the Economic Order*. Routledge.

HAYEK, F. (1960) *The Constitution of Liberty*. Routledge & Kegan Paul.

HAYEK, F. (1973) *Law, Legislation and Liberty*. Routledge & Kegan Paul.

HEARNSHAW, F. J. C. (1933) *Conservatism in England*. Dawsons.

HILL, R. L. (1929) *Toryism and the People*. Constable.

HILTON, B. (1979) 'Peel: a reappraisal', *Historical Journal*, **30**.

HOFFMAN, J. D. (1966) *The Conservative Party in Opposition, 1945–51*. Macgibbon & Kee.

HOFFMANN, R. and LEVACK, P. (1949) (eds) *Burke's Politics*. New York.

HOGG, Q. (1947) *The Case for Conservatism*. Penguin.

HUNTINGTON, S. (1957) 'Conservatism as an ideology', *American Review of Political Science*, 6.

JAMES, R. R. (1959) *Lord Randolph Churchill*. Weidenfeld & Nicolson.

JAMES R. R. (1969) *Memoirs of a Conservative: J. C. C. Davidson's Memoirs and Papers, 1910–37*. Weidenfeld & Nicolson.

JESSOP, B. (1974) *Traditionalism, Conservatism and British Political Culture*. Allen & Unwin.

JONES, W. D. (1956) *Lord Derby and Victorian Conservatism*. Blackwell.

JOSEPH, SIR K. (1975) *Reversing the Trend*. Conservative Political Centre.

JOSEPH, SIR K. and SUMPTION, J. (1979) *Equality*. Centre for Policy Studies.

KEDOURIE, E. 'Tory ideologue: Lord Salisbury', *Encounter*, (June 1972).

KENNEDY, A. (1953) *Salisbury: Portrait of a Statesman*. Murray.

KIRK, R. (1953) *The Conservative Mind: from Burke to Santayana*. H. Regnery Co., New York.

KIRK, R. (1982) *The Portable Conservative Reader*. H. Regnery Co., New York.

KRAMNICK, I. (1968) *Bolingbroke and his Circle*. Harvard U.P.

KRAMNICK, I. (1974) *The Rage of Edmund Burke*. Basic Books, New York.

LANGFORD, P. (1980) 'Old Whigs, Old Tories and the American Revolution' in P. Marshall and G. Williams (eds.) *The British Atlantic Empire before the American Revolution*. Frank Cass.

LARKIN, P. (1930) *Property in the Eighteenth Century*. Cork U.P.

LAYTON-HENRY, Z. (1980) *Conservative Party Politics*. Macmillan.

LINDSAY, T. and HARRINGTON, M. (1974) *The Conservative Party, 1918–1979*. Macmillan.

MACDOWELL, R. (1959) *British Conservatism, 1832–1914*. Faber.

MACKENZIE, J. (1984) *Propaganda and Empire: the Manipulation of British Public Opinion, 1880–1960*. Manchester U.P.

MACMILLAN, H. (1938) *The Middle Way*. Macmillan.

MACPHERSON, C. B. (1980) *Edmund Burke*. Oxford U.P.

MANNHEIM, K. (1936) *Ideology and Utopia: Introduction to the Sociology of Knowledge.* Routledge.

MANNHEIM, K. (1953) *Essays in Sociology and Social Psychology.* Routledge.

MARSH, P. T. (1978) *The Discipline of Popular Government: Lord Salisbury's Domestic Statecraft, 1881–1902.* Harvester.

MARSH, P. T. (ed.) (1979) *The Conscience of the Victorian State.* Harvester.

MERTON, K. (1957) *Social Theory and Social Structure* . Glencoe Free Press.

MIDDLEMAS, K. and BARNES, J. (1969) *Baldwin.* Weidenfeld & Nicalson.

MILLER, D. (1981) *Philosophy and Ideology in Hume's Thought* Clarendon Press.

NELSON, J. M. (1977) 'Ideology in search of a context: eighteenth century political thought and the loyalists of the American Revolution', *Historical Journal,* **20.**

NEWBOULD, I. (1983) 'Sir Robert Peel and the Conservative Party, 1832–1841: a study in failure', *English Historical Review,* **98.**

NORTON, P. and AUGHEY, A. (1981) *Conservatives and Conservatism.* Temple Smith.

NUGENT, N. and KING, R. (1977) *The British Right: Conservative and Right Wing Politics in Britain.* Saxon House.

OAKESHOTT, M. (1962) *Rationalism in Politics.* Methuen.

O'GORMAN, F. (1973) *Edmund Burke: His Political Philosophy.* George Allen & Unwin.

O'GORMAN, F. (1982) *The Emergence of the British Two-Party System, 1760–1832.* Edward Arnold

O'SULLIVAN, N. (1976) *Conservatism.* Dent.

PARKIN, C. (1956) *The Moral Basis of Burke's Political Thought.* Cambridge U.P.

PARKIN, F. (1967) 'Working class Conservatives', *British Journal of Sociology,* **18.**

PHILLIPS, G. D. (1980) 'Lord Willoughby de Broke and the politics of radical toryism, 1909–14', *Journal of British Studies,* **20.**

PINTO-DUSCHINSKY, M. (1967) *The Political Thought of Lord Salisbury, 1854–68.* Constable.

POCOCK, J. G. A. (1960), 'Burke and the Ancient Constitution', *Historical Journal,* **3.**

POCOCK, J. G. A. (1965) 'Machiavelli, Harrington and English political ideologies in the eighteenth century', *William and Mary*

Quarterly, 3rd Series, **22**.

POCOCK, J. G. A. (1982), 'The political economy of Edmund Burke's analysis of the French Revolution', *Historical Journal*, **25**.

PUGH, M. (1982) *The Making of Modern British Politics, 1867–1939*. Basil Blackwell.

QUINAULT, R. E. (1979) 'Lord Randolph Churchill and Tory Democracy', *Historical Journal*, **22**.

QUINTON, A. (1978) *The Politics of Imperfection*. Faber.

RAMSDEN, J. (1978) *The Age of Balfour and Baldwin, 1902–40*. Longman.

RIPLEY, R. (1965) 'Adams, Burke and Conservatism,' *Political Science Quarterly*, **80**.

ROBB, J. (1942) *The Primrose League, 1883–1906*. Columbia U.P.

ROBERTS, D. (1958) 'Tory paternalism and social reform in early Victorican England', *American Historical Review*, **64**.

SCHENK, H. G. (1966) *The Mind of the European Romantics*. Constable.

SCHUMANN, H-G (1978) 'The problem of Conservatism: some notes on methodology', *Journal of Contemporary History*, **13**.

SCRUTON, R. (1980, 1984) *The Meaning of Conservatism*. Pelican.

SMITH, P. (1967) *Disraelian Conservatism and Social Reform*. Routledge.

SMITH, P. (1972) *Lord Salisbury on Politics*. Cambridge U.P.

SOUTHGATE, D. (1974) *The Conservative Leadership, 1832–1932*. Macmillan.

STANLIS, P. (1958) *Edmund Burke and the Natural Law*. Michigan U.P.

STANNAGE, T. (1980) *Baldwin Thwarts the Opposition*. Croom Helm.

STEWART, R. (1978) *The Foundations of the Conservative Party, 1832–67*. Longman.

STRAUSS, L. (1953) *Natural Right and History*. University of Chicago Press.

THOMPSON, G. C. (1886) *Public Opinion and Lord Beaconsfield, 1876–60* (2 vols.) Macmillan.

UTLEY, T. E. (1949) *Essays in Conservatism*. Writers & their work.

UTLEY, T. E. (1968) *Enoch Powell: the Man and his Thinking*. Kimber.

VIERECK, P. (1965) *Conservatism Revisited*. Lehmann.

WATSON, G. (1973) *The English Ideology: Studies in the Language of Victorian Politics*. Allen Lane.

WEISS, J. (1977) *Conservatism in Europe, 1770–1945*. Thames & Hudson.

WHIBLEY, C. (1925) *Lord John Manners and his Friends* (2 vols).

WHITE, R. J. (1950) *The Conservative Tradition*. N. Kaye.

WOLFF, M. *et al.* (1965) *The Conservative Opportunity*. Conservative Political Centre.

WOLIN, S. S. (1954) 'Hume and Conservatism', *American Political Science Review*, 48.